盈成

WIN SON PRESENTS
A TAIWANESE AMERICAN
★ ★ COOKBOOK ★ ★

JOSH KU and **TRIGG BROWN** of Win Son

with **CATHY ERWAY**

盈成

Photographs by **LAURA MURRAY**

ABRAMS, NEW YORK

TABLE OF CONTENTS

LEFT: Pan-Griddled Pork Buns (page 171)

★ ★ ★

Prologue:
★ THE TAIWANESE AMERICAN DREAM ·

IN AUGUST 2015, I RECEIVED A BIZARRE EMAIL. It was from a producer at Heritage Radio Network, where I hosted a podcast, and the subject line was "Taiwanese Food Connection!"

The content was brief: "Trigg, a friend of the network and former cook at Craft and current chef at Upland, is looking to possibly open a Taiwanese restaurant in Brooklyn. I wanted to introduce you two and maybe Trigg could pick your brain sometime! He read your book and loved it."

I couldn't believe what I was reading. I had just spent the last few months promoting the launch of my cookbook, *The Food of Taiwan*, which was one of the first US-published cookbooks to explore the island-nation's cuisine. And I had spent the last several months before that searching for US-based Taiwanese chefs, experts, and other Taiwanese American community organizers who I could partner with on events for the cookbook's launch. I became friendly with a few Taiwanese American food professionals who participated in things like panel events with me, and I visited Taiwanese American organizations from city to city.

It was a lot of fun. When I first shopped that book proposal around, in 2010 and 2011, nobody wanted to touch it. I learned then that a lot of Americans had no idea what or where Taiwan was. Uncomfortable meetings with agents and editors ensued. Then, over the next few years, Taiwanese food and culture slowly became more recognizable in popular culture. This was thanks in no small part to Eddie Huang, whose hit restaurant Baohaus helped launch a multifaceted, and highly visible, film and television career. Other young Taiwanese American pop culture sensations, like basketball player Jeremy Lin and fashion designer Jason Wu, proudly branded themselves as Taiwanese American, too. This was all exciting— and yes, I persevered and finally got that cookbook deal. But through all these discussions, meetings, and events that I had after its publication, I began to sense that there was something missing in the current landscape of Taiwanese food culture in the United States.

At this time, a lot of the Taiwanese restaurants I encountered in New York City and New Jersey, where I grew up, seemed intent on recreating some of the island's greatest street foods, for a mostly Taiwanese American audience. Many others were clandestinely Taiwanese — bearing no trace of the word "Taiwanese" on their menus or in their names — like A & J Bistro in East Hanover, New Jersey, where my mom and I would often go for Taiwanese beef noodle soup and fried pork chops over rice. There didn't seem to be too many restaurants at the time that fashioned themselves as being self-aware of both their Taiwanese and American identities — that is, restaurants that strove to really celebrate the changes to a cuisine that occur in a diaspora, rather than hide them. Those changes might be due to having a different set of accessible ingredients, different lifestyle or dining-out habits, or just different preferences; they might even incorporate ideas from elsewhere, based on the chef's unique lived experiences in America. In short, I was looking for food that was proudly Taiwanese *American*.

But what did "looking to possibly open a Taiwanese restaurant in Brooklyn" mean? Looking back at the email from my friend, what did this chef from Craft and Upland, two New American restaurants in New York City with a local-seasonal bent and European core, have to do with any of that? And what kind of a name was Trigg?

Trigg Brown was the full name. We exchanged a few emails that summer, before he headed off to Taiwan for a while. The next thing I knew, it was February 2016, and Trigg reached out to me to ask if I would like to collaborate on a soft-opening pop-up event at his soon-to-be restaurant. He saw that I

had recently helped out with an event by Yumpling, a Taiwanese American pop-up (now a restaurant and food truck), and he invited them to participate as well. The restaurant wouldn't be opening until later that spring, but we could serve a collaborative menu for friends and family for a few nights, he suggested. It sounded fun. But one thing: "What is your restaurant going to be called?" I asked.

Trigg responded: "The restaurant was Winsome, but some LA breakfast joint trademarked the name last year so we're figuring out a new one. Sucks because it was Josh's grandfather's company, Winsome, that inspired our name, and we've been branding as Winsome for a while now."

Josh Ku was the restaurant's cofounder. By that time I had gathered that he was the Taiwanese American of the two of them, whereas Trigg was a white guy. And they were best friends. I met them both in person shortly after, at their work-in-progress restaurant on a corner of East Williamsburg jammed with bodegas, honking traffic, and hipsters. There were no chic New American restaurants in earshot, and there weren't any Asian restaurants either, besides Chinese takeout. Meeting the two friends in their space and talking over our pop-up plans, it was clear that these weren't your average restaurant owners. For one, they were both in their mid-twenties and had never run a restaurant before.

Josh was slinky and tall as a beanstalk—he was probably the tallest East Asian guy I'd ever seen in person. Frequently topped with a Mets cap, he had an infectious

The corner of Graham and Montrose Avenues in Brooklyn in 2001 when El Brillante first occupied the restaurant space, compared to 2021. Win Son Bakery opened across the street (see pages 12–13).

cackle and was prone to deadpanning answers to long questions with one syllable. A Queens and Long Island native, he had a chill, laid-back demeanor, calmly assessing the action from his tall perch and letting his partner do much of the talking while he did much of the behind-the-scenes work.

Clad in well-worn cooking clogs and a few dishrags at a time, Trigg was a cook's cook, a kitchen quarterback-turned-entrepreneur with aspirations of running a neighborhood restaurant. He was also a food history nerd and could talk endlessly about a dish if you asked him about it. Bred in Virginia, he spoke with a slight tinge of drawl and was exceedingly polite, prone to making unnecessary apologies.

Together, they exuded a genuine warmth and optimism that seemed so rare for the hospitality industry. They didn't take themselves too seriously—but they were very serious about learning and sharing the art of Taiwanese food through their soon-to-be restaurant. They reminded me of Bill and Ted embarking into the unknown on their Excellent Adventure. Yet the whole thing sounded like an unlikely proposition—two buddies with disparate backgrounds, cooking *Taiwanese* food in East Williamsburg? But once they shoved a plate of food in front of me, any hesitations I had came to an abrupt halt.

The first food of theirs I remember eating was the Nutritious Sandwich. In his typical, nutty-history-professor-meets-cool-uncle way of explaining things, Trigg reeled out a long story about how it was sort-of-but-not-really inspired by a sandwich in Taiwan called just that in English, which was made popular by Keelung's night market scene.

I wasn't paying enough attention to the story of the sandwich because it was so good. The bread was hot and glistening from having been freshly deep-fried, and its crust gave way with the tiniest hint of crunch as I tore through to its sweet, soft

center. In between were magical layers of pan-fried shrimp patty, ham, and pickled pineapple, flanked by oozing mayo and slivered scallions. It was the kind of thing that you had to keep eating another bite of until the last dollop of mayonnaise was licked clean from your fingertips. I didn't know at the time that theirs had digressed from the way nutritious sandwiches were usually presented in Taiwan. But then again, different vendors in Taiwan were evolving that dish, and basically every other one that existed, with their own takes on it, too.

Next, I tried their Guohua Street Salad. This was named for an actual street in Taiwan and doesn't reference a traditional salad. In fact, raw, fresh vegetables are scarce in Taiwanese cuisine, especially the kinds with leafy greens. Their Guohua Street Salad was inspired by a spring roll famous in Tainan, the southern Taiwanese city and former capital where the street is located. But instead of having cooked cabbage and slivered veggies tucked inside the roll, here they were dressed and piled with a million other things, including a procession of shrimp on a skewer, creating a symphony of flavors and textures that rang differently with every bite. Together, it was such a balanced and entertaining dish, though you would have no idea that it had anything to do with spring rolls or Taiwan if you weren't told.

And on and on it went. I'll let this book tell the rest of the many revelations in food that Win Son has offered, challenging the notions of Taiwanese *and* American food by marrying them in weird and sometimes convoluted and nonsensical ways. But always with delicious results.

When Win Son opened in the spring of 2016, they proudly billed their cuisine "Taiwanese American food," painted right on the awning. Win Son was not their initial name, however; as mentioned, Josh's grandfather's business, which was originally a textile company based in Taiwan, had been called Winsome. Like so many of the Taiwanese-influenced dishes that they produce, it isn't a direct translation from the original. Bringing it to life in a new home required a fresh imagination and new branding—not as Taiwanese anymore, but Taiwanese American.

In a 2018 review titled "Taiwanese American Win Son Delivers One of NYC's Most Thrilling Meals," *Eater NY* food critic Ryan Sutton declared, "Win Son is where you should be eating now." In 2019, Josh and Trigg opened their sister all-day café, Win Son Bakery, working with pastry chef Danielle Spencer to satisfy the nostalgic Taiwanese American's longing for fan tuan and homemade Taiwanese pastries in a part of Brooklyn where you couldn't get any, and to meet the neighborhood's need for a nice coffee shop. In 2020, Trigg and Josh were named semifinalists for the James Beard Award, and Trigg was named one of *Food & Wine*'s Best New Chefs.

What's more, Taiwanese American food culture has since flourished. As if right on cue, I began hearing about and exploring new and clever takes on Taiwanese food from coast to coast—from the Taiwanese-inspired cuisine by Joanne Chang at Myers + Chang in Boston to the playful dumplings by Hannah and Marian Cheng of Mimi Cheng's in NYC to the fresh and seasonal focus of Vivian Ku's Pine & Crane and Joy in LA to the incredible tasting menu honoring Taiwanese flavors by Jon Yao at Kato. And also, the homey noodle soups by Rich Ho at Ho Foods and the updated Taiwanese classics at 886 by Eric Sze, both in New York City. The close friendship formed among Rich, Eric, Josh, and Trigg over their shared experiences of running Taiwanese restaurants in America has been truly inspiring to watch as well. They're far from alone, as more and more Taiwanese Americans have taken to food to express their identity and passions on a plate.

Today, Win Son and Win Son Bakery are Taiwanese American food institutions that continue to expand the meaning of Taiwanese American food today. The stories behind what makes the food special are all shared in this book. And of course, the recipes themselves are irresistible. From the cacophony of spring alliums, fermented black beans, and chiles that is a dish called Flies' Head (page 73) to the Fried Milk Dough Sundaes with Peanuts and Cilantro-Mint Sauce (page 227), we hope the creativity wrought from classic Taiwanese favorites, reinvented for a Brooklyn audience, will inspire home cooks everywhere to explore their own versions of what Taiwanese American food can be.

CATHY ERWAY

✦ A WORD FROM JOSH

HELLO! I'M JOSH. I am a coauthor of this book about Taiwanese American food, and the co-owner of Win Son and Win Son Bakery in Brooklyn. I'm a native New Yorker, and I grew up in Long Island and Queens. Since I was a kid, my mother would take my sisters and me to Taiwan once every few years to spend time with family. It was during those early visits when I developed a curiosity toward my heritage and Taiwanese culture.

On those trips I loved hearing about my grandfather, my mom's dad. Being the oldest of twelve kids, he left the countryside to work in the city and support the family when he was fourteen. Our restaurant name, Win Son, was inspired by his eventual sweater manufacturing company, Winsome, in Taiwan. His success is a source of pride for me, but even more, the patience and dedication to his wife and family are his true strengths and have become my learning tree. When I was visiting, I'd hear the way he talked to his family and the way my aunts and uncles responded, and that made a great impact on me. Win Son is our romanization of the Chinese name, 盈成, which translates to "success and abundance of profit" but is also representative of the example we hope to follow.

The term "Taiwanese American," though simple, can have a multiplicity of meanings, which we explore throughout this book. For us, it's our restaurant's identity and the reflection of my relationship with my business partner and chef. We almost opened an Italian restaurant. Trigg's background was mostly steeped in New American cuisine, and out of a desire to give ourselves the best chance in a difficult industry, we considered it quite seriously. The more we talked about it though, the more the concept veered toward Taiwanese cuisine.

We were drawn to Taiwanese cuisine initially through our trips to Main Street Imperial (or *Bei Gan*, as it is called by the regulars), a Taiwanese restaurant in Flushing, Queens. Those times we shared and the conversations about food became the impetus to forming the ideas that would bring Win Son to life. We saw a growing interest in regional Asian cuisines, marked by more and more friends venturing out to the Chinatowns in Queens and in Brooklyn. And there were already restaurants like Baohaus, a Taiwanese xiao che and steamed bun shop by Eddie Huang, and Xi'an Famous Foods, a Western Chinese restaurant by Jason Wang; we were inspired by them showcasing the foods of their heritage and wanted to do the same.

With the ink barely dry on our new lease for the restaurant space in Brooklyn, Trigg and I took two weeks off to go to Taiwan. At that time, my mom was primarily based in Taiwan—in Tainan, where she took care of her father half of the year. We were able to spend our days with her and my cousin Eric; they toured us around the island showing us anything they enjoyed themselves or thought we would enjoy. A crash course you might say, but really, the focus was more on experiencing the island rather than force-feeding Trigg every dish Taiwan had to offer. It was on this initial trip that the menu for Win Son started to take shape beyond the skeleton menu derived from what we enjoyed in New York.

Whatever you want to call it, the food we serve is what makes sense to us—a Taiwanese American guy raised in New York, and a white dude from Virginia who can cook lu rou fan better than your mom. Though we're not trying to say our way is any better or worse than what you'd find in Taiwan, we do feel that it's true to our

experience, and it's something that our community has, thankfully, also embraced.

Flies' Head (page 73) is probably my favorite dish that we serve. It's something that my dad would always order when we went out to eat. This dish mostly consists of diced budding chives, quickly stir-fried with ground pork, garlic, chiles, and fermented black beans. It wasn't until I started college when I really began to appreciate and understand the dish and why my dad enjoyed it so much. When we would spend time together, it would most often be eating out. Watching him shovel the mixture of rice and budding chives into his mouth with chopsticks, half choking and half eating, I would often react in confusion and disgust. I later understood that it was just that good and worth the embarrassment that ensued if eaten too quickly.

My dad's family came from mainland China to Taiwan at the end of the 1940s, but my mom's family had been in Taiwan for thirteen generations. Her family was originally from Fujian province, and they made their way over during the seventeenth century, like so many others from that region. Today, Taiwan is a mixed society of descendants from this period and others. Most of its population came with the latter group. A large proportion of the population can trace their roots to the Hakka people from China, and there are also over twenty-five indigenous tribes in Taiwan that have maintained some of their culture through all the changes. Nowadays, Trigg can speak to a lot of the history of Taiwan much better than I can—his affinity for studying cuisine and history is quite strong. While being a white chef cooking Taiwanese food may be enough incentive, he goes above and beyond, which is one of the reasons why the food is amazing and continues to get better.

OPENING WIN SON WAS AN ENTIRELY SELFISH ENDEAVOR THAT I CAN EXPLOIT TO CONTINUALLY FULFILL MY FOOD MOODS.

I went to high school in Long Island, where there were only a handful of Asian kids in my class. We all bonded over our "otherness," of course, and it connected me to the broader Asian-American diaspora. The church I was raised in also provided me with a lot of experiences that have contributed to my identity and our restaurant today. Largely consisting of Chinese Taiwanese members, the church allowed me to experience and learn more about myself, where my parents are from, and my further connection to this Taiwanese American identity.

My fondest memories are the food memories of Taiwan: the breakfasts with dan bing and sweet soy milk (just kill me now); Xiao Guai Guai (aka Kuai Kuai), a puffed corn snack with a sweet coconut flavor (used as a behavioral tool to keep me in line and ready to mop the floor); and lastly, family dinners on my mother's side that always featured my favorite fish, a pan-fried milk fish flayed open on its back. In a sense, opening Win Son was an entirely selfish endeavor that I can exploit to continually fulfill my food moods.

It's insane to think that someone I don't know could be reading these words, and for that I feel confused and excited—but mostly proud. I'm proud that we've been able to contribute to a platform where thoughts and ideas are more freely exchanged, and I am appreciative of those with the same goals who are also contributing, and to those who have paved the way before us. Lastly, I'm grateful for the experience that building this restaurant has given me, helping me find my own way and my own identity as I grow. As happy-go-lucky as I want to be, running Win Son does bear a responsibility beyond building our team and business. Our accessibility relies on educating our guests and expressing our identity as a Taiwanese American restaurant.

It's no secret that New York City has some of the greatest food in the world, all within a hop, skip, and jump away. So when we decided to do Taiwanese cuisine, we were drawn to it with a desire to share something we found to be exciting and fun. What I love about running Win Son is how much it symbolizes the growth of our partnership as well as our relationships with all the people we've gotten to meet and work with, from food vendors to employees and guests. It has allowed us to share something very personal to us.

I'm passionate about being a great collaborator and am lucky to work with someone who shares the same commitment and goals. Thank you for reading, and I hope you'll enjoy our recipes and stories along the way.

A WORD FROM TRIGG

I WAS WORKING THROUGH THE LINE AT COLICCHIO & SONS IN 2012 WHEN JOSH AND I MET. My roommates and I were doing regular barbecues in our backyard in Bed-Stuy, and Josh's best friend lived upstairs. One Memorial Day, C&S was closed. Having days off in common with normal people is rare for line cooks, so my non-restaurant industry roommates and I threw a party. It was soft-shell crab season. We rigged up some electric fryers with extension cords, and when people started showing up, we fried crabs continuously—ten dozen of them throughout the afternoon. We got a good mix of people: different folks from different places getting to know one another over good food. We also fried chicken thighs to bulk up the offerings. Martin's Potato Rolls held crispy proteins with lime-Espelette aioli and ramp pickles. There was some significance beyond the indulging and imbibing, though. Josh regularly attended our food-oriented get-togethers from that point on. This friendship took a course I never expected it to, and his confidence in my ability to please people with my food enabled me to do things I never thought possible.

Josh has a knack for teaching himself something and executing dutifully. As our friendship developed, he asked a lot of questions about cooking, how I prepared something or where I learned it, and what my job was like. In turn, I learned that he ran his own property management company and that his folks were from Taiwan. We bonded over things we had in common: riding motorcycles, working odd and demanding hours, and an interest in Taiwanese food—mine an outsider's curiosity and his rooted in family history and heritage. Our friendship grew during our trips to Flushing, Queens, to load up on Taiwanese food.

We talked shit about the grind on the way out to Flushing. We commemorated the free time with small feasts, and then returned to the grind. It was a simple, gratifying cycle that provided an escape and an opportunity to dream about something bigger. Josh often took me to this Taiwanese place he particularly loved. By that time, I had moved from Colicchio & Sons to Craft, where I was on the vegetable station. My world was vegetables, so when we were eating the *cang ying tou*, or Flies' Head (page 73), one of Josh's favorite dishes, it hit home for me. It was a perfectly balanced, vegetable-forward dish with some pork, but mostly green budding chives. The perfect cook on the chives had me hooked and intent on learning more.

At this time, the thought of opening a restaurant was laughable. I was a line cook with no credit who considered a raise from $10.50 an hour to $11.50 an hour good. Opening a restaurant just wasn't in the cards for me. After a couple years of

CLOCKWISE FROM TOP LEFT: Josh and Trigg; specialities from the bakery, including the mochi donut, bolo bao, custard toast, and sun cookie; Josh, Cathy, Trigg and his dog Ophelia; Win Son socks by Lucky Honey; Trigg in the bakery with Laura Montes, Zulma Cepeda, and Lucia Apolo.

getting to know Josh, though, he started working on a space in one of his dad's properties that he managed. Incidentally, my friend Alex called me and said I could have their family stove on the sole condition that I removed it from their home. It was a Garland commercial range from the seventies. The lady who owned their house before them ran a catering business out of her kitchen, but since then it had been out of commission. I called Josh immediately and said, "Listen, this sounds crazy, but we should go get this stove and put it in that spot you're working on, and maybe it'll sweeten the deal for a tenant or maybe we could even sell the stove on eBay and split it." We joked about opening a restaurant with it ourselves.

I didn't go to culinary school. I started washing dishes when I was fifteen for gas money. We lived outside of Richmond, Virginia, and driving was the only way to get anywhere. I worked that dish job for a year and then I started cooking on the line after that. I loved it. Growing up, the only cooking TV I watched was reruns of the OG *Iron Chef* with my older brother, Merrill. We loved making sandwiches together and also had fun watching this hilariously dubbed reality cooking show. There wasn't this crazy media obsession with food at that time. I guess it was becoming cool, but at that time it wasn't a thing; I was just doing it as a job and I happened to really enjoy it.

When I was about to graduate high school, I bounced the idea of culinary school off some of my coworkers. Cooks, servers, and bartenders—they were all career restaurant industry people and advised against it. They told me to go to school and get a real job. I sort of listened. I went to the University of Virginia (writing my entrance essay on the club sandwich) and studied English, but I kept cooking throughout college. I worked at a handful of restaurants while I was in school, and I began to learn better knife skills, basic vinaigrettes and sauces, and how to take myself more seriously. Under the mentorship of Pei Chang at the Keswick Clubhouse, I realized just how undereducated, underprepared, and underdeveloped I was as a cook and a person. I kept working for Pei throughout college and ended up taking a chef management job under his wing, but one summer, I took a break to live on my brother's couch in New York and work at Craft for free.

At nineteen, I was working from the early morning to close, just doing whatever I could to help and not be in the way. It was like being in college for cooking. The restaurant operated on a higher level than I had ever seen. The copper pots and the French suite, the prep cooks and the porters, the professional demeanor—it was all new to me, and I loved the immersive experience. I told my chef there, James Tracey, I'd quit college and start working for him immediately, but he advised me to finish school and come back, which I did.

These technique- and ingredients-driven restaurants helped frame my culinary perspective while Josh and I were pilgrimaging out to Flushing for *cang ying tou* (flies' head), *o a jian* (oyster omelet), *san bei ji* (three-cup chicken), and more. Eating Taiwanese food with Josh was an education in and of itself. I encountered dishes that contained lessons on Taiwanese food and history. It made me realize how similar Taiwanese food is to American food in its melting-pot nature. I dedicated myself to learning as much as

I could about Taiwanese history, politics, and culture. I read *Island in the Stream* by April C. J. Lin and Jerome F. Keating, and of course, *The Food of Taiwan* by Cathy Erway, our coauthor. I traveled to Taiwan with Josh and his mom for weeks at a time, eating pretty much everything we came across. Josh's family directed my education in Taiwanese food—his mom, Auntie Leah, his cousin Eric, and his aunts and uncles. I could never thank them enough, so I hope Win Son makes them happy and full!

Josh and I appreciate how Taiwanese food has impacted our friendship and changed our lives as we have built a neighborhood business and community around it. Six years after opening Win Son and three years after opening Win Son Bakery, I could never remove Taiwanese influence from my culinary perspective even if I wanted to, and we've been fortunate to continue to learn about Taiwanese food and culture, especially through relationships with some amazing people, some of whom you'll meet throughout

WE WANTED THE FOOD TO EXPRESS THE CULINARY CULTURAL IMPRESSION TAIWAN HAS MADE ON US.

By 2015, Josh and I had converted years of inadvertent research into a distinctly American-based perspective on Taiwanese food. We hoped that our restaurant, though unique in serving some Taiwan-inspired dishes, would serve our neighborhood in East Williamsburg, that its price point would be inclusive enough to bring folks together, and that we could put a few new spins on dishes that we loved and articulate them clearly on the plate. With a good lease, Josh's ability to project manage on a budget, and a Kickstarter campaign, we were able to get Win Son's doors open at 159 Graham Avenue in the spring of 2016. At the beginning, various food writers wanted to call us a "Taiwanese street food restaurant" or "Taiwanese soul food"—labels that just didn't seem to fit. We came up with "Taiwanese American food" because we didn't want to purport authenticity and we didn't want to say "fusion" either. We wanted the food to express the culinary cultural impression Taiwan has made on us.

this book: Ho Chie Tsai, founder of TaiwaneseAmerican.org; Katy Hui-wen Hung, coauthor of *A Culinary History of Taipei*; Lisa Cheng Smith, founder of Yun Hai Taiwanese Pantry; Auntie Leah; and of course, my mentor, Pei Chang.

I am honored to help direct Win Son alongside Josh Ku and our incredible team, some of whom have been with us since the beginning. Others have started their own businesses or moved on to other industries, but without every one of those people, Win Son wouldn't be what it is today. Cooking and eating Taiwanese food brought us together. I hope the menu we serve at Win Son and the recipes in this book offer access both to delicious food and Taiwanese culture. We think it's important to raise awareness, and food tells stories better than any other medium we know.

CLOCKWISE FROM TOP: Braised Beef Shanks (page 102), Lu Rou Fan (page 151), Whole Roasted Fish with Garlic-Ginger Sauce (page 131), Roasted Peanuts with Chinese Five-Spice and Sichuan Peppercorn (page 38).

PANTRY RECOMMENDATIONS

KOMBU CHA   **SHIRO DASHI**   **DARK SOY SAUCE**   **SOY PASTE**   **KECAP MAN**

ONE OF OUR GOALS WITH THIS COOKBOOK IS TO INTRODUCE HOME COOKS TO THE TRUE INGREDIENTS THAT WE USE IN OUR KITCHENS, EVEN IF THEY MIGHT BE A LITTLE OBSCURE FOR THE AVERAGE SUPERMARKET. Thanks to e-commerce sites like Mercato, Weee!, and our favorite destination for Taiwanese ingredients, Yun Hai, there are a lot more international food products that you can have shipped to your door anywhere in the States now. And if you live close to a big city, you can always stock up at any Asian grocery store.

CLEAR RICE WINE　　　RED RICE WINE　　　BLACK RICE VINEGAR　　　LIGHT SOY SAUCE　　　CHILI OIL

You may notice that some the ingredients below have Japanese origins. Given that Taiwan was under Japanese rule during a formative half of the twentieth century, Japanese ingredients and techniques are still commonly used in Taiwanese cooking today. At Win Son, our food and techniques have always had one foot in Japanese cuisine, too, thanks to Trigg's training at a Japanese restaurant under the tutelage of a Taiwanese American chef, Pei Chang. But we also want to nod to the enduring Japanese influences in Taiwanese cuisine by including them in a lot of our cooking.

We hope you enjoy exploring these ingredients if they're new to you, and that you learn more about the cuisine on a deeper level. We guarantee they will fire up your home cooking, so don't be shy about using them liberally outside these recipes. We wouldn't be so stubborn about telling you to buy and use them if we weren't confident that they will.

CHILE FLAKES

There are tons of types of chile flakes—Calabrian chile flakes from Italy, Sichuan dried chiles and flakes, and gochugaru, chile flakes from Korea that are slightly sweeter in flavor. We like to use a mixture of gochugaru and Sichuan chile flakes, because the gochugaru helps cut the spiciness of the hotter Sichuan chile flakes. Taiwanese food isn't particularly spicy—you might get a bird's-eye chile sautéed into the flies' head, for instance, but it's not characteristic of the cuisine. Honestly, you can use any type of chile flakes wherever they're called for in these recipes, depending on your spice tolerance.

CHILI OIL

Whether it's got crispy, frizzled onions and garlic and a potpourri of spices or just chile flakes at the bottom, a bright-red chili oil is an essential condiment in much of Asia. It is not as ubiquitous in Taiwan as on the mainland, but it is a Win Son essential. It's not that spicy, so it's a handy way to layer flavor and a bit of peppery heat, but not a super spicy heat. The varieties with more crunchy stuff often go by the name chili crisp, and their popularity has exploded in recent years. You can find all kinds of them, often from small-batch makers. So when stocking your home kitchen, it might be helpful to think of it in two categories: the stuff you cook with every day and the stuff you only use as a nice condiment, like an affordable cooking olive oil versus a high-end extra-virgin olive oil for finishing a dish. Your nice chili oil could be mixed into some vegetables or used to dress a salad to give it an extra kick. We would actually put it on everything: dumplings, eggs, veggies, chicken, and fish. Trigg has been marinating mushrooms with chili oil (sort of like in our Grilled Whole Mushrooms with Chili Oil, page 94) for ages. In these contexts, it's great to use your top-shelf chili oil or to make your own, like our House Chili Oil (page 258). However, if you're cooking for a group or don't have time to make chili oil, get some Lao Gan Ma brand Spicy Chili Crisp. It's the Heinz 57 of chili oil. Not only is it always going to be perfectly consistent and super affordable, but it's insanely delicious. There is no occasion where we are going to be sad or disappointed that we're using Lao Gan Ma. One thing we strive to do with this book is to introduce you to all the ingredients—high-end and low-end, homemade and store-bought.

FERMENTED TOFU/DOU FU RU

These little cubes of tofu in a jar pack a big umami punch. They're fermented with salt and other seasonings, and there are different variations of it throughout China. The version we stick with is preserved in chile dressing. It's usually called "Fermented Tofu with Chili" on the small glass jars. Its flavor is funky and somewhat cheesy, and it is sometimes dubbed "Chinese cheese" in English, which is kind of weird. But take out one or two of these cubes and dissolve it into a stir-fry and it's amazing. We sneak it into condiments at Win Son, like the mayo in our Big Chicken Bun (page 155) and our Ginger Deluxe Sauce (page 258). You can't always pick it out in the sauces, but it lends a unique—and totally vegan—hit of savory funk.

FRIED SHALLOTS

This quintessential ingredient in Taiwan is used a lot at Win Son—as a garnish, a thickener to sauces (like the lu rou), and as a crunchy complement to greens, noodles, and salads. It's also a prominent element in our chili oil. Fried shallots are also a building block of other Taiwanese staples: *shacha*, a chunky infused oil made with dried seafood and chiles, and shallot sauce, an oil with crispy shallots, chiles, and spices. The oil from frying the shallots is a powerful tool as well, as it can be used as a flavorful finishing oil for noodles and other dishes. Upgrading the quality of that oil is encouraged, like using schmaltz (duck or goose fat), which is common in Taiwan. You can either fry shallots at home or purchase

them premade, and while the goose fat–fried variety is rare in the US, you can easily find fried shallots, in addition to shallot sauce and shacha sauce made by the Bulls Head brand, in Asian markets or online.

KOMBU CHA (KELP TEA POWDER)

Ground kombu, or seaweed, is combined with seasonings like salt, sugar, and MSG to make an incredible secret weapon that we love to deploy for a kelp-y umami in dishes that happens to keep them vegetarian. For example, in our Pea Shoot Salad (page 69), it's sprinkled in along with crushed-up nori snacks to really underline the seaweed flavor. It's also laced into our "Chicken" Spice Mix (page 254), which is ideal for fried chicken.

MSG

Monosodium glutamate is one of the most wrongly maligned ingredients of our times. Unfortunately, it really stems from its association with Chinese cuisine— the typical pejorative is something like, *Oh, I must be sick because I got beef with broccoli from a Chinese takeout place.* Never mind that MSG is in Doritos and ranch dressing and just about everything you're going to see on the grocery store shelves. There's also this negative association that it's a Chinese "cheat" ingredient, or that it causes migraines or your body to

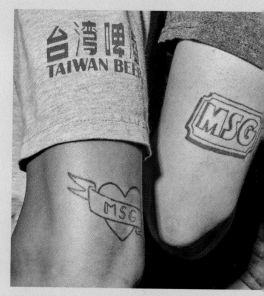

LEFT: Bonnie's chef and former Win Son chef Calvin Eng's tattoo. RIGHT: Trigg's tattoo.

swell or your hair to fall out. We have no intention of invaliding anything someone may be feeling. But we just know that if you utilize MSG in the same way that you utilize salt or butter to enhance flavor, there's nothing wrong with using it in moderation. We also totally support efforts to rehabilitate the bad rap that MSG has gotten over the years, like Ajinomoto's #KnowMSG campaign. (Ajinomoto is a 112-year-old Japanese company that has been selling its patented MSG powder made from wheat for culinary uses ever since it started; it's used in households as well as restaurants throughout Asia—where people aren't sick all the time.) We love how MSG wakes up fried slices of eggplant, or how it

SHIO KOJI

**FERMENTED TOFU/
DOU FU RU**

**PICKLED MUSTARD
GREENS**

MSG

CHILI FLAKES

works with salt and sugar in a subtle and distinct way. We're not suggesting you go crazy with it like the stuff that's dusted all over Cheetos. We're just asking that you give it a try, without scrutinizing it like you wouldn't with an extra tablespoon of butter or pinch of salt. It's just an ingredient. Too much salt or butter is bad for you. So is beer.

PICKLED MUSTARD GREENS

Lacto-fermented mustard greens are an everyday addition to noodle soups, stir-fries, bento meals, and more in Taiwan. At Win Son, they're an essential component of our Garlic Ginger Sauce with Pickled Mustard Greens (page 257).

RICE VINEGAR

There are two main categories of rice vinegar used in Taiwan: clear or "white" rice vinegar, which has a mellow acidity and slightly sweet flavor profile, and black vinegar, which comes in many varieties of its own. In Taiwan, the black vinegar is often infused with fruit and vegetables for added dimension. We love black vinegar as a component in sauces (like our Chile Vinaigrette dipping sauce, page 255) and to help balance the richness of meaty dishes like Lu Rou Fan (page 151) in very small doses. White rice vinegar can be used as an alternative, though with more subtle

effects; we prefer Japanese clear rice vinegars for seasoning because they're often sweeter and balanced.

RICE WINE

This is a must-have ingredient in many Taiwanese dishes, and sorry, but using dry grape wine like sherry is not a good substitute. Rice wine comes from fermented rice, so it has a totally different flavor profile. And everyone cooks with it in Taiwan. One of the interesting relics of Japanese colonial rule in Taiwan is a state-owned manufacturer of liquor and tobacco, the Taiwan Tobacco and Liquor Corporation (TTL). It's now privatized, but it had pretty much been a monopoly until around the millennium, and it still makes many popular brands of booze, including the iconic Taiwan Beer label. It also makes rice wine for cooking, known as *mijiu* or *michiu*. There're roughly two categories of mijiu: white and red. The white, which is really clear, has a more alcoholic and subtle taste. The red, which is amber-colored, has a stronger, sweeter taste. The TTL-owned brand of rice wines is marketed as Oriental Mascot in the Western world—you can find it in most Asian supermarkets. This imparts a classic taste of Taiwanese cooking in dishes and is the nostalgic choice if you're chasing after that flavor. But increasingly,

Shaoxing rice wine, another amber-colored variety of rice wine from China, is used in Taiwan as well, but it is saltier. Use Shaoxing rice wine interchangeably with Taiwanese red rice wine in these recipes. If you really need a substitute, try dry sake, a Japanese rice wine. Just don't go for the sherry.

SESAME OIL

A must-have in Taiwanese pantries which adds fragrance and nutty depth to dishes; it should be amber-colored as it's made from toasted sesame seeds, and therefore stronger in taste and aroma than light sesame oil. A lot of times we'll mix shiro dashi and sesame oil as a last-minute seasoning for noodles, like in our Danzai Noodles (107).

SHIO KOJI

This is a great marinade popular in Japanese cuisine, adding savory depth to meats like Grilled Pork Collar (page 97) or chicken breast. The main ingredient is *koji*, or *qú* in Chinese, which is fermented rice, and the rest is water and salt, usually, depending on the producer. Given that the rice is inoculated with the same bacteria that gives you soy sauce or miso paste, you could think of it as a thinner, chunkier miso, but made with rice rather than soybeans. You can also puree shio koji to add it as a secret (and totally vegan) boost of umami to just about anything. Some chefs will stock liquid shio koji, which is a pressed, liquid version, and keep it in their pantry to enhance vinaigrettes, marinades, and pickles. This product is pretty hyped in restaurant kitchens nowadays, but it's a simple and ages-old ingredient used not just in Japanese cuisine but around the world. Look for it in Asian markets, organic markets, or online.

SHIRO DASHI

An essential building block in Japanese cuisine, dashi can instantly boost a dish's umami and give it an oceany depth of flavor. But instead of making dashi the proper way, by soaking high-quality bonito flakes and kombu (see page 256), a lot of home cooks in Japan opt for granules of instant dashi bouillon, like the brand Ajinomoto's Hondashi soup stock base, for convenience. We fully support that, but if you can get your hands on Shiro Dashi, this liquid in a bottle is the crème de la crème of dashi and soy sauce, combined. It's a much more concentrated version of dashi than what you'd make at home, seasoned with white soy. We use a ton of it in our cooking. It doesn't overpower anything. You can't really pick it out among the bold flavors in, say, the Flies' Head (page 73), with all those chiles and garlic. It instead acts as a stealth flavor enhancer, adding a smoky, salty, almost

nostalgic flavor to everything it touches. We like the shiro dashi from the brand Yamaki Kappo, which comes in a glass bottle, but there's no shame in using a teaspoon or two of Hondashi or another type of instant dashi bouillon dissolved in a quarter-cup of water as a substitute.

SOY SAUCE

Home pantries should contain both light and dark soy sauces, which are used for different purposes. LIGHT: Light soy sauce is the typical "soy sauce" that you see in grocery stores across America—under brand names like Kikkoman (even though that's a Japanese type of soy sauce technically called shoyu) or La Choy (pretty sure this one has more additives like food coloring, and is made using less traditional processes). These are easily found in American supermarkets, but if you can get to an Asian market, look out for brands like Kimlan, or shop online at YunHai.shop to get other Taiwanese brands of soy sauce. It's an everyday seasoning like salt you use at home, and it's also used sparingly with some add-ons like garlic, white pepper, and sesame oil as a condiment, for example as a dip for dumplings. DARK: You're more likely to use dark soy sauce during the beginning stages of a long-simmered braise or stew, like Lu Rou Fan (page 151), or to add color or depth of flavor to a stir-fry. It's more concentrated and

slightly thicker in body, so it'll be saltier, and you'll want to take care so as to not over-season your food with it. Dark soy sauce can be found in any Asian supermarket.

TAIWANESE SOY PASTE

Also known as thick soy sauce, soy paste is an ingredient that's singular to Taiwanese cuisine. It's essentially a starch-thickened, diluted soy sauce with some sweetness and other flavor notes often added. So it makes a great dipping sauce or condiment for things like dumplings or the Beef Roll (page 188). Many home cooks also shake it into their stir-fries and braises, like in Three-Cup Chicken (page 145) to give a one-two punch of sweet and salty along with a little thickness. Given all that, this condiment is akin to oyster sauce in Cantonese cuisine or kecap manis in Indonesian cuisine, and both are apt substitutes if you can't find soy paste. But keep in mind that even brands of the same type of sauce will vary a lot in flavor and saltiness, so you always want to check and taste for seasoning levels. Thanks to e-tailers like Yun Hai, today it is much easier to access artisanal brands of soy paste. We love the Firewood Soy Paste from Yu Ding Xing.

A CHIVE GUIDE: Flat Chives & Budding Chives

We're kind of obsessed with green alliums at Win Son. We love getting our hands on ramps when they're in season during that short window in spring and adding them to sauces or fermenting them (page 46). Some of our favorite Taiwanese dishes are very allium-forward, like the Flies' Head (page 73) and the Pan-Fried Chive Pockets (page 176). But it's important to distinguish between the types of alliums. Flat chives (*jiu cai*) are a long and flat-leafed type of Chinese chive that's very fragrant, soft, and delicate, seen on the right in this image. This is what you want in your juicy chive pocket or sealed inside dumplings with pork or shrimp. Then there are the long, hollow-stemmed budding chives (*jiu cai hua*), which are famous for being stir-fried in dishes like flies' head because they retain some crispness after being tossed in a hot wok.

A Conversation with
Josh, Trigg, and Lisa Cheng Smith of Yun Hai
OUR FAVORITE TAIWANESE INGREDIENTS

LISA CHENG SMITH is a co-founder of Yun Hai, an e-commerce site that imports artisanal ingredients from Taiwan, like terra-cotta-aged soy sauces and cold-pressed sesame oils. She's become a friend and collaborator of ours. We hopped on a video call together in the summer of 2021 for this talk.

CATHY: What ingredients do you think best represent Taiwanese cuisine to you?

JOSH: For me, I guess chives. And I think basil. I don't know, when you ask the question that way, I think about early experiences in Taiwan as a kid and what I'd eat there. But then the adult me thinks I should talk about ingredients that are more consistent in Taiwanese dishes overall, and I really don't know too much about that. I guess sesame oil is something that's around a lot. Rice wine.

LISA: I think that question is really tough to answer for the same reason. There isn't any one ingredient that's like, only Taiwanese—they're pretty much present in Chinese or other Asian diasporic foods. But I definitely think there are some distinct combinations. Garlic, red chile— a not too spicy one—and rice vinegar, that all feels super familiar and is so present at so many meals in Taiwan. And cilantro and sesame oil, too. The aroma together feels super familiar. I wouldn't just say cilantro or just sesame oil, but that combo together.

I think textures, like sweet potato starch and taro starch and all these root-based starches that create this texture that's Q or QQ (Taiwanese parlance for "bouncy" or "springy")—that's important, too, because Taiwan is an island that grew no wheat, so all the starch they had grew from tropical roots, initially. And there's the type of sweet potato starch that's coarsely ground, which I haven't encountered anywhere else. It's about where these ingredients originate. The rice wine in Taiwan, it's different from the ones you'll find in China. The *tian mian jiang* (a sauce used to make zhajiangmian, page 115) is different in Taiwan, too. There's this interpretation of ingredients that are maybe Sichuanese or something else in origin, and for whatever reason it has evolved in Taiwan. So maybe it's sesame oil, cilantro, red chile, taro, and all these types of sauces and foods that are made on the island in their way.

JOSH: You said garlic, right?

LISA: Yes, and all the starches.

JOSH: Yeah, I don't know what I'm saying. Whatever Lisa's saying, that's what I'm saying.

TRIGG: I can speak to something else rather than specific ingredients, like an overall flavor profile, I would say Taiwan to me is subtle, clean, sweet flavors. When I think of Taiwan and my time there traveling with Josh's family I think of sweet Almond Milk Yulu (page 242) in the summer. There's a sweet tooth in Tainan, whether it's the sugared peanuts or sweet soy milk or almond milk yulu, and because that's where Josh and I spent a lot of time and it's where his family is based, those kinds of flavors are the ones I think of when I think of Taiwan. Even the squid soup has levels of sweetness to it.

LISA: What just came to mind when Trigg was just talking is also produce. Like bamboo—it's hard to get here, because really fresh, amazing bamboo is just hard to find. But if I think of the ba-wan [a Taiwanese dumpling with a clear rice starch wrapper filled with minced pork and bamboo], with pork and bamboo and rice starch, that to me has a quintessential flavor profile that's very Taiwan to me. And maybe with roots that go back further than just recent migration.

JOSH: Isn't sea cucumber really Taiwanese?

LISA: I was also going to say the seafood. All this stuff you can't get here but in Taiwan it's a daily thing, like, I'm going to sit by the seaside and have this amazing dish. And it's stuff that I can't get because it's impossible to import.

TRIGG: That's what I was trying to get at a little earlier, too. You see a lot of menu similarities when it comes to Taiwanese restaurants in America. You see a lot of different restaurants throughout New York doing what they're doing because at the end of the day, we're embracing the bounty of what's at the Greenmarket, or what's local and in season. What Lisa's bringing to the table with Yun Hai has expanded the whole situation. Like now, you're not relegated to just Kimlan soy paste anymore. You're getting more ingredients from Taiwan, and that's changing the game.

JOSH: You are. I hate to relate this back to karaoke, but it's like going to Taiwan to sing karaoke but you only know Western music. But of the Western songs they have on their karaoke lists it's only thirty songs, and it's like, Britney Spears and Backstreet Boys and you don't want to sing that shit, but then you have to because that's all they got.

LISA: I actually wanted to mention licorice root. I always put it in my five-spice powder and it always makes my soy-braised chicken taste more like Taiwan to me. There's also this dip of soy paste, licorice powder, and sugar, and it's served with fresh-cut tomatoes and you stir it up with chopsticks and dip the tomato in.

JOSH: I feel like I can taste it in my mouth as you're describing it.

LISA: It's kind of a taste of old-time Taiwan. Like *gu zao wei*, which means "old-fashioned Taiwanese flavor" in Mandarin.

JOSH: That's like wuyuzi, too [see page 117].

LISA: The bottarga is definitely old school.

JOSH: Lisa, when are you gonna open a freaking restaurant?

TRIGG: I will eat there all the time.

LISA: I will never open a restaurant.

TRIGG: Smart.

CHAPTER 1
SNACKS AND APPETIZERS

MARINATED CUKES

Serves 4 to 6

INGREDIENTS

1½ pounds (680 g) medium cucumbers (about 3)

2 cloves garlic, minced

2 teaspoons kosher salt, plus more as needed

1½ teaspoons toasted sesame oil, plus more as needed

½ teaspoon MSG (optional)

Fresh cilantro leaves with tender stems

Store-bought fried shallots

About ½ ounce (14 g) wuyuzi or Taiwanese cured mullet roe, finely grated (optional)

WE COMPARE THESE CUKES TO POTATO CHIPS: IF THEY'RE THERE IN FRONT OF YOU, YOU CAN'T STOP EATING THEM. We were fans of Nan Xiang Xiao Long Bao, a great soup dumpling spot in Flushing, Queens, and we ate there a lot when we were coming up with the concept for Win Son. This is an ode to their simple cucumber and cilantro salad. We sprinkle ours with fried shallots for some crunch. As an additional option, top it off with a small pile of *wuyuzi*—shaved puffs of cured mullet roe, known in Italian as *bottarga* and enjoyed in Taiwan, too (see page 117). It's highly recommended for some extra savory ocean flavor, especially if you're trying to be fancy.

Peel the cucumbers and slice crosswise into 2½-inch-thick (6 cm) pieces. Cut the pieces lengthwise into quarters. Remove and discard the seeds.

Place the cucumbers in a sieve and toss with the garlic, salt, sesame oil, and MSG, if using. Set the sieve over a bowl and chill, tossing occasionally, for at least 1 hour and up to 2 days. Taste the cucumbers before serving; they might need a bit more salt or sesame oil to bring them back to life.

Drain the liquid from the cucumbers and transfer to a serving dish. Sprinkle with a handful each of cilantro and fried shallots, finish with the grated wuyuzi, if using, and serve immediately.

ROASTED PEANUTS
WITH CHINESE FIVE-SPICE AND SICHUAN PEPPERCORN

Makes about 1 quart (960 ml); serves about 12

HOT NUTS ARE THE PERFECT SNACK TO GET YOUR PALATE READY FOR A GREAT MULTI-COURSE MEAL. We have been serving five-spice peanuts since some of our earliest days at Win Son—actually, since before we opened up. For a soft-opening launch party, we collaborated with our good friend Jeff Fann, who owns Yumpling, a Taiwanese food truck and now restaurant in Long Island City, Queens, and Cathy Erway, our cookbook guru, on a special menu for friends and family. Warm, hot, and slippery five-spice peanuts were the amuse-bouche that went out to everyone's table to kick things off. We've spiced up our nuts a bit more since then, adding garlic and scallions and a cacophony of dried spices that'll tickle your nose.

INGREDIENTS

1 teaspoon green cardamom pods, skins removed

1 teaspoon Sichuan peppercorns

1 star anise

1 pound (455 g) raw unsalted peanuts (see Note)

3 tablespoons neutral oil, such as soybean

1 teaspoon Chinese five-spice powder

1 teaspoon cayenne pepper

1 teaspoon salt

½ teaspoon MSG

3 cloves garlic, minced

4 scallions, finely chopped

2 tablespoons Chinese black vinegar

2 tablespoons shiro dashi

1 teaspoon toasted sesame oil

Lime wedges, for spritzing

Preheat the oven to 325°F (165°C). In a dry pan over medium heat, toast the cardamom, Sichuan peppercorns, and star anise, shaking the pan frequently, for 1 to 2 minutes, until very fragrant. Transfer to a bowl. Let cool a few moments, then transfer to a spice grinder or food processor and pulse several times, until the mixture is a fine dust.

On a sheet pan, toss the nuts with the oil to coat evenly and place in the oven. Check after 20 minutes of roasting, and remove from the oven if the nuts are sizzling and gently browned; if they're not quite there yet, shake the pan and return to the oven for 1 to 2 minutes longer. Be sure to remove them from the oven as soon as they appear golden brown and before they start turning too dark.

Immediately after removing the peanuts from the oven (do not let them cool), transfer to a bowl and toss with the ground toasted spice mixture, the Chinese five-spice powder, cayenne pepper, salt, and MSG. While still hot, add the minced garlic and scallions and stir until fragrant. Finally, stir in the black vinegar, shiro dashi, and sesame oil. Serve in small bowls along with a lime wedge for spritzing. Keep the nuts in a jar or airtight container in the refrigerator for up to a week.

NOTE: This recipe would work with other types of nuts, such as almonds or cashews instead of peanuts. For best results, go with all one type of nut, so they cook evenly.

BUTTER-FRIED PEANUTS

Makes 1 pint (375 g)

INGREDIENTS

1 pint (375 g) roasted unsalted peanuts

½ cup (1 stick) unsalted butter

1 tablespoon neutral cooking oil, such as soybean

IN TAIWAN, A SPRINKLE OF PEANUT POWDER CAN BE FOUND ON EVERYTHING FROM PORK BELLY BAO TO A PILE OF SAUTÉED GREENS. It's often blended with a little sugar, providing that finishing dust of texture and savory-sweet something extra. At Win Son, we like to cook chopped peanuts in butter, stirring until it froths up, which transforms each piece into a super-crunchy, tasty granule of goodness. It's really easy to do at home, and makes for a nice garnish for just about anything—including the Fried Milk Dough Sundae with Peanuts and Cilantro-Mint Sauce (page 227).

NOTE: *While we typically use these crushed peanuts as a buttery and crunchy topping, you could also leave them whole or substitute walnuts, pistachios, or pine nuts.*

Place the nuts in a food processor and gently pulse a few times until they are evenly chopped to about the size and texture of small pebbles, or Grape-Nuts.

Line a sheet pan with 3 layers of paper towels. Position a strainer over a mixing bowl and set aside.

In a medium saucepan, add the butter and oil and melt over medium-high heat. Add the chopped nuts and stir constantly. The butter will start to foam and the milk solids will caramelize as the peanuts fry. It will be super fragrant. Keep stirring until they are just turning golden brown, 3 to 4 minutes. Pour the mixture into the strainer to drain, then transfer the nuts to the paper towels and let cool for several minutes. Store in a sealed container in the refrigerator for up to 3 weeks.

LISA'S TEA EGGS
Makes 6

INGREDIENTS

FOR THE CHINESE FIVE-SPICE SACHET:

1 bay leaf

1 star anise

½ teaspoon fennel or anise seeds

¼ cassia bark stick or ½ cinnamon stick

½ teaspoon Sichuan peppercorns

½ teaspoon ground white pepper (optional)

Muslin bags or cheesecloth (optional)

(Or, substitute all of the above with 1 tablespoon Chinese five-spice powder.)

FOR THE EGGS:

¼ cup (2 ounces/50 g) Chinese rock sugar or if unavailable, demerara or light brown sugar

4 cups (960 ml) hot water

2 heaping tablespoons (3 ounces) or 4 teabags strong oolong tea, such as tieguanyin

6 eggs

1 tablespoon salt

¼ cup (60 ml) soy sauce

LISA CHENG SMITH IS THE COFOUNDER OF YUN HAI, AN E-COMMERCE BUSINESS THAT IMPORTS REALLY FANTASTIC FOOD PRODUCTS FROM TAIWAN TO THE US. (See our conversation on Taiwanese ingredients, page 32.) She's also a great home cook, and we hounded her to contribute a recipe of her own for this book. She didn't disappoint. A little background on tea eggs: These are eggs that have been boiled and soaked in a steeping liquid made from tea, spices, and soy sauce. After boiling but before steeping, the shells are crackled all over, giving the eggs a marbled appearance after their soak. Lisa says they always remind her of the way a celadon teacup ages as it's exposed over and over again to tea—the glaze on the delicate porcelain cracks with each use, taking on the color of the tea over time.

Tea eggs are ubiquitous snacks throughout Taiwan, and they're pretty easy to make at home. Lisa's version is a bit different than the kind you'll find in just about every grocery and convenience store in Taiwan, though; the eggs are soft-boiled to result in more custardy yolks. If you don't prefer that, just boil the eggs a bit longer. This recipe also doesn't have as much soy sauce as many recipes might, in order to allow the flavor of the oolong tea to shine. Dark soy sauce is often employed in tea eggs to give them more color, but in this method, caramelized sugar is used, lending color, fragrance, and a bonus luster on the eggshells.

Add the peeled eggs to noodle soups or ramen, or just eat them plain as a snack, as is done daily in Taiwan.

MAKE THE CHINESE FIVE-SPICE SACHET: In a small bowl, combine the bay leaf, star anise, fennel seeds, cassia, peppercorns, and white pepper (or use pre-made five-spice powder). For easy removal, secure the five-spice mixture in a cheesecloth or muslin bag.

MAKE THE EGGS: In a small saucepan, pour in the rock sugar and ¼ cup (60 ml) water and heat over medium-low. Stir frequently until dissolved. Once the sugar has dissolved, let the sugar syrup bubble until it becomes a classic golden caramel color, stirring constantly, about 5 minutes. (The darker the caramel, the darker the color of the eggs will be.) It's easy to burn, so watch it closely.

As soon as the sugar reaches your desired color, turn off the heat. Partially cover the pan with a lid while you slowly pour the hot water in to stop the caramelization. Stir to combine. Add the five-spice sachet to the caramelized liquid (or add the loose five-spice powder). Simmer covered for 15 minutes. Add the tea in a muslin bag or tea ball (or loose) and simmer for 15 more minutes.

Meanwhile, clean the eggs well in room temperature water, gently rubbing their shells to remove any debris. (Because we'll be steeping the eggs in their shells, it's very important to get them clean, especially if you are using farm fresh eggs.)

Tap the rounded (as opposed to tapered) end of each egg with the back of a spoon to make a small crack. This releases air from within the egg, which prevents breakage when cooked in boiling water.

Remove the five-spice sachet and discard. Strain the steeping liquid and discard the tea. Stir in the salt and soy sauce. Gently spoon the eggs in. Bring back up to a boil.

For a custardy yolk, simmer for 6 minutes. This would normally result in very runny yolks, but since we're soaking the eggs in warm liquid after this step, they will firm up a bit more to achieve that custardy texture. (Simmer for 30 seconds to a minute longer if you aren't a fan of soft yolks.) Using a slotted spoon or a skimmer, remove the eggs and put them into a cold water bath. Remove the steeping liquid from the heat but cover the pot to keep it warm.

Once the eggs are just cool to the touch on the outside, tap them all over with the back of a spoon to crackle the shells. Don't be afraid to crack them significantly. We want to create places for the steeping liquid to enter and bathe the eggs.

Return the eggs to the steeping liquid and cover. Let sit for 24 hours. (You can transfer to a fridge after the liquid has cooled completely if you like.)

Once the eggs are done, they should be richly colored. Depending on the tea you used and how much you cracked your eggs, the marbleization of the peeled egg may be light or dark, but it should have captured the fragrance of tea, along with the subtle sweet taste of the caramelized sugar and the savoriness of the soy sauce. The yolks should be custardy on the outside with a runny center and slightly greenish-brown edges, having absorbed some of the tea essence. You can store the tea steeping liquid in the freezer to make your next batch. Store the cooked eggs in an airtight container in the refrigerator for up to one week. Peel just before eating.

MARINATED EGGS

Makes 12

INGREDIENTS

12 eggs

1/4 cup (60 ml) light soy sauce

1/4 cup (60 ml) shiro dashi

1/4 cup (60 ml) mirin

2 tablespoons rice wine

Chili Oil (page 258, optional)

IT'S ALWAYS GOOD TO HAVE SOME SOY-SAUCE-MARINATED SIX-MINUTE EGGS AROUND YOUR KITCHEN. From these, you can create filling and delicious dishes with little more than some leftover rice. These tan-colored eggs are often served as a side to another protein, floating beside a piece of meat in a noodle soup, or resting beside a heap of minced pork in our Lu Rou Fan (page 151). But they can easily take the starring role in simple meals. Here's our favorite way to prepare them.

Prepare an ice bath in a large bowl.

In a pot, bring 3 quarts (2.8 L) of water to a rippling boil. Using a slotted spoon or spider, carefully lower and submerge the eggs in the boiling water and leave them in there for 6 minutes exactly.

Remove the eggs from the boiling water and immediately submerge them into an ice bath. Leave them in there for 15 to 20 minutes, until the eggs have completely cooled down. Peel the eggs carefully (it's easier if you peel them right in the water that they're cooled down in) and place in a baking tray or a dish that fits them nicely in one layer.

In a bowl, combine the soy sauce, shiro dashi, mirin, and rice wine. Drape the eggs with one layer of paper towels to cover and pour the marinade over the top, being sure to soak the paper towels thoroughly. Remove as much air from between the eggs and the towels as possible, pressing the towels down so they cling to the eggs. Refrigerate for 1 hour, pausing for 30 minutes to turn the eggs over. Strain the liquid and discard. Top with Chili Oil, if using. These eggs will have the best texture when eaten on the day they are prepared, but they can be kept refrigerated in an airtight container for up to one week.

CHARRED FERMENTED SCALLIONS OR RAMPS

Makes 1 pint (200 g)

WE LOVE ALL KINDS OF ONIONS—THEY'RE MAYBE OUR FAVORITE INGREDIENT—BUT IF YOU HAVE SCALLIONS OR RAMPS ON HAND, THIS IS ONE WAY TO REALLY ENJOY THEM. A ramp is just a very nuanced onion that tastes a little garlicky. People overhype them during their short season, but they *are* really good. We like to get them in mid-to-late-April, when you can still find bulbs that are skinny and delicate, so that they don't require much additional cooking. If they're big fat bulbs, the leaves and the bulbs cook unevenly, and the pickling process becomes a little more complicated.

We wanted to preserve the younger ramps we were getting in right as soft-shell crabs were coming in season. So, we fried soft-shell crabs, put them on a milk bun (page 185), and topped them with tofu mayo and fermented ramps. The doubanjiang and rice vinegar combo is so good, though, that we kept using it to ferment charred scallions to pair with the soft-shell crabs and all kinds of dishes, like Lu Rou Fan (page 151), too.

INGREDIENTS

1 tablespoon white toasted sesame seeds

1 tablespoon red chile flakes, such as gochugaru or Sichuan chile flakes

1 teaspoon *doubanjiang* (aka chili bean sauce; can be found in Asian markets)

¼ cup (60 ml) rice vinegar

2 teaspoons salt

8 ounces (225 g) scallions or ramps (about 2 bunches)

1 tablespoon neutral oil, such as soybean, for pan-frying

In a sanitized glass or ceramic dish with a flat bottom (such as a small casserole or baking dish), combine the sesame seeds, gochugaru, doubanjiang, rice vinegar, and salt with ¼ cup (60 ml) water. Stir until well incorporated.

Trim the root ends from the scallions and any wilted or yellowing tips on the shoots. Chop the scallions or ramps into 4- to 6-inch (10 to 15 cm) batons.

Heat a large wok or cast-iron pan with the neutral oil until it's searing hot. Add the white parts of the scallions or ramps, spreading them so each one has direct contact with the pan. (Work in batches if they do not all fit.) Don't move the scallions or ramps for 30 seconds to a minute, or until the bottoms are well-charred. Turn them with tongs and don't move, to sear another side. Repeat until all sides are well-charred and remove them from the pan. Add the green batons to the pan and char on both sides as well. (This will take much less time than the white batons.) Scallions are sturdier and more fibrous than delicate ramps, so snip the charred scallion pieces into manageable ¾-inch (2 cm) batons. Transfer all the charred scallions to the dish with the marinating mixture. Toss to coat thoroughly, then press down a piece of plastic wrap over the entire surface of the scallions to submerge them in the liquid entirely, squeezing out any air pockets that might form in between.

Cover the dish with a cloth towel and let sit at room temperature for 2 to 3 days, until the mixture appears slightly bubbly and the taste is pleasantly sour. Then refrigerate and enjoy for up to 2 months.

47

FERMENTED CHINESE BROCCOLI

Makes about 1 quart (650 g)

THE TAIWANESE MINCED PORK MEAT SAUCE LU ROU FAN (PAGE 151) WAS ALWAYS PART OF THE MENU AT WIN SON, BUT WHEN IT LANDED IN THE DINING ROOM IN THE FIRST FEW MONTHS, PEOPLE DIDN'T SEEM TO GET IT. Was it an appetizer? A share-worthy entrée? In Taiwan, only a very small ladle of this meat sauce is spread over a bowl of white rice, either as a small meal or snack, or as part of a larger, multicourse meal. We didn't want to compromise the integrity of the dish, but we decided to round it out with more flavors and vegetables to complement it and increase the portion size to an entrée. So we added a marinated egg on the side and cut some of the richness of the pork belly with black vinegar. We were trying to be sensitive to how the food would land in our neighborhood.

The one thing that was missing was a pickle. Pickled daikon is a common accompaniment, but Trigg had been roasting Chinese broccoli (*jiè lán*, a leafy brassica variety) and dousing it in chile vinaigrette as a vegetable side dish, and one of our line cooks, Matt Valerio, thought it would be cool to ferment the roasted Chinese broccoli. We started grilling the broccoli in Trigg's backyard, then tossed it with salt and spiked it with some ginger. Turns out, it's a great pickle and now a staple ingredient at Win Son. It can be enjoyed alongside any hearty entrée, not just lu rou fan, or it can help open your palate to a multicourse meal.

4 bunches Chinese broccoli

¼ cup (60 ml) neutral oil, such as soybean

1½ teaspoons salt

½ teaspoon MSG

1 head garlic

4-inch (10 cm) piece fresh ginger

½ cup (120 ml) House Chili Oil (page 258) or your favorite chili oil, such as Lao Gan Ma Spicy Chili Crisp

1 tablespoon Chinese black vinegar

1 tablespoon light soy sauce

1 tablespoon mirin

Trim the stems of the Chinese broccoli, but otherwise keep the pieces whole and intact. Pat them dry well, then toss in a bowl with the oil, ½ teaspoon salt, and the MSG.

Heat an outdoor grill or just a cast-iron griddle until very hot. Place the Chinese broccoli bunches down and don't move them for 2 minutes. Once the bottoms are nicely charred, move them around and flip them over to lightly char the other sides. Do this a couple more times to char the Chinese broccoli all over, being careful not to burn too much of it, so that you have a good mix of pieces that are totally green along with some that are black. Remove from the heat and let cool for a few minutes. Chop the broccoli bunches along their length into segments about 2 inches (5 cm) long.

Peel and trim the garlic cloves and the ginger, and cut the ginger into coarse slices. Transfer to a food processor and pulse several times, stopping to scrape down the sides, until they're well chopped. (You can also mince both by hand instead.)

In a large bowl, toss the charred Chinese broccoli with the minced garlic and ginger, chili oil, black vinegar, soy sauce, mirin, and the remaining teaspoon salt. Using tongs or chopsticks, stuff the Chinese broccoli into a large sterilized 1-quart (950 ml) mason jar, pressing the pieces down to remove any air pockets. Pour in the remaining liquid mixture that the Chinese broccoli was tossed with. Cover the top with a piece of parchment paper and if necessary, a heavy object to weigh it down and ensure the liquid comes to the top. Drape a clean kitchen towel over the jar and keep away from sunlight at room temperature for 3 days, checking each day to make sure the greens are still submerged in liquid, pressing them down with clean tongs or chopsticks if need be. After 3 days, they should be extra-pungent in flavor. Refrigerate in an airtight container for up to 2 months.

SNACKS AND APPETIZERS

O A JIAN
Serves 1

O A JIAN IS USUALLY TRANSLATED TO ENGLISH AS "OYSTER OMELET" OR "OYSTER PAN-CAKE." It looks more like an omelet, but we would argue that pancake is a more apt name, as it's mostly the sweet potato starch slurry that binds the oysters, egg, bean sprouts, and greens that are tossed in the pan. It's a savory pancake, though, and it's smothered with a sweet and tangy Sea Mountain Sauce (page 260).

In Tainan, the stall we go to makes them with a ton of fresh oysters. They're a dark and meaty local variety, and they sit, pre-shucked, in a pile over an ice block right next to the large wok-burner skillet. Taking notes from our good friend Eric Sze, owner of 886, a Taiwanese restaurant in New York, we eventually added shrimp to our o a jian at Win Son, in addition to the oysters. They cook quickly and gently like oysters, and add more variety to the mix.

But aside from that, we haven't strayed from the classic formula. The texture of o a jian is incredibly gooey, wet, and messy—pretty different from a Western-style pancake or omelet. The eggs, oysters, and the sweet potato starch (which solidifies into a clear gel in the pan) share a similar, jiggly texture. In Tainan, you pretty much slurp this up from your plate, so we didn't change that texture one bit. There's a description of this texture in Taiwan that goes by the name of Q or QQ. A tapioca ball is one example of that bouncy, chewy texture. O a jian is another.

NOTE: *If you don't like the chewier texture, you can whip the starch into the eggs to make the texture fluffier and more uniform, but if you like the stretchy side of Q, keep the ingredients separate so you can slurp the o a jian up like a wet, soggy noodle.*

INGREDIENTS

2 eggs

2 tablespoons shiro dashi

1 tablespoon toasted sesame oil

2 tablespoons fine sweet potato starch

3 tablespoons neutral oil, such as soybean

4 shrimp, peeled, deveined, and sliced in half lengthwise

4 oysters, shucked

Sea Mountain Sauce (page 260) or Charred Scallion Sauce (page 254; optional)

Thai basil leaves, chopped scallions, and crispy shallots, for garnish (optional)

In a medium bowl, whisk the eggs with the shiro dashi and sesame oil.

Put the sweet potato starch into a small bowl. Whisk in 2 tablespoons water. Make sure you give it a stir just before making the omelet, to ensure the starch doesn't settle on the bottom.

Heat the neutral oil in a nonstick pan over medium-high heat until hot. Add the shrimp and cook for about 10 seconds, stirring. Pour the egg mixture into the pan. Tilt the pan to spread the egg all around, and once the edges of the egg start to set, quickly pour the sweet potato starch and water slurry all around the egg. Arrange the oysters on top.

Loosen the edges of the omelet all around with a silicone spatula and shake the omelet around in the pan. Use a large spatula (or two) to flip the entire omelet over, or, if you're confident enough, give the pan a quick jerk to flip it over without help. (It's OK if it doesn't land perfectly.) Cook the opposite side for just a few more seconds to cook the oyster and crisp the edges a little. Transfer immediately to a serving plate. Top with your choice of sauce and preferred garnishes, if using.

SHRIMP CAKES

Makes 6

WE CAME UP WITH THIS SAVORY SHRIMP CAKE WHEN WE WERE CREATING OUR TWIST ON THE TAIWANESE NIGHT MARKET FAVORITE KNOWN AS THE NUTRITIOUS SANDWICH (PAGE 182). Classic versions of the sandwich in Taiwan typically feature a fried-dough sandwich bun encasing ham, tomato, cucumber, and mayo, which is delicious and crushable as is. But our version evolved to include a seared slab of this shrimp cake, which is a lot simpler than it might sound. As you'll see from the ingredients, it's essentially fresh shrimp, folded with starch, eggs, and a few seasonings, molded together and pan-fried (sort of like the Turnip Cake, page 54). Make a big batch of this to freeze for later uses, wrapping up individual patties of the shrimp cake in plastic before storing. It's delicious stuffed inside a steamed bun, scallion pancake, or milk bun, or on its own with a dab of oyster sauce or Taiwanese soy paste.

INGREDIENTS

1 pound (455 g) frozen shrimp, any size

⅜ cup (45 g) fine sweet potato starch

¼ cup (60 ml) shiro dashi

1 egg, beaten

3 to 4 tablespoons neutral oil, such as soybean

If the shrimp are already peeled and deveined, then thaw only halfway; they will be slightly easier to grind. If the shrimp need to be peeled, thaw them completely and then devein them.

Working in batches, if need be, depending on the size of your food processor, place the shrimp, starch, shiro dashi, and egg in a food processor and pulse several times, stopping to scrape down the sides, until a nice paste forms. Alternately, you can mince the shrimp by hand and mix it with the rest of the ingredients in a bowl.

Grease a sheet pan with a tablespoon or two of the oil. Form the shrimp mixture into 6 tight, round patties, 3 to 4 inches (7.5 to 10 cm) in diameter, shaping them by hand as you would a hamburger. Place them on the oiled sheet.

Heat a fry pan with a couple tablespoons of oil over medium-high heat. Working in batches, if need be, place the patties in the pan with room in between each and don't move them for 2 minutes, or until they're gently browned across the bottom. Reduce the heat to medium. Carefully flip each patty and brown the opposite sides. The patties should also turn from translucent to opaque as they're cooking. Once they're cooked through and browned on both sides, remove from the heat and serve, or cool and freeze as described in the headnote.

TURNIP CAKES

Makes 1 (8½ by 4¼-inch / 21.5 by 11-cm) loaf; serves 8

TURNIP CAKES ARE BELOVED IN TAIWAN, AS WELL AS THROUGHOUT MUCH OF CHINA. In Taiwan, they're a common breakfast food, often found in the breakfast cafes along with Fresh Soy Milk (page 218) and breakfast goodies like the Dan Bing (page 206). We serve them at Win Son Bakery crisped up and golden brown so that they almost resemble neat little rectangles of hash browns. Ours are also studded with thick-cut bacon morsels for a savory edge. We love to dunk these into Sweet Soy Dipping Sauce (page 261).

6 shiitake mushrooms, dried or fresh, chopped

2 tablespoons dried baby shrimp (optional)

1½ pounds (680 g) daikon radish, grated (about 2 medium radishes; makes about 4 cups/440 g)

2 teaspoons salt

4 ounces (115 g) bacon, chopped (about 4 thick-cut strips; optional)

2 scallions, chopped

1 large clove garlic, minced

1½ cups (220 g) rice flour (NOTE: You cannot substitute with glutinous rice flour.)

Neutral oil, such as soybean, as needed

If using dried shiitakes, cover the whole mushrooms with 2 cups (480 ml) water and let sit for at least 40 minutes or up to overnight, until softened. Squeeze out and retain 1 cup (240 ml) of the liquid; strain the shiitakes. Remove the tough stems before chopping. If using dried baby shrimp, cover in 1 cup (240 ml) water and let sit for 20 minutes, or until softened.

In a large bowl, toss the grated daikon with the salt and let sit for 30 minutes. Using cheesecloth or a clean cloth towel, wring out the daikon, reserving 1 cup (240 ml) of the liquid.

Heat a medium saucepan over medium-high heat and add the bacon, if using. Cook over low heat, stirring occasionally, until browned and crispy throughout, about 4 minutes. If not using bacon, add 2 tablespoons neutral oil. In the same pan, cook the shiitakes, scallions, garlic, and strained baby shrimp, if using, over low heat, stirring occasionally, until the scallions are well-softened, about 4 minutes.

Whisk together the 1 cup (240 ml) reserved daikon liquid and 1 cup (240 ml) reserved mushroom liquid (or 1 cup/240 ml water, if using fresh shiitakes) with the rice flour. Stir the squeezed-out grated daikon into the pan with the shiitakes, etc. Cook over medium-high heat,

stirring, for 2 to 3 minutes. Add the rice flour slurry and stir well to combine; the mixture will be thick.

Turn the mixture out into a well-oiled loaf pan. Place the pan in a steamer or in a large wok with a lid, so that it fits inside without losing any steam. (If needed, use foil to make sure there are no gaps where the steam can escape.) Add several inches of water to the bottom of the steamer or wok, bring to a boil, and cover. Steam the loaf for 1 hour, making sure to check that there is always water boiling on the bottom and adding more if needed.

Remove the foil, if using, and let cool for at least 15 minutes. Turn the cake onto a cutting board and slice into 1-inch (2.5-cm) slabs. Heat a fry pan with 2 tablespoons neutral oil and pan-fry the slices for 2 to 3 minutes per side, until golden brown. (Work in batches to allow room for the slices to brown thoroughly on each side.) Add additional oil as necessary to avoid sticking or if the pan seems dry. Turnip cakes can keep for up to 1 week refrigerated; wrap the loaf with plastic wrap to retain moisture.

NOTE: Making turnip cake at home is a bit of a chore, so it's great for special occasions like a holiday spread.

A Conversation with
Josh, Trigg, Cathy, Eric Sze, Rich Ho, and Calvin Eng
WHAT IS TAIWANESE FOOD IN AMERICA?

ERIC SZE and RICH HO are fellow Taiwanese American restauranteurs who've been friends with Josh and Trigg since opening their respective restaurants, 886 and Ho Foods, in New York City's East Village in 2018. CALVIN ENG is a former chef de cuisine of Win Son who went on to open his own Cantonese restaurant, Bonnie's, in Brooklyn, named after his mother. We all sat down for dinner one night in February 2020 at Main Street Imperial (Bei Gan), a Taiwanese restaurant in Flushing, Queens. Afterward, we went to sing karaoke.

TRIGG [to Josh, who is speaking with the waiter, menu in hand]: You start ordering and we'll start shouting at you.

ERIC: Xianggan rou si [slivered pork stir-fry]!

RICH: Is spicy OK?

ERIC: Do you have *si gua* tofu [braised tofu with loofah squash]?

TRIGG: Did you get the *o a mi sua* [thin noodles with intestine]?

ERIC: O a mi sua!

RICH: Any seafood?

CATHY: *San bei you yu* [Three-Cup Squid]?

TRIGG: Sick.

RICH: What's that Taiwanese noodle dish, the fried noodle?

ERIC: Chou mifen?

JOSH: You guys want Three-Cup Chicken?

CALVIN: What's that on the picture [pointing to a poster of menu items written in Chinese characters and images]? My eyes are bad but it looks like pineapple pizza.

JOSH: OK, they're gonna give it to us.

ERIC: How about the preserved radish omelet?

ERIC: So she's suggesting we get the tea-braised pork ribs.

JOSH: What do we have for *cai* [vegetables]?

CATHY: We have the si gua tofu and I guess that's it. Should we get a green vegetable?

FROM LEFT TO RIGHT: Eric singing karaoke at the Bushwick bar Heaven or Las Vegas; clams and basil at Main Street Imperial in Flushing; Josh, Cathy, Trigg, Eric, Calvin, and Rich at Main Street Imperial; reaching for san bei ji (three-cup chicken); Josh at Heaven or Las Vegas.

TRIGG: Water spinach.

JOSH: She said it's cool now, she said we have everything we need.

CALVIN: I love how you guys say *you mei you* [Mandarin for "Do you have or not have?"].

TRIGG: It's one of those phrases that apply to any words after it. I feel like I can communicate so much with that.

RICH: There's no shame in it. It's exactly what you want to say, and no more.

CATHY: What about Flies' Head, did we get that? [To Josh] Isn't that your favorite dish?

JOSH: That's my favorite dish of all time. The first time I had it I was like, *What the fuck is this?* My dad would always order it here. He'd order it and we'd eat it, and we just, like, would not talk. And then we'd start talking again after it was done. With Trigg, we would always order when we came here, too.

CALVIN: That's funny you said you guys stopped talking but then you'd continue to talk afterwards.

JOSH: My dad doesn't talk much anyway.

ERIC: All my dad does is talk.

TRIGG: When my dad talks to me, you know, he's very quiet.

CATHY: What about food? Did your dad like to talk about food?

TRIGG: Eh . . .

RICH: My dad would talk *only* about food. Very opinionated. For better or for worse.

ERIC: I feel like Taiwanese dads, or Asian dads in general, for them it's like, food is the flex. And now there's kind of this transition into knowing red wine, for some reason. It's a little weird, but like, I'll see my dad hanging out with his friends schmoozing over red wine. Growing up, my dad would be going to joints and pigging out but now it's like, *I've got five bottles,* and I'm like, *Man . . . it's not you!* It's like, *Stop hanging out with these people!*

[Food starts coming to the table, and there is a scramble to find enough space to put it all down.]

CALVIN: [pointing at the *rou si doufu gan,* or slivered pork and dry tofu stir-fry]: That's my favorite Taiwanese dish. My mom would teach me how to make it, and she would slice the pork really thin.

CATHY: [to Rich] Do you have a favorite Taiwanese food? Is it beef noodle soup, because you have a beef noodle soup shop?

RICH: No. No!

ERIC: I know what mine is, it's the Hakka steamed cups of starch.

TRIGG: Oh, are they weirdly called rice cakes sometimes?

ERIC: No, that's migao. These are wa gui— let's see if I can find it . . .

TRIGG: Yeah, we had this in Tainan.

ERIC: It's like a blob of steamed starch.

RICH: It's a blob?

TRIGG: There's a sweet sauce on the side, like you put it on?

ERIC: Yes, yes, because you break it, then you pour it in.

RICH: It's like a turnip cake.

TRIGG: Here you go, Rich . . . that's the *o a mi sua* [intestine noodle].

CATHY: What do you guys think is the most Taiwanese thing here?

JOSH: Trigg? I think Trigg is.

RICH: Maybe the o a mi sua.

CATHY: What makes something Taiwanese? Is it the fact that it's only found in Taiwan? Does that help?

ERIC: I think that helps.

TRIGG: Yeah, I mean like, the zhajiangmian [noodles with fried bean sauce, page 115] we have at Win Son—it was something that me and Josh would see in Taiwan a lot but it's almost more iconic in Korea and China.

ERIC: Zhajiangmian is one of the dishes that kind of achieved stardom in each region that it went to. Like it achieved stardom when it was in Shandong, and then it was so close to Korea, they're, like, right next to each other. But then Beijing is also, like, the most famous place for zhajiangmian, but then Taiwan is also famous for zhajiangmian, and Korea is also famous for zhajiangmian . . . I don't know. I guess the Cantonese aren't really famous for zhajiangmian. But that's just their cuisine.

CATHY: In Taiwan a lot of people think the *xiao long bao,* or soup dumplings, are better than in Shanghai, even though that's where they were from.

ERIC: The funny thing is that the most famous restaurant in Taiwan is Din Tai Fung, and nothing on the menu is Taiwanese. Like, absolutely nothing. I was thinking about this the other day when I was in the shower. I was going through a mental checklist and was like, goddamn, they have Sichuan, Beijing, Shanghai, some Japanese dishes, but no Taiwanese dishes.

RICH: I don't know if you guys feel this way but for us growing up here and being Taiwanese, whenever we went to a Taiwanese restaurant here, we thought all those dishes were Taiwanese.

JOSH: Yeah. Except for dim sum. That's obviously not Taiwanese.

TRIGG: That's kind of how I feel eating with Josh at Taiwanese restaurants sometimes. It's like, OK, this is a Taiwanese restaurant, so everything's Taiwanese . . . but then there's all these places in China where the food really originated, before it got to Taiwan.

RICH: Yeah, so I think in my experience, growing up in Los Angeles, Taiwanese American kids grew up thinking that certain foods were Taiwanese—but that's mostly because there were, like, three Taiwanese restaurants around us, and that's what they serve.

JOSH: And those are the same kids that come to your restaurant now and are all like, *Hey, that's not Taiwanese!* [laughs]

RICH: [laughs] Well, I don't know where the kids all come from but, yeah, that happens sometimes.

CHAPTER 2

VEGETABLES

FRIED EGGPLANT WITH BLACK VINEGAR, LABNEH AND SPICED CASHEWS

Serves 3 to 4

WE REALLY LOVE THE EGGPLANT YOU FIND IN MARKETPLACES IN TAIWAN. It's usually steamed or fried, then marinated and served cold along with dishes like tricolor steamed egg, marinated baby squids, pig ear salad, and cucumbers. It's a *xiao che*, or "small eats"—a chilled dish you can grab and eat just by itself or while waiting for hot stuff. Trigg could eat bowls of it, which is why he wanted to find a way to feature it on our menu—he decided to make it the base for a hearty vegetarian dish that is served hot. Labneh makes a creamy sauce, a liberal amount of cilantro adds its distinct flavor, and a strong black vinegar gastrique literally glues the whole dish together, keeping the spiced cashews in place. While the labneh isn't very Taiwanese, it pairs well with the sweet-and-sour gastrique, and Taiwan is no stranger to yogurt. The cashews are coated with cayenne pepper and Chinese five-spice powder.

4 large Chinese eggplants (see Note)

4 tablespoons salt, plus more for serving

1 cup (200 g) sugar

1 cup (240 ml) Chinese black vinegar

1 cup (140 g) raw cashews, chopped into large chunks

1 teaespoon Chinese five-spice powder, plus more for serving

1 teaspoon cayenne pepper, plus more for serving

½ cup (120 ml) labneh or full-fat Greek yogurt

Neutral oil, such as soybean, for frying (about 4 cups/960 ml)

2 cups (480 ml) rice flour, for dredging

Pinches of MSG (optional, but strongly recommended)

1 bunch fresh cilantro, leaves and stems finely chopped

NOTE: Chinese eggplant is the long purple emoji eggplant. This recipe involves letting the eggplant sit overnight to extract as much liquid as possible. Plan ahead.

Lob the ends off of each eggplant. Cut each eggplant crosswise into thirds if they're short or fourths if they're long, and then quarter each section lengthwise. Put in a bowl and toss with 3 tablespoons of the salt to draw out the bitterness and the water from the eggplant. This also enables the vegetable to fry more quickly and become crispier. Let sit overnight, or for at least 4 hours.

Sprinkle the sugar over the bottom of a large pot and set over medium-high heat. When the sugar begins to melt, stir constantly with a heatproof spatula so the caramel develops evenly. When the caramel is smooth and light brown, very slowly and carefully whisk in the vinegar. It is important that you add a very small amount of vinegar at first because the caramel will react furiously, billowing steam that can burn you. Also, if you add too much at first, the caramel will cool down and it will be hard to incorporate the vinegar. When you've added all the vinegar, let it simmer, whisking, until reduced by half. Remove the black vinegar gastrique from the heat.

Put the cashews in a bowl and season with the Chinese five-spice powder, cayenne pepper, and remaining 1 tablespoon salt.

In a bowl, stir the labneh with 1 teaspoon of the oil, so it shines and spreads easily.

When you're ready to cook, fill a wok or a large wide pot halfway with oil and set over medium-high heat. Use a candy thermometer to make sure the oil is at 350°F (175°C). You can also test the temperature of the oil by inserting a chopstick: The oil is ready when it bubbles all around the chopstick. Have ready a wire rack set over a rimmed sheet pan.

Gently squeeze out the water thoroughly from the eggplant pieces by grabbing a handful at a time, and transfer the eggplant to a bowl. Toss with the rice flour to coat. The eggplant should be generously covered in rice flour, but make sure the excess is shaken off by using a strainer or a sieve.

Working in batches to prevent the pieces from sticking together, gently drop the eggplant into the hot oil and cook, stirring once halfway, for 1 full minute. Carefully remove the fried eggplant from the oil with a slotted spoon or spider and transfer to the wire rack. Season while they're hot with a pinch each of salt and MSG.

Smear the labneh generously across the bottom of a bowl. Sprinkle a little Chinese five-spice powder and cayenne onto the yogurt. Arrange the eggplant over the labneh. Top with a big handful of chopped fresh cilantro and drizzle with liberal amounts of the black vinegar gastrique. Finish with the spiced cashews.

CHARRED CHINESE BROCCOLI "SALAD"

Serves 4 to 6

A PLATTER OF DEEP-GREEN CHINESE BROCCOLI, OR *JIÈ LÁN*, OFTEN MAKES AN APPEARANCE ON HOME DINNER TABLES AND IN RESTAURANT BANQUET MEALS ALIKE. It's a great vegetable complement for meaty dishes, like the Lu Rou Fan (page 151). We even created a Fermented Chinese Broccoli (page 48) to go with that dish at Win Son, but that takes a bit more time and planning ahead. If you're cooking for a few people (for a potluck, for example), we like to char it, chop it, and mix in Taiwanese soy paste, basil, cilantro, and mint. It's an insanely delicious chopped salad of sorts that goes well with anything. We served it once at a charity barbecue hosted by the restaurant Olmsted and had never seen so many people excited by the vegetables at a barbecue before.

INGREDIENTS

2 bunches Chinese broccoli (aka *jiè lán*)

2 tablespoons neutral oil, such as soybean

¼ teaspoon salt

¼ cup (60 ml) Taiwanese soy paste

1 cup (20 g) packed Thai basil leaves

1 cup (16 g) packed fresh cilantro, both leaves and stems, chopped

1 cup (30 g) packed mint leaves

½ lime, for spritzing

Trim the stems of the Chinese broccoli, but otherwise keep the pieces whole and intact. Pat them dry well, then toss in a bowl with the oil and salt.

Heat an outdoor grill or just a cast-iron griddle until very hot. Place the Chinese broccoli bunches down and don't move them for 2 minutes. Once the bottoms are nicely charred, move them around and flip them over to lightly char the other sides. Do this a couple more times to char all over the Chinese broccoli, being careful not to burn too much of it, so that you have a good mix of pieces that are totally green along with some that are black. Remove from the heat and let cool for a few minutes.

Chop the Chinese broccoli into bite-size pieces, about 1 inch (2.5 cm) in length, and transfer to a large bowl. Toss with the soy paste to coat thoroughly, then toss in the basil, cilantro, and mint. Serve the lime alongside for spritzing.

SESAME CAESAR SALAD

Serves 6 to 8

A THICK, CREAMY DRESSING TOSSED WITH RAW ROMAINE LETTUCE IS PROBABLY NOT SOMETHING YOU'D FIND ANYWHERE IN TAIWAN, EXCEPT MAYBE STARBUCKS. But we love the contrast of creamy richness and crisp freshness that is Caesar salad, so we put this salad on our menu at Win Son Bakery, where it fits right in with the dinner menu. It's got anchovy paste and plenty of garlic like the original, but also a thick Asian sesame paste for an incredible nutty depth of flavor. Make it your new go-to.

FOR THE BREADCRUMBS:

1 cup (80 g) panko breadcrumbs

2 tablespoons unsalted butter

1 to 2 teaspoons garlic powder

Pinch of salt

MSG

FOR THE DRESSING:

1 tablespoon Wadaman Golden Sesame Paste or toasted white sesame paste

¼ cup (60 ml) Kewpie mayonnaise

1 tablespoon Dijon mustard

1 clove garlic, grated or smashed and finely minced

1 tablespoon anchovy paste, or 2 anchovies, finely minced

1 tablespoon red wine vinegar

2 tablespoons cracked black pepper

2 teaspoons fresh lemon juice

½ cup (50 g) grated Parmigiano-Reggiano, plus more for serving

FOR THE SALAD:

1 small head leafy lettuce, such as little gem, leaves separated

Salt and cracked black pepper

2 tablespoons olive oil or neutral oil, such as soybean

1 tablespoon toasted white sesame seeds

1 tablespoon store-bought fried shallots

MAKE THE BREADCRUMBS: Preheat the oven to 325°F (165°C). Place the panko breadcrumbs in a food processor and pulse for several seconds, until no larger chunks can be seen and the mixture resembles coarse sand.

Melt the butter in a medium, oven-safe saucepan. Reduce the heat to low and add the finely ground breadcrumbs and the garlic powder. Stir constantly over low heat for 2 minutes, or until the breadcrumbs have become slightly golden brown in color. Transfer the pan to the oven and cook for 15 minutes, or until the crumbs are about the color of caramel. (Check in after 10 minutes and give it a toss, or remove from the oven early.) Season with a pinch of salt and MSG to taste.

MAKE THE DRESSING: Stir the sesame paste to combine the oil that settles at the top before measuring it out. In a medium bowl, whisk it together with the mayo, Dijon, garlic, anchovy paste, vinegar, black pepper, lemon juice, and half the grated Parmigiano-Reggiano.

MAKE THE SALAD: In a large bowl, dress the lettuce with a pinch of salt, a crack of black pepper, and the olive oil. Then gently coat the leaves with the Caesar dressing, mixing with your hands to thoroughly dress the salad. Transfer to a serving bowl and top with a couple extra dollops of dressing, the breadcrumbs, more grated Parm, the sesame seeds, fried shallots, and a crack of black pepper. Serve immediately.

VEGETABLES

GREEN SOYBEAN, TOFU SKIN, AND PEA SHOOT SALAD

Serves 6 to 8

THIS IS A PRIME EXAMPLE OF TAIWANESE-STYLE VEGETABLES, SIMPLY SEASONED AND FRESH, AND SO GOOD AND REFRESHING ALONGSIDE AN ORDER OF DUMPLINGS OR A BOWL OF NOODLES. Young, green soybeans (*mao dou* in Mandarin or *edamame* in Japanese) can be found shelled and frozen in the freezer section of any Asian grocery. While there, look for sheets of tofu skin (*dou fu pi* in Mandarin or *yuba* in Japanese) in the refrigerated section, alongside the tofu. This salad is a classic cold dish or appetizer in Taiwan and many parts of China, but with mustard greens instead of pea shoots. Since we typically have lots of pea shoots (*dou miao* in Mandarin) in our kitchen at Win Son, we went with them instead, and they lend the dish a sweeter flavor. We also added roasted nori snacks, crushed up, for a little more umami.

INGREDIENTS

Salt

1 pound (455 g) pea shoot tendrils (can be found in Asian produce markets)

10 to 12 ounces (280 to 340 g) frozen shelled green soybeans or edamame

12 to 14 ounces (340 to 400 g) tofu skins

3 tablespoons toasted sesame oil

½ teaspoon ground white pepper

4 ounces (115 g) roasted seaweed snacks, crushed

2 tablespoons kombu cha (powdered seaweed seasoning; optional)

2 tablespoon toasted white sesame seeds

Bring a large pot of well-salted water to a boil. Meanwhile, prepare a large bowl with an ice bath. Once the water is boiling, submerge the pea shoots and blanch for 1 minute. Transfer with tongs immediately to the ice bath to cool thoroughly. Drain well, squeeze out the leaves, and pat dry.

You can use the same pot of hot water and bring it to a boil again to blanch the frozen green soybeans. Prepare another ice bath on the side. Once boiling, add the soybeans and cook for 2 to 3 minutes, until tender. Drain and transfer the soybeans to the ice bath to cool thoroughly. Drain well and pat dry.

Slice the tofu skins into ¼-inch (6-mm) strips. Chop the squeezed-out pea shoots into ½-inch (12-mm) pieces. Combine them in a large bowl with the soybeans, sesame oil, white pepper, seaweed snacks, kombu cha seasoning, if using, and sesame seeds. If desired, season with salt.

SAUTÉED PEA SHOOTS OR WATER SPINACH

Serves 6 to 8

INGREDIENTS

1 pound (455 g) pea shoot greens or water spinach (can be found in Asian markets)

2 tablespoons neutral cooking oil, such as soybean

1 teaspoon salt

MSG

2 large cloves garlic, chopped

2 teaspoons toasted sesame oil

Store-bought crispy shallots (optional)

Taiwanese soy paste, for serving (optional)

Sautéed pea shoots have been on the menu at Win Son since we opened. These are the tendrils from pea plants, with leaves and shoots that feature a delicate texture and sweet pea-like flavor. We love a simple sautéed green on the table with any meal. Water spinach is another green that's really popular in Taiwan, and it has a great texture thanks to its crisp, hollow stems. Keep these things in mind when you're sautéing either one at home: First, work in batches to ensure that the greens cook evenly and quickly, and get seasoned nicely throughout. Second, you just want to wilt them gently, with lots of garlic. Once they're plated, we love to drizzle on some Taiwanese soy paste, like Yun Hai's Firewood Soy Paste.

Wash the greens and drain them. Pat dry well with paper towels. If using pea shoots, just leave them whole and divide into two piles to cook one at a time. If using water spinach, cut into 3- to 4-inch (7.5 to 10 cm) sections and separate the parts with the most stems; you'll cook that batch first.

In a large wok or chef's pan, heat 1 tablespoon of the oil over high heat.

If cooking pea shoots, add the first batch to the pan along with a pinch of salt and MSG and cook, stirring frequently, for 1 minute before adding half the garlic. Continue cooking for 30 seconds to a minute longer. Taste for seasoning, adding more salt and MSG as needed. Toss with

1 teaspoon of the sesame oil and remove from the pan. Repeat the process with the second batch.

If cooking water spinach, add the stems along with a pinch of salt and MSG to the hot oil. Cook, stirring frequently, until they just become tender, about 2 minutes. Then add the leaves, another pinch of salt and MSG, and half the garlic, and stir for another 30 seconds to a minute. Taste for seasoning, adding more salt and MSG as needed. Toss with 1 teaspoon of the sesame oil and remove from the pan. Repeat the process with the second batch.

Transfer the greens to a plate, sprinkle with the shallots, drizzle with the soy paste, if using, and serve.

FLIES' HEAD
Serves about 4

THIS DISH MIGHT HAVE BEEN THE FOOD CATALYST TO OUR PARTNERSHIP AND PURSUIT OF STARTING A RESTAURANT. It was Josh's father's favorite dish to order at *Bei Gan*, or Main Street Imperial Taiwanese restaurant in Flushing. So it was one of the first things Trigg sampled when Josh took him to the place.

It's a light, chive-centric dish that's served over rice. It is called *flies' head* because the pork and fermented black beans that stud the green chives are tiny, like flies' heads. The pork adds an unctuous savory note, enhanced by the shiro dashi (a soy-dashi concentrated soup base, which you can find in Japanese markets), funky beans, and garlic, but there are more chives than there is pork in this dish. At Win Son, we also make a vegetarian-friendly version with minced dry tofu, or *doufu gan*, instead of the pork, which is explained in the variation on the next page.

Whichever you go with, just be sure to serve this with rice. Not only do the ingredients match the rice grains in size, but the sauce from the glazed chive buds causes the pork, vegetables, and rice grains to cluster together like molecules, creating something greater than the sum of its parts. The combination of flavors and textures really makes it hard to not shovel this into your mouth. If you've put your chopsticks down while there's still some left, it's because you're getting more rice to eat it with.

1 pound (455 g) budding chives (aka garlic chives or flowering chives, see page 31)

4 to 6 fresh red bird's-eye chiles, thinly sliced (see Note)

4 to 6 cloves garlic, minced

¼ cup (45 g) dried fermented black beans (see Note)

2 tablespoons neutral oil, such as soybean

8 ounces (225 g) ground pork shoulder (or leave this out and see the Vegetarian Variation with Dry Tofu below)

½ cup (120 ml) mirin

¼ cup (60 ml) shiro dashi

¼ cup (60 ml) rice wine, preferably Taiwanese, or use Shaoxing rice wine as a substitute

2 teaspoons cornstarch mixed with 2 teaspoons water

2 tablespoons Bull Head Shallot Sauce

¼ cup (60 ml) toasted sesame oil

Trim any very tough, light green or white stems from the budding chives. Finely chop the budding chives. (You can snip off the buds with scissors and reserve them or stir-fry into the dish, whichever you prefer.) In a bowl, combine the chives, chiles, garlic, and fermented black beans. Make sure you have all of your ingredients prepped and ready to go, because the cooking process is quick.

In a wok or large wide pot, heat the neutral oil over high heat. Add the pork and break it up as the fat renders and the meat cooks. When the pork is just cooked, after about 2 minutes, add the mirin, shiro dashi, and rice wine, and let the mixture bubble for another 2 minutes. Stir in the cornstarch and water slurry and allow it to gently thicken the sauce for another minute.

Turn down the heat to medium-low and quickly add the chive mixture and the shallot sauce. Mix thoroughly with a spoon or by using a tossing motion with the pan—you are more or less dressing the vegetables with the glazed meat and warming them in the pan. Add the toasted sesame oil. After a few tosses, and about 30 seconds to a minute, the mixture needs to come out of the pan and into a serving bowl. The chives should be just barely cooked, still bright green, and dressed from the hot, glazed pork. (Don't overcook.) Adjust the seasonings; the stir-fry should be flavorful and balanced (salty, sweet, spicy). Serve immediately.

VEGETARIAN VARIATION WITH DRY TOFU: Replace the ground pork with 8 ounces (225 g) dry tofu (aka *doufu gan*), which may be five-spice flavored or smoked. (Look for it in the refrigerated aisle of Chinese markets.) Mince the tofu before starting the recipe, and use in place of the pork for the rest of the steps.

NOTE: Red bird's-eye chiles get spicier as they get smaller. If the chiles are large, maybe use six, and if they are smaller, maybe only go for four. Not to be confused with black turtle beans, dried fermented black beans usually appear sticky and are very savory. We prefer the whole, loose beans, which usually come in a 1-pound (455 g) bag, to the type that come in jars mashed up or in a salty brine, but either will work here.

SAUTÉED CABBAGE WITH BACON

Serves 3 to 4

WE LOVE A SIMPLE SAUTÉED CABBAGE AS A SIDE DISH, BUT TO MAKE IT EVEN MORE TASTY, LITTLE MORSELS OF UMAMI BOMBS CAN BE TOSSED INTO THE PAN ALONG WITH THE LEAVES. We went with bacon in this version, and instead of the dried baby shrimp that you might see studding many sautéed cabbage dishes in Taiwan, we've created a shrimp powder to incorporate the salty, fishy flavors more evenly throughout the mixture. (If you don't want to make the powder, you can substitute dried baby shrimp that have soaked in water to soften and been drained.) If you're shopping for veggies in an Asian produce market, look for the flattened heads of green cabbage often called Taiwanese cabbage; these have tender leaves and are quicker to sauté than the slightly denser regular green cabbage. Or, if you're shopping in a farmers' market or gourmet grocery, you might find Savoy or Caraflex cabbage, both of which are suitable substitutes. But if needed, just go with regular old green cabbage for this one, and you won't be dissatisfied.

INGREDIENTS

6 dried shiitake mushrooms

½ pound (225 g) green cabbage

4 thick slices of bacon

3 tablespoons neutral oil, such as soybean

½ teaspoon salt

¼ teaspoon sugar

¼ teaspoon MSG

2 teaspoons Shrimp Powder (page 260)

¼ cup (60 ml) chicken stock

2 tablespoons butter (optional)

Red chile flakes such as gochugaru or Sichuan chile flakes (optional)

To rehydrate the dried shiitakes, cover with 2 cups (480 ml) of water and let sit for at least 40 minutes or up to overnight, until softened. Squeeze out and retain 1 cup (240 ml) of the liquid; strain the shiitakes. Remove the tough stems before slicing into thin slivers.

Chop the cabbage roughly into 6-inch (15-cm) wedges and set aside. Cut the bacon into fat, square pieces, ½ to 1 inch (12 mm to 2.5 cm) around.

In a large chef's pan or wok, heat a couple tablespoons of oil over medium-low heat. Add the bacon pieces and slowly render, stirring occasionally, until the pieces are uniformly lightly browned and crisp and the fat appears translucent.

Stir in the cabbage and season with the salt, sugar, MSG, and shrimp powder. Add the chicken stock. Cover and continue cooking at medium-low heat until the cabbage is softened and steamed through, 3 to 4 minutes, stirring occasionally. Add the butter, if using, and toss until the cabbage appears glazed. Transfer to a serving plate and garnish with a pinch of the gochugaru or Sichuan chile flakes, if desired.

SUNGOLD AND PEACH SALAD
Serves 6 to 8

HERE'S A LIGHT AND TANGY SALAD THAT MAKES IT ONTO THE MENU AT WIN SON BAKERY WHEN PEACHES AND TOMATOES ARE IN PEAK SEASON, IN MID TO LATE SUMMER. In Taiwan, tomatoes are enjoyed in many ways. Sometimes, you can even find sliced cherry tomatoes topping an ice cream sundae with a bunch of other fresh fruit. They're sweet and juicy enough to go both sweet and savory routes. Sungolds are some of the sweetest varieties around, and the honey-like flavor pairs well with ripe and tangy yellow peaches.

Here's a trick to slice many of these little tomatoes in half at once: Use the lids from two plastic containers to hold the tomatoes in place (one on top and one on bottom; sometimes placing each lid upside down holds the tomatoes in place better) and gently slice through the middle of the tomatoes with a sharp knife.

INGREDIENTS

FOR THE SALAD:
4 ripe peaches

1 bunch scallions, thinly sliced

2 pints (580 g) Sungold tomatoes, halved

Small pinch salt

Small pinch ground white pepper

1 cup (20 g) packed Thai basil leaves, slivered, plus more left whole for garnish

FOR THE DRESSING:
1 egg yolk

1 clove garlic, smashed and roughly chopped

2 teaspoons Dijon mustard

⅓ cup (75 ml) rice vinegar

½ cup (120 ml) grapeseed oil

3 tablespoons white soy sauce (aka *shiro*)

Toasted white sesame seeds

MAKE THE SALAD: Halve the peaches; remove the pits. Slice the peaches into wedges and chop the wedges into fourths. Place the fourths in a bowl. Add the scallions and halved Sungolds and gently toss to combine. Season with a tiny pinch of salt and white pepper.

MAKE THE DRESSING: In a blender, place the egg yolk, garlic, Dijon mustard, and rice vinegar. Start the blender at low speed to bring the mixture together. Slowly drizzle in the grapeseed oil to emulsify. Add the white soy sauce and taste for seasoning. The emulsification will break, so if you're making this vinaigrette ahead or for later use, just shake it to bring it back together.

When you're ready to serve, drizzle the tomatoes and peaches with the white soy vinaigrette and toss in the fresh Thai basil (reserve a few whole leaves for the garnish). You may have more dressing than you need; store any remaining dressing in the refrigerator for up to 1 month. Serve immediately or keep chilled for up to 1 day. Garnish with whole Thai basil leaves and sesame seeds right before serving.

WOOD EAR MUSHROOM SALAD

Serves 6 to 8

INGREDIENTS

2 ounces (55 g) dried wood ear mushrooms (aka black fungus)

½ cup (120 ml) shiro dashi

1 tablespoon soy sauce

1 tablespoon rice vinegar, plus more as desired (can be clear or Chinese black vinegar)

½ teaspoon toasted sesame oil

½ teaspoon Chinese five-spice powder

½ teaspoon ground white pepper

2 teaspoons sugar

1 to 2 teaspoons chili oil, such as House Chili Oil (page 258; optional)

1 bunch fresh cilantro, both stems and leaves, chopped

THIS IS A REALLY FRESH AND DELICIOUS CHILLED SALAD THAT MAKES A GREAT SIDE, OR *XIAO CHE*—IT'S SUPER SIMPLE AND SO REFRESHING. It's all about the fun, crunchy texture of wood ear mushrooms, and the balance of bright flavors in the seasonings. Wood ear mushrooms (aka Chinese black fungus) are a curly type of mushroom that grows from the bottom of trees, so they sort of resemble ears growing from a trunk. They're sold dried, in bags, like certain kelp or seaweed varieties, and they are common in Chinese and Taiwanese pantries. Look for them in Asian markets or online. The smaller ones are easiest to prepare at home.

Place the wood ear mushrooms in a clean, empty French press or a large bowl. Bring 2 cups (480 ml) water and the shiro dashi to a boil and pour over the dried wood ear mushrooms; press the mushrooms down with the French press or a plate to ensure the mushrooms stay submerged while they soak. After approximately 20 minutes, they should be completely hydrated and pliable.

Remove the mushrooms from the liquid. Trim the tough stems off the mushrooms and discard. Put the rest of the mushrooms in a large bowl and toss with the soy sauce, vinegar, sesame oil, Chinese five-spice powder, white pepper, sugar, and chili oil, if using. The salad can be served immediately or chilled up to a day ahead. Top with the chopped cilantro to serve.

GUOHUA STREET SALAD
Serves 6

GUOHUA STREET IS A STREET REVERED FOR ITS FOOD IN TAINAN, THE CITY IN SOUTH-ERN TAIWAN WHERE JOSH'S MOM LIVES AND MUCH OF HIS FAMILY IS BASED. It runs right along several open-air markets with a slew of independent fruit and vegetable vendors, squid soup shops, hand-ground espresso stalls, and famous little street-side restaurants (like Fu Sheng Hao, renowned for its rice cakes). When we're down there, Josh's mom makes sure we stop by the best mango salesman, almond milk maker, and *o a jian* (oyster omelet) specialist.

On a Guohua Street corner, there is a cart with a team of ladies selling Taiwanese spring rolls (*twin jen or chwen jien*); the assemblers stuff thin flour skins with shredded cabbage, carrots, shrimp, tofu, beans, roast pork, raw garlic, cilantro, sliced egg omelet, and sugared peanuts. We opened Win Son with a salad inspired by the delicious components of this roll, including pork and eggs. When persimmons came in season that fall, we thought it would be fun to add fruit to the mix, highlighting the abundant fresh fruit and often sweet flavor profiles of Tainan. We eventually pared down the proteins, leaving just shrimp. This made the dish lighter and also pescatarian friendly. When persimmon is not in season, we happily use mangoes instead. You can use either fruit or both, as you prefer.

FOR THE PICKLED RAISINS:
2 tablespoons golden raisins

1 tablespoon mirin

1 tablespoon rice vinegar

FOR THE DRESSING:
¼ cup (60 ml) smooth peanut butter

2 tablespoons rice vinegar

1 tablespoon soy sauce

1 tablespoon mirin

FOR THE SHRIMP:
1 pound (455 g) large shrimp, peeled and deveined

2 teaspoons toasted sesame oil

½ teaspoon salt

¼ teaspoon ground white pepper

FOR THE SALAD:
5 cups (450 g) loosely packed shredded Napa cabbage

1 cup (90 g) shredded carrots

1 tablespoon House Chili Oil (page 258) or your favorite chili oil, such as Lao Gan Ma Spicy Chili Crisp

¼ teaspoon salt

¼ teaspoon sugar

¼ teaspoon MSG

½ tablespoon Shrimp Powder (page 260; optional)

1 tablespoon store-bought fried shallots

1 tablespoon toasted white sesame seeds

1 ripe mango or persimmon, peeled and diced into ½-inch (12-mm) cubes

1 cup smoked or five-spice dry tofu (aka *dou fu gan*), diced into ¼-inch (6-mm) cubes

1 lime, halved

¼ cup (4 g) packed chopped fresh cilantro leaves and tender stems

¼ cup (7.5 g) packed fresh mint leaves

¼ cup (5 g) packed fresh Thai basil leaves

½ cup (55 g) Butter-Fried Peanuts (page 40)

PICKLE THE RAISINS: In a small saucepan, combine the golden raisins, mirin, and rice vinegar and heat over medium heat, stirring occasionally, until it just comes to a boil. Remove from the heat and let sit uncovered to cool slightly as the raisins plump up and you prepare the rest of the components. (The raisins can be pickled the day before and refrigerated overnight.) Reserve the pickling liquid.

MAKE THE DRESSING: In a small bowl using a fork, mix together the peanut butter, vinegar, soy sauce, and mirin with 2 tablespoons water and set aside.

COOK THE SHRIMP: In a small bowl, season the shrimp with the sesame oil, salt, and white pepper and toss to coat. Skewer about 4 shrimp. (If using bamboo skewers, soak them in water for at least an hour or overnight, or use metal skewers.) Place the skewers on a well-heated gas or charcoal grill, or cast-iron grill pan, and don't move for 2 to 3 minutes, until the shrimp is nicely charred on one side. Flip the skewers and

char the opposite sides for another 2 minutes or so, until the shrimp is just fully cooked and charred on both sides. Set aside.

MAKE THE SALAD: In a large bowl, mix the Napa cabbage and carrots with the pickled raisins and 1 tablespoon of their pickling liquid, the chili oil, salt, sugar, MSG, and shrimp powder, if using. Sprinkle in the fried shallots and sesame seeds.

Next, gently toss the salad with the peanut butter dressing and give it a taste, adding a splash more rice vinegar if you think it's too sweet or salty. Transfer to a serving dish or bowl.

In the same bowl the cabbage and carrots were tossed in, combine the mangoes and the dry tofu with the juice from half the lime. Toss well, and layer on top of the salad in the serving dish.

Cover with the cilantro, mint, Thai basil, and fried peanuts. Arrange the shrimp skewers on top and the remaining lime half on the side, to squeeze liberally all over the salad before serving.

GATHERING 'ROUND THE GRILL

TRIGG HERE. In Brooklyn, apartments are tight and kitchens are small, so I've always done a lot of grilling to compensate for that. From fire escapes to roof-tops to backyards, I'm usually the one running the grill. Gas grills are great and I have no beef with them, but I have to recommend charcoal. If you have a konro grill, that's great. A big, wide charcoal grill is even better. I like to keep a few logs under the grill and throw 'em on when needed—it allows you to maintain heat control by adding a "turn up" option. This is great for long parties and evenings, so you don't have to relight the grill every time someone wants to throw an extra hot dog on it.

There are a lot of dishes in Taiwan that just wouldn't be the same without an out-door grill, too—street foods like grilled corn that's been slathered with a sticky-sweet glaze, or Taiwanese sausages that acquire a little char on their sides. Grilling is a univer-sally loved pastime, we think. So with these recipes, we created a full menu for a great barbecue for plenty of people. Feel free to mix and match with other appetizers and veggie-forward dishes, of course. These grilled entrées are pretty easy, but impressive enough for a nice occasion. And if you're going to make it all together like we did, in my backyard in the summer while working on this book, here are a few tips and recommen-dations I have for you—or whoever's the grill master at your fest.

Don't be afraid to use a lot of charcoal to start out. Here's how I do it: Pile the charcoal all on one side of the grill, and light it up with the help of lighter fluid. Let the charcoal flame up. When the flame starts to settle, I throw a log on. When the coals are white hot and the wood is smoldering, start adding the chicken (page 90) to the side of the grill with the indirect heat (no coals underneath). That's because chicken bombs your coals with fat drippings and will cause a grease fire. Be sure to place the chicken with the fat-tiest skin side facing the grill; this will prevent the meat from drying out.

Once your chicken is organized on the non-hot side of the grill, start throwing the vegetables (for the Grilled Vegetables with Black Sesame Sauce, page 91) on the super-hot side, with a plan to evacuate them to a more stable area once they become charred. (Don't place the vegetables directly over the coals and the wood, but very close to the heat source.) Place the mushrooms (page 94) upside-down (so that their caps fill up with juices as they warm), the summer squash and zucchini skin-side down, and the cipollini onions farther away, closer to the chicken. The longer the cipollinis cook, slow and low, the better. Like the mushrooms, the onions will cook in their own juice, while the outsides slowly caramelize.

After the vegetables are organized and doing their thing, throw the pork (page 97) on the hot side of the grill. Remember, as all this is happening, you will want to pay attention to your chicken and rotate the pieces to ensure each cooks thoroughly. No need to flip them over from their fatty sides, though—the more browning on that side, the tastier it will be.

The pork fat will be just as flammable as the chicken fat, but searing these pork collar chops is the goal, so it's OK if the flames go a little crazy at times. Go aggressive with the salt and pepper; that's all you need. Get good color on both sides of the steaks, then pull them back over by the chicken and let them render for a while. You can eat these steaks medium-rare like a beef rib eye, but even with a rib eye, I'm more of a medium fan. I like to let that fat render slowly so that each buttery bite from the fat cap almost melts in your mouth at the end. Take the pork off the grill and let it rest for ten minutes.

While the pork is resting, you can now clear away the hot section of the grill for the shrimp skewers (page 95). These take the least time, effort, and skill to cook. Just be sure not to leave them on there for too long or they'll overcook.

After checking on your slow-roasting chicken and vegetables, you can get ready to serve. Slice the pork into long strips across the grain. Pile the chicken pieces onto a platter and add a lime half for spritzing. Smear the black sesame sauce all over another platter and spread your grilled vegetables on top.

At this point, you can serve everything together, or maybe hold a few pieces of the chicken and pork for seconds or for people who are showing up later. Barbecues can get big. Maybe you expected four to six people, but twelve people came over all at different times. That's fine. Place the meats you don't wish to serve immediately on a sheet pan with a rack close to the grill. If it's rainy or cold, I'll turn my oven on inside at a low temp and hold things in there. When the serving platters are nearly empty, bring out the reinforcements and keep the party going.

RIGHT: Friends and family in Trigg's backyard

CHAPTER 3
GRILL OUT

GRILLED CHICKEN WITH GARLIC AND RICE VINEGAR

Serves 8

WE THINK CHICKEN IS ONE OF THE MOST IMPORTANT MEATS TO PURCHASE A HIGH-QUALITY VERSION OF, WITH REGARD TO TASTE. Look for air-chilled birds, which aren't dunked in water with suspect chemicals. For this recipe, we like to use the wings, legs, and thighs. If you want to make all wings, go for it. Love thighs? Go for all thighs. And so on. Our preference is for dark meat, a preference that is shared in Taiwan.

With dark meat, low and slow grilling is key to cooking it thoroughly to the bone. Since breasts are only protected with a thin layer of skin and need to cook through all the way to the bone on the other side, they can dry out on the grill pretty easily. Dark chicken meat has more bone to meat, and there is more fat, skin, and cartilage—the longer you cook dark-meat chicken on a low flame, the softer and more supple those parts become, while the skin gets as crispy as if it came out of the fryer (as long as you don't get the grill too hot).

We've kept this recipe pretty simple when it comes to the marinade—an aggressive amount of garlic, and then just salt, Chinese five-spice powder, and cracked black pepper. These flavors absorb into the chicken overnight with olive oil. We also have a basting spritz that you can keep spraying or spooning onto the chicken as it cooks slow and low on the grill. If you want it spicier, you can add a couple tablespoons of Sichuan chile flakes or gochugaru to the marinade, or just sprinkle them on for a finishing touch when it's done. See more tips on how to cook the chicken in "Gathering 'Round the Grill," page 83. If you are thinking about making just one grilled vegetable, we particularly love serving this with cipollini onions (see page 91).

FOR THE CHICKEN AND MARINADE:

4 pounds (1.8 kg) skin-on, bone-in chicken thighs, drumsticks, and/or whole wings

1 head garlic, cloves peeled and minced or chopped in a food processor

¼ cup (60 ml) olive oil

2 tablespoons kosher salt

1 tablespoon cracked black pepper

1 teaspoon ground white pepper

1 teaspoon Chinese five-spice powder

1 tablespoon Sichuan chile flakes

FOR THE BASTING SPRITZ:

½ cup (120 ml) rice vinegar

½ cup (120 ml) rice wine, preferably Taiwanese, or use Shaoxing rice wine as a substitute

1 tablespoon shiro dashi

1 tablespoon toasted sesame oil

FOR THE GARNISH:

2 limes

1 small red onion, sliced to thin slivers

1 cup (16 g) loosely packed fresh cilantro leaves and stems

Red chile flakes, such as gochugaru or Sichuan chile flakes (optional)

MARINATE THE CHICKEN: Combine the chicken with the garlic, olive oil, salt, black pepper, white pepper, Chinese five-spice powder, and Sichuan chile flakes and rub to distribute evenly. In a large bowl or baking dish, marinate the chicken. Cover the bowl or baking dish with plastic wrap and let marinate in the refrigerator for at least 4 hours or up to 2 days.

MAKE THE BASTING SPRITZ: Mix together the rice vinegar, rice wine, shiro dashi, and sesame oil in a spray bottle, or if that's unavailable, just mix them in a bowl and have a spoon or brush ready to baste the chicken with later on.

If using a gas grill, heat over medium-high until it reaches 450°F (230°C). Typically gas grills have three burners across a rectangular surface of grates. Keep the left side high and reduce the center and right burner flames to medium-low then place the chicken pieces skin side down on the grills.

If using a charcoal grill, keep the charcoal contained to just one-half of the grill rack. Let the coals flame for 20 minutes or so until the flames die down and the coals are white-hot. You don't want to see black charcoal or your food will taste like fuel. Rub the grates with a brush or towel

before placing the chicken pieces down on the sides with the thickest, fattest skin on the grills.

Watch the chicken and move the pieces around on the grill to ensure that no piece becomes too charred (but don't flip them). Spray or brush all the pieces with the basting mixture. Continue this process of moving the chicken around and spraying or brushing them with the baste until the bottoms of the chicken pieces are dark golden brown and the pieces are cooked through, about 40 minutes. (There's no need to flip over and cook on the sides with less skin and fat, as this can dry the meat out.) If some pieces become too charred early on, that's fine, but try to control the charring later on in the process. To check if the chicken is cooked through, insert a thermometer into the thickest part of the meat close to the bone and ensure that it reaches 160°F (70°C) before removing it from the grill.

GARNISH THE CHICKEN AND SERVE: Halve the lime and squeeze the juice from one-half into a bowl. Toss the thinly sliced red onions in the lime juice to let them pickle ever so slightly. Transfer the grilled chicken pieces to a serving platter. Spritz or brush them all again, then scatter the red onion, cilantro, and more chile flakes, if using, on top. Serve with the extra lime half on the side.

GRILLED VEGETABLES
WITH BLACK SESAME SAUCE
Serves 4 to 6

OUR SAUCE FROM THE BLACK SESAME NOODLES WITH MUSHROOMS (PAGE 112) ISN'T JUST FOR NOODLES. It makes a great complement for grilled vegetables, or even raw vegetables. We like to spread this thick sauce on a plate then pile the grilled vegetables on top of it, so you can smear it on any piece that you pick up. Sweet cippolini onions, with their flattened shape, are perfect for grilling whole and slowly caramelizing. Zucchini and summer squashes are a classic for summer grill-outs, as are bell peppers in a rainbow of colors. Bring any of your favorite vegetables to the mix, or whatever looks good in season.

INGREDIENTS

4 to 6 cipollini onions, all around the same size

2 or 3 summer squashes, such as zucchini and yellow squash

2 or 3 bell peppers, any color

4 tablespoons olive oil

1 teaspoon salt

1 teaspoon cracked black pepper

1 cup (240 ml) sauce from Black Sesame Noodles with Mushrooms (page 112)

Trim the ends from the onions and cut the squashes into 1-inch-thick (2.5 cm) slices across their length, so that you have very big, flat pieces. Halve the bell peppers, then remove their seed pockets, pith, and caps. Keep halved if on the smaller side, or cut into quarters if large. The key is to have evenly sized pieces of each type of vegetable. If you find smaller peppers like shishito or Italian frying peppers, keep them whole.

If using a charcoal grill, bring it to a high flame, then let the fire die down, so that the coals are white-hot. If using a gas grill, heat over a medium-high flame.

In a large bowl, toss the cut vegetables with the olive oil, salt, and black pepper. Arrange on the grill and let them cook at medium-low temperature for several minutes, keeping watch. Rearrange the pieces as needed—if some are burning or cooking much more quickly than others, swap places using tongs. Once the pieces are gently browned on one side, flip them over and continue the process. The vegetables should be gently cooked and softened, and super concentrated in flavor with this slow and long way of grilling them. It should take around 20 to 30 minutes.

Pour the sesame sauce into the center of a large serving platter. Using the back of a large serving spoon, spread it all around the bottom of the platter. Pile the vegetables on top and serve.

FROM TOP LEFT CLOCKWISE: Grilled Pork Collar with Shio Koji and Chili Oil (page 97), Grilled Shrimp with Chili Butter and Cilantro (page 95), Grilled Whole Mushrooms with Chili Oil (page 94), Grilled Chicken with Garlic and Rice Wine (page 88), Marinated Cukes (page 37), Grilled Vegetables with Black Sesame Sauce (page 91).

GRILLED WHOLE MUSHROOMS WITH CHILI OIL

INGREDIENTS

½ pound (230 g) fresh mushrooms, such as cremini, button, and shiitake, with tough stems removed

1 tablespoon olive oil

¼ teaspoon salt

¼ teaspoon cracked black pepper

2 tablespoons House Chili Oil (page 258) or your favorite chili oil, such as Lao Gan Ma Spicy Chili Crisp

Chopped fresh cilantro and/or scallions, for garnish (optional)

THIS IS TRIGG'S FAVORITE WAY TO COOK MUSHROOMS—THEY'RE LIKE LITTLE FLAVOR BOMBS. Just toss them in the marinade and then grill them upside-down, until they start bubbling on the underside of the mushrooms. (Before turning them over, be sure to pour this flavorful mushroom juice on anything else you're grilling beside it, like chicken.) Cremini, button, white mushrooms—whatever the grocery store has will work fine. These mushrooms are great on their own and make a perfect complement to a roasted or grilled piece of fish.

Rinse the mushrooms and wipe clean to remove any dirt. Dry well. Place in a bowl and toss with the olive oil, salt, pepper, and chili oil. Let marinate for 15 minutes.

When the grill is very hot, place the mushrooms cap side down on the grill racks, allowing space in between each one. Pour any remaining juice from the marinade into the caps of the mushrooms as they grill. Don't move for 2 to 3 minutes, until the bottoms become nicely charred. Then gently flip each mushroom to char the opposite side, another 2 minutes or so. Transfer to a serving dish and top with the fresh cilantro and scallions, if using.

GRILLED SHRIMP with CHILI BUTTER and CILANTRO

Serves 3 to 4

THIS IS A REALLY SIMPLE CROWD-PLEASER THAT TAKES ALMOST NO TIME TO COOK. Look for head-on wild shrimp or prawns, and let them soak up our Garlic-Ginger Sauce with Pickled Mustard Greens overnight. This condiment-turned-marinade is turned into a condiment once again after the shrimp are grilled. See more tips on how to cook it in "Gathering 'Round the Grill" (page 83).

INGREDIENTS

1 pound (455 g) head-on shrimp or prawns, preferably wild

FOR THE MARINADE:
2 tablespoons Garlic-Ginger Sauce with Pickled Mustard Greens (page 257)

2 tablespoons shiro dashi

½ teaspoon salt

¼ teaspoon cracked black pepper

FOR THE CHILI BUTTER:
4 tablespoons (½ stick) unsalted butter

1 tablespoon House Chili Oil (page 258) or your favorite chili oil, such as Lao Gan Ma Spicy Chili Crisp

1 tablespoon shiro dashi

1 tablespoon Garlic-Ginger Sauce with Pickled Mustard Greens (page 257)

TO SERVE:
Handful fresh cilantro leaves

MARINATE THE SHRIMP: Rinse the shrimp and pat dry. Leave the shell on the head and leave the tail on, but remove the peel on the body by inserting scissors just below the back of the head and gently snipping to the tail. Toss in a large bowl with the garlic-ginger sauce, shiro dashi, salt, and pepper. Let marinate for at least 30 minutes or up to overnight. If using bamboo skewers, be sure to soak them for at least 1 hour before using (or overnight).

MAKE THE CHILI BUTTER: Place the butter, chili oil, shiro dashi, and garlic-ginger sauce in a small saucepan, and if you have space on the grill, allow the butter to melt alongside the shrimp skewers right on the grill; otherwise, heat over low heat on the stovetop until the butter has just melted. Stir to combine.

COOK THE SHRIMP: Heat a charcoal grill over a medium-high flame or a gas grill to medium heat. Skewer the shrimp four or five to a stick and place on the grills. Let cook for about 2 minutes, until slightly charred on one side, and flip. Let char and turn pink on the opposite side, another 2 to 3 minutes.

TO ASSEMBLE AND SERVE: Transfer the skewers to a serving platter. Spoon the chili butter all over and put the remaining chili butter in a dish on the side. Garnish with the cilantro leaves and serve.

GRILLED PORK COLLAR
with SHIO KOJI and CHILI OIL
Serves 8 to 12

THE PORK COLLAR IS LIKE THE RIB EYE OF THE PIG. It's a widely utilized cut in Korean barbecue as well as Japanese, Chinese, and Taiwanese cuisines. If you can get a whole pork collar, you can portion it out into steaks or chops by cutting across the muscle, which is seamed out of the shoulder up against the collar bone, and slicing steaks about the size of your index finger. Before butchering, you can throw it in the freezer for 20 minutes to firm it up and make the process a little easier—that way you can use a bread knife to slice it into chops easily. See more tips on how to cook it in "Gathering 'Round the Grill," page 83.

INGREDIENTS

1 (3- to 4-pound/1.4 to 1.8 kg) full pork collar, or 8 pork collar chops (aka CT butt or coppa steaks)

FOR THE MARINADE:
2 tablespoons shio koji

2 cloves garlic, grated

1 (2-inch/5 cm) piece fresh ginger, peeled and grated

1 cup (240 ml) light soy sauce

1 cup (240 ml) mirin

TO SERVE:
½ cup (120 ml) House Chili Oil (page 258) or your favorite chili oil, such as Lao Gan Ma Spicy Chili Crisp

If using a full pork collar, slice the collar into about eight 1½-inch-thick (4 cm) chops.

MAKE THE MARINADE: In a large bowl, combine all the ingredients.

Heat a charcoal grill to a medium flame or a gas grill to medium heat. Place the chops on the grill, with about an inch in between each piece. Let them cook over medium heat until dark grill marks appear on one side, about 2 minutes, rotating as you please.

We like to make sure there aren't crisscross grill marks. You can avoid this by rotating the meat in a circle so the grill marks cover the surface of the meat completely, rather than in corny box or diamond shapes. Be careful to move pieces away from an area that's too hot so that they develop a char more gradually. Keep grilling, turning the chops often, until a golden brown color starts to develop, about 10 minutes.

Right before the pork is done, using tongs, dip the steaks in the marinade and then let the chops finish on the grill, just 1 to 2 minutes per side so the sugar can start to caramelize, but not burn.

Once the chops are golden brown, transfer to a plate or tray. Let rest for 8 to 10 minutes.

TO SERVE: Slice into long strips against the grain and transfer to a serving dish. Drizzle liberally with the chili oil.

WHO ARE TAIWANESE AMERICANS?

HOCHIE IS A TRUE BADASS AND PIONEER OF THE TAIWANESE AMERICAN COMMUNITY. Originally from Kao-hsiung, Taiwan, he grew up in the Midwest in the 1970s and 1980s and helped run Taiwanese American youth summer camp programs. He went on to medical school and became a doctor, founding one of the first Taiwanese American student organizations at his university. Then in 2006, he founded TaiwaneseAmerican.org, a grassroots organization highlighting news, events, and individuals in the Taiwanese American community. He's done so much to support and celebrate Taiwanese American identity, and we're humbled to call HoChie a friend. We got on a Zoom call with him to catch up.

CATHY: So what's new with Taiwanese American.org?

HOCHIE: Our mission has been the same since we started TaiwaneseAmerican.org fifteen years ago, which is to highlight events, organizations, individuals, and the things that are happening in Taiwanese America—basically capturing a slice of Taiwanese America as it is now. So I will also add that I feel like I'm in transition because I've been doing this work in the community for so long. But in the past several years, I elevated my editor-in-chief to do a lot more things, so she's basically running the show now and I'm so happy to see her doing that. So she's essentially the next generation of our second generation.

TRIGG: That's success, right? We sometimes say that if we were opening Win Son today, we probably wouldn't do it the same way, not at all. At least from an outsider's perspective, it seems like Taiwanese American culture is in a different place now, even compared to where it was five years ago.

HOCHIE: Yeah. If I had to put a rough measurement to it, every five or seven years it seems our community has matured or changed in a way. It just seems like [there are] a broader, more diverse set of viewpoints that comprise Taiwanese America versus the time when I started the website and versus fifteen years before that.

Taiwanese culture—what is it? It's always changing.

But it's like, when people immigrate to the US, it puts them into a time capsule. Their idea of what Taiwan is will always be the way it was when they left. The Waishengren ["foreigners," in Taiwan] who came to Taiwan in the 1940s, they always thought of themselves as Chinese, sure. But their kids and their kids'—they don't see it the same way. Regardless of the background, they associate their sense of Taiwanese Americanness as this sense of land, culture, and shared history. So it doesn't matter where your parents are from. If you can tie your lineage to Taiwan, you can embrace that.

JOSH: My mom's family has been in Taiwan for over ten generations. But she also says, *Look, we are from Taiwan but we are Chinese.* I understand what she's saying. But maybe Americans don't necessarily tie things together the way others might.

HOCHIE: When we say "Taiwanese American," it doesn't exclude people who say their ethnic identity is Chinese or national identity is Chinese. It is whatever you make of it and it's a kind of melting pot now.

I will say that the Taiwanese folks I knew growing up did not have a positive light at all on Chiang Kai-shek and what he was doing with democracy. They saw themselves as more Japanese.

JOSH: I think it's a great point because from my grandfather's perspective, he grew up under Japanese rule and learned Japanese as a main language and then learned Chinese Mandarin after. There

was almost a preference for Japanese rule rather than when Chiang Kai-shek came.

HOCHIE: Many of the Taiwanese people I know hang on to things that are Japanese. One thing that comes to mind is hot pot, but we'd always call it *sukiyaki* when I was growing up. When people started calling it "hot pot" in the nineties, it seemed kind of weird to me.

CATHY: What about shabu-shabu?

HOCHIE: Yeah, I never heard of that in the Midwest.

JOSH: It's a rebranding—make it hot again.

TRIGG: I love that recipe book you gave me.

HOCHIE: The original North American Taiwanese American Women's Association cookbook [*Homestyle Cooking of Taiwan*]! It's like, all the moms' recipes. It first came out in 1994 or 1995 and was updated nine or ten years ago.

TRIGG: When you came to Win Son the first time, for us it was really exciting that you were having a fun meal there and you felt accepted.

HOCHIE: I'm a second-generation and I appreciated the evolving of things that you have on the menu. But if I brought a parent, they might not want it. They'd ask for the "secret menu" stuff.

You will always come across traditionalists who will say Taiwanese food is one thing. But then there's the evolution of the Taiwanese American community. You represent where our second generation and onward is going.

CHAPTER 4
NOODLES AND SOUPS

BRAISED BEEF SHANKS

Serves 8, plus makes broth for Niu Rou Mian
(Beef Noodle Soup, page 104)

BEEF SHANKS ARE AN AMAZING CUT. They are the muscles in a cow's leg, which have clear tendons and swirling ligaments running through them. Once braised, these soften and add a nice textural contrast to the meat, and when you slice the braised shanks against the grain, the pieces are really beautiful, streaked with gelatinous tendons and flavorful fatty bits. Braised beef shanks are the classic topping for a proper bowl of *niu rou mian* (Taiwanese beef noodle soup) and are also the starting point for the Beef Roll (page 188). Or, you can just slice the shanks up and serve them chilled or warm with a few garnishes, as described here, as part of a multicourse, family-style meal. Boneless shanks can be found in Asian markets, but if you can't find them, debone beef shanks and save the bones in your freezer for the next time you want to make stock (see page 262).

2 tablespoons neutral cooking oil, such as soybean, plus more to brown the aromatics

2 boneless beef shanks (about 2 pounds/910 g total)

4-inch (10-cm) piece fresh ginger, peeled and coarsely chopped or sliced

1 head garlic, peeled and smashed

1 bunch scallions, both white and green parts, chopped to 2-inch (5-cm) segments

4 cups (960 ml) rice wine, preferably Taiwanese, or use Shaoxing rice wine as a substitute

1 cup (240 ml) soy sauce

2 teaspoons green and/or black cardamom pods (preferably 1 teaspoon each)

1 teaspoon Sichuan green peppercorns

1 teaspoon coriander seeds

1 tablespoon dried orange peel (can be found in Asian markets) or fresh orange zest

OPTIONAL GARNISHES, FOR SERVING:

House Chili Oil (page 258) or your favorite chili oil, such as Lao Gan Ma Spicy Chili Crisp

Toasted sesame oil

Taiwanese soy paste or soy sauce

Chopped fresh cilantro

Crushed peanuts

Preheat the oven to 325°F (165°C). In a 6-quart (5.7 L) or larger Dutch oven or stockpot, heat the neutral oil. Once the oil is popping, place the shanks fatty side down in the pot. Sear until golden brown, about 1 minute. Flip and sear the opposite sides of the shanks. Remove the beef from the pot and set aside on a plate.

In the same Dutch oven or pot that you seared the beef in, add a little more of the neutral oil, then the ginger, garlic, and scallions and stir, scraping up the browned bits in the pan. Cook over medium-high heat, stirring frequently, until the aromatics are slightly browned, about 2 minutes. Add the rice wine and bring to a boil. Then add the soy sauce and 1 quart (960 ml) plus 2 cups (480 ml) water and bring up to a boil again. Return the beef shanks to the pot and submerge them in the liquid. Place the cardamom, peppercorns, coriander, and orange peel in cheesecloth and secure as a sachet (or pack it into a tea ball), then add it to the pot.

Cover with a lid. (Or if unavailable, create a cartouche by cutting a piece of parchment paper to fit across the top.)

Braise for 4 to 6 hours in the oven. Check on the shanks at 4 hours and ensure that the meat is becoming tender but not falling apart into the broth. You want it to be just firm enough to be sliceable. Once done, allow the braise to come to room temperature before chilling. Strain the braising liquid through a fine-mesh sieve first and use for Niu Rou Mian (page 104), or as a stock for any soup you want to make. You should have about 3 quarts (2.8 L) liquid in the end. Keep for up to 1 week refrigerated in airtight containers, or freeze.

The beef shanks can be served chilled or warm. Slice them and arrange on a platter. Drizzle with the chili oil, sesame oil, and/or Taiwanese soy paste, and sprinkle with the cilantro and peanuts, if using.

NIU ROU MIAN (BEEF NOODLE SOUP)

Serves 4 to 6

BEEF NOODLE SOUP REIGNS SUPREME IN TAIWAN. Infused with warm spices, enriched with tomato, and accented with a hint of Sichuan peppercorns, this classic noodle soup will warm you to your bones. The highlight is the Braised Beef Shanks (page 102) that are placed on each bowl, which also appear in our Beef Roll (page 188). And we decided to get a bit more creative with our soup toppings, introducing some oxtail, which shares a similar gelatinous quality that shanks have when braised. For a special, we once even made beef noodle soup using sous-vided boneless short ribs, which we then speared onto a trompo to shave off like shawarma. That's all to say that in the event that you can't find beef shanks for this dish, you can use another cut of beef, it just won't have the signature texture of the classic.

NOTE: Use both beef shanks and oxtail or go with just one or the other. As much as we love boneless beef shanks, we know that they can be difficult to find if you don't live close to an Asian butcher shop. Oxtails can provide that collagen-rich, texturally interesting quality in place of shanks, if not the same visual appeal, but we love a bowl with both shanks and oxtails. If using bone-in shanks, debone them and save the bones in your freezer for the next time you want to make stock.

1 whole, boneless beef shank (about 1 pound/455 g total)

1 pound (455 g) oxtails, cut to ½-inch (12 mm) pieces (optional; see Note)

2 tablespoons tomato paste

2 tablespoons neutral cooking oil, such as soybean

1 red onion, quartered

4-inch (10-cm) piece fresh ginger, peeled and coarsely chopped or sliced

1 head garlic, peeled and smashed

1 bunch scallions, both white and green parts, chopped to 2-inch (5-cm) segments

4 cups (960 ml) rice wine, preferably Taiwanese, or use Shaoxing rice wine as a substitute

1 cup (240 ml) soy sauce

2 teaspoons green and/or black cardamom pods (preferably 1 teaspoon each)

1 teaspoon Sichuan green peppercorns

1 teaspoon coriander seeds

1 tablespoon dried orange peel (can be found in Asian markets) or fresh orange zest

2 pounds (910 g) Asian dried wheat noodles, preferably a wide and flat type

1 cup (60 g) packed pea shoots or another fresh leafy green, rinsed and cut to bite-size pieces

½ cup (55 g) chopped scallions and/or fresh cilantro

OPTIONAL GARNISHES:
4 Marinated Eggs or Lisa's Tea Eggs (page 45 or 41), halved

House Chili Oil (page 258) or your favorite chili oil, such as Lao Gan Ma Spicy Chili Crisp

Preheat the oven to 425°F (220°C). Rub the shanks and oxtails, if using, in the tomato paste to coat all over. Place on an oiled sheet pan and roast for 10 minutes. Remove from the oven and let cool.

In a 6-quart (5.7 L) or larger Dutch oven or stockpot, heat the neutral oil. Toss in the red onion, ginger, garlic, and scallions. Stir and cook over low heat until the aromatics are very fragrant, about 1 minute. Add the rice wine and bring to a boil. Then add the soy sauce, 1 quart (960 ml) plus 2 cups (480 ml) water, the shank, and the oxtails to the pan. Bring up to a boil again, then reduce the heat to a low simmer. Place the cardamom, peppercorns, coriander, and orange peel in cheesecloth and secure as a sachet (or pack it into a tea ball), then add it to the pot.

Cover with a lid and ensure the simmer is a very gentle but steady bubble, typically as low as the heat will go without turning off. Check on the shanks and oxtails at 4 hours and ensure that the meat is becoming tender but not falling

apart into the broth. You want the shanks to be just firm enough to be sliceable, and all the oxtail pieces intact but just about to fall out of their bones. Remove the shanks and oxtails when they are tender enough and place in separate containers. Discard the spice sachet. Strain the liquid with a fine-mesh strainer. Taste the broth for seasoning, adding a touch of soy sauce, if desired. You should have about 3 quarts (2.8 L) liquid in the end.

Bring a large pot of water to a boil and cook the noodles according to the directions on the package.

Divide the noodles among four to six serving bowls. Pour about 2 cups (480 ml) of the hot broth into each bowl and immediately stir the noodles with chopsticks in the hot broth. Divide the pea shoots, if using, among each bowl, submerging them in the broth to gently poach them. Arrange the braised beef shank slices and the oxtails, if using, in each bowl, followed by the scallions, eggs, and chili oil, if using, and serve immediately.

DANZAI MIAN

Serves 4

DANZAI MIAN IS AN OLD SCHOOL TAIWANESE NOODLE SOUP THAT'S A CLASSIC OF THE CUISINE. The story goes that it was created and sold by fishermen, during their off-season. It has a spoonful of sauce from Lu Rou Fan (page 151) atop the bowl, and a lone shrimp—it's simple, yet soul soothing.

There's a place in Taiwan that Josh would go to a lot whenever visiting family during college. He'd take the high-speed rail straight to Tainan after landing in Taoyuan International Airport, and his third uncle would be there to pick him up. Then, they'd go to Du Hsiao Yueh, a famous danzai noodle shop, before heading to Ah Gong's house. It was an "eating before arriving" tradition that carried on over the years, with Trigg joining Josh on some of those trips later on, too. Du Hsiao Yueh is a popular franchise now, but these older shops still offer a high-quality experience. The noodle soup is prepared in the middle of the dining room, where you can see a clay pot of soup broth sitting atop a flame. We're told that the broth never leaves the clay pot, and the same master broth keeps on going, which deepens the flavor.

We've kept it straightforward and respectful to the classic. But feel free to top it with your choice of garnishes, like our House Chili Oil (page 258) or Marinated Eggs (page 45), in addition to or instead of the classic topping of shrimp and pork sauce.

INGREDIENTS

4 shrimp or prawns, peeled and deveined

Pinch each salt and ground white pepper

1 tablespoon neutral oil, such as soybean

4 individual-size bundles dried Asian wheat noodles

1 bunch (about 2 cups/ 225 g) bean sprouts

A splash plus 4 tablespoons shiro dashi

2 tablespoons toasted sesame oil

1 quart (950 ml) Superior Broth (page 261) or chicken broth

1 teaspoon Shrimp Powder (page 260)

2 tablespoons butter, cut into 4 small cubes

4 tablespoons Lu Rou Fan (page 151)

4 teaspoons pureed Garlic Confit (page 256; about 6 to 8 cloves)

1 bunch fresh cilantro, both leaves and stems, chopped

Chili oil, red chile flakes such as gochugaru or Sichuan chili flakes, for garnish (optional)

Seaweed and/or chopped scallions, for garnish (optional)

Toss the shrimp with the salt, white pepper, and neutral oil. Heat a grill or cast-iron grill pan and add, once very hot over medium high, the shrimp. Don't move them for 1 minute, then flip over to cook the opposite sides. Let cook until they're pink on both sides and have browned lightly.

Boil a large pot of water. Drop the noodles in and stir so they don't clump together. Add the bean sprouts right before the noodles are finished and, using a strainer or spider, strain out both. Set the noodles and sprouts into a metal bowl and stir with a splash of shiro dashi and the sesame oil, then divide evenly among four bowls.

In a saucepan, bring the broth up to a boil, stir in the shiro dashi, shrimp powder, and butter, and divide the seasoned broth among the four bowls.

On top of the noodles that should now be forming a small island in the center of the bowls, put 1 tablespoon lu rou fan, 1 teaspoon garlic confit, and a grilled shrimp on each portion. Encircle the shrimp with generous finger pinches of cilantro and your choice of chili oil, gochugaru, chile flakes, seaweed, or scallions, if using.

COLD SESAME NOODLES
Serves 4 to 6

THE BEST FOOD IS OFTEN THE SIMPLEST FOOD, IN ANY CULTURE. Taiwanese cold sesame noodles are a great example: super-simple and insanely delicious. But it's all about the sauce. We've had them in various ways and have also made a lot of variations on this. But two distinct sauces stick out in memory.

One was from a roadside stall in Tainan, where the cold noodles were served in a bowl and covered with a big ladle of deep tan–colored and slightly grainy sesame sauce. The other was at a place dedicated to black sesame paste noodles, with add-on options like wontons and fish balls. It was kind of a wild place, thick with the rusted, nutty aroma of sesame paste and filled with old and young people, all facedown in big bowls of noodles.

Both versions were incredible and we were inspired to make two recipes: one using sesame sauce made with toasted white sesame seeds—sometimes called white sesame paste, though it is brown from the seeds being toasted—served cold, and the following recipe (page 112) using black sesame sauce, served warm. We've used variations of both these sauces for cold noodle specials, high-end tasting-style dinners, and as a dipping sauce mixed with fermented bean curd for hot pot. (Shout out to Eric Sze of 886 restaurant, who helped us understand hot pot culture and the role of sesame paste in dipping sauces for it.)

For this classic version, add on an array of toppings such as sliced avocado, poached shrimp, snow pea leaves, soybeans, and bean sprouts, and it's the best summer dish for a fresh meal or late-night hangover cure.

Also, it's easy to make this recipe vegetarian by subbing out the chicken stock for water or vegetable broth (no shame in water!) and the shiro dashi for light soy.

1 pound (455 g) dry Asian wheat noodles, preferably thick and flat types

2 tablespoons toasted sesame oil

1 cup (240 ml) Wadaman Golden Sesame Paste or toasted white sesame paste

½ cup (120 ml) chicken stock (or water), plus more as needed

2 tablespoons shiro dashi

1 tablespoon dark soy sauce, plus more as needed

2 tablespoons Chinese black vinegar, plus more as needed

1 tablespoon mirin

1 tablespoon sugar, plus more as needed

1 clove garlic, grated

1 tablespoon pureed Garlic Confit (page 256; about 3 to 4 cloves)

2 tablespoons Kewpie mayonnaise

OPTIONAL GARNISH SUGGES-TIONS, PER SERVING BOWL:

1 fried or soft-boiled egg

1 half avocado, thinly sliced

1 handful fresh bean sprouts

1 heaping spoonful fresh corn kernels

1 heaping spoonful fresh soybeans or edamame

A few poached shrimp

1 handful blanched snow pea leaves

Gochugaru or Sichuan chile flakes

A drizzle of House Chili Oil (page 258) or your favorite chili oil, such as Lao Gan Ma Spicy Chili Crisp

Toasted white sesame seeds

Cook the noodles according to the directions on the package. Set up an ice water bath. Once the noodles are cooked, drain and transfer them to the ice water; let sit for 1 to 2 minutes, until cool, then drain. Toss with the toasted sesame oil in a large bowl.

Mix the sesame paste in its bottle with a fork to incorporate the oils that separate and rise to the top (place a medium bowl beneath it to catch any spills). Pour the sesame paste in the bowl and add the chicken stock; mix with a fork. Stir in the shiro dashi, dark soy sauce, black vinegar, mirin, sugar, grated garlic, and garlic confit and combine until smooth. Stir in the Kewpie mayonnaise last. If it looks a little thick, add more stock or water to create a thinner consistency. Taste for seasoning, adding any additional vinegar, sugar, or soy sauce as desired.

When you're ready to serve, cover the noodles with the sauce mixture and toss to evenly coat. Transfer the noodles to serving bowls and top each with your choice of the garnishes, if using, and serve.

BLACK SESAME NOODLES
with MUSHROOMS

Serves 4

THIS IS OUR TAKE ON SESAME NOODLES THAT WE SERVE AT WIN SON, AND IT'S ONE OF OUR BESTSELLING DISHES. In contrast to the Cold Sesame Noodles (page 109), this black sesame sauce incorporates dried and blended mushrooms for a totally vegetarian boost of umami. It's served with a big tangle of sautéed mushrooms and pea shoots, so it makes for a great vegetarian entrée.

1 head garlic

3 tablespoons neutral oil, such as soybean, plus more for drizzling

½ cup (½ ounce/14 g) dried black trumpet mushrooms

½ cup (120 ml) boiling water

¼ cup (60 ml) black sesame paste

1 tablespoon Wadaman Golden Sesame Paste or toasted white sesame paste

¼ teaspoon salt, plus more for seasoning

1 pound (455 g) Asian wheat noodles, fresh or dried

3 to 4 ounces (85 to 115 g) fresh mushrooms, preferably maitake, oyster, or beech, stems trimmed and mushrooms separated into bite-size pieces

3 to 4 ounces (85 to 115 g) fresh pea shoots or spinach

Cracked black pepper

1 tablespoon House Chili Oil (page 258) or your favorite chili oil, such as Lao Gan Ma Spicy Chili Crisp

1 tablespoon toasted sesame oil

1 teaspoon mirin

1 teaspoon soy sauce

1 teaspoon Chinese black vinegar

1 to 2 scallions, chopped

Sprinkle of Butter-Fried Peanuts (page 40; optional)

Black sesame seeds (optional)

Preheat the oven to 275°F (135°C). Slice off the stem of the garlic head, just enough to expose the cloves. Drizzle the exposed part with a little bit of the neutral oil. Wrap the garlic head tightly with foil and place directly on the oven rack to roast for 1 hour. Remove from the oven and let cool.

Meanwhile, place the black trumpet mushrooms in a small bowl and cover with the boiling water. Let soak for at least 20 minutes, until fully softened.

Once the garlic is cool enough to handle, remove the roasted cloves from the skins. Place in a blender or food processor along with the mushrooms and their soaking water, the black sesame paste, the golden sesame paste, ¼ cup (60 ml) water, and the salt. Blend or process until smooth. Taste for seasoning, adding extra salt if desired.

Cook the noodles according to the directions on the package. Drain in a colander and, if desired, run the noodles under cold water to cool them down. Shake off excess water to drain.

Heat a wok or pan over high heat with 2 tablespoons of the neutral oil and once the oil is very hot, add the fresh mushrooms. Season with a generous pinch of salt and don't move the mushrooms for about 30 seconds to gently sear them. Stir and let cook for several more seconds to sear the other side. Depending on how large the mushrooms are, cook, stirring occasionally, until they are softened and gently browned on all sides, then remove from the pan and set aside. Heat another tablespoon of neutral oil in the same pan and add the pea shoots. Season with a pinch each of salt and pepper. Let cook, stirring occasionally, until the greens are just wilted, about 1 minute. Remove from the pan and set aside.

In a large bowl, mix together the chili oil, sesame oil, mirin, soy sauce, and black vinegar. Add the noodles and toss to coat thoroughly.

To serve, spread the black sesame mixture onto the bottom of a serving dish. Arrange the noodles on top, followed by the sautéed mushrooms and greens, and garnish with chopped scallions, butter-fried peanuts, and black sesame seeds.

NOODLES AND SOUPS

ZHAJIANGMIAN with LAMB AND CILANTRO-MINT SAUCE
Serves 4

ZHAJIANGMIAN ORIGINATED IN CHINA, BUT IT'S POPULAR THROUGHOUT TAIWAN. It's traditionally made with ground pork that's smothered with a sweet and savory fermented bean paste called *tianmianjiang* ("sweet bean sauce" in English). Taiwan's version of zhajiangmian has its own unique quirks that distinguish it from versions of the dish you'd find in Northern China and elsewhere in the world. (It's popular in Korea and Japan, too.) Often there's chopped vegetables in it, or dry tofu. Ours has a few more twists, too. We went with ground lamb instead of pork—the heady, savory, and gamey flavor of lamb really holds up well to all the spices going on in this dish. But in this recipe, you can use either.

INGREDIENTS

1 pound (455 g) lamb or pork shoulder

2 tablespoons minced garlic

1 tablespoon peeled and minced fresh ginger

2 teaspoons toasted white sesame seeds

2 teaspoons red chile flakes, such as gochugaru or Sichuan chile flakes

1 teaspoon salt

4 large dried shiitake mushrooms

3 to 4 tablespoons neutral oil, such as soybean

¼ cup (60 ml) tianmianjiang (sweet bean sauce)

1 tablespoon shiro (white) miso paste

2 cups (480 ml) Superior Broth (page 26`) or chicken broth

2 teaspoons cornstarch

Soy sauce

1 pound (455 g) thick Asian wheat noodles, preferably fresh

2 scallions, chopped

½ cup Cilantro-Mint Sauce (page 255)

OPTIONAL GARNISHES:
Julienned cucumber

Fresh cilantro

Slivered scallions

Cut the lamb into ½-inch (12 mm) cubes. (Ideally, get bone-in meat and roast the bones to use for Superior Broth, page 261). In a large bowl, toss the meat with 1 tablespoon of the garlic, the ginger, sesame seeds, chile flakes, and salt. Cover and chill for at least 6 hours, or overnight.

Place the shiitake mushrooms in 2 cups (480 ml) water, cover, and let soak for at least 30 minutes, until softened (can be done overnight). Once fully softened, squeeze out the mushrooms, retaining all the soaking liquid. De-stem the mushrooms and finely chop. Strain the soaking liquid through a fine-mesh strainer.

In a large heavy-bottomed pot or Dutch oven, heat 2 tablespoons of the neutral oil over high heat until it's sputtering. Working in batches, add the cubed lamb or pork in a single layer, with at least half an inch of space in between the pieces, and let sear until browned on the bottom, about 2 minutes. Flip and brown the opposite sides. Transfer them to a bowl once all the batches have been nicely browned, adding more neutral oil to the pan for the next batch as necessary. (They do not need to be fully cooked at this point.)

In the same pan, add another tablespoon of the oil and heat over medium-high. Add the remaining 1 tablespoon minced garlic and the chopped shiitakes. Cook, stirring occasionally, for 1 to 2 minutes, until the garlic is fragrant and the mushrooms have slightly browned in parts. Add the tianmianjiang and miso paste and stir for another 1 to 2 minutes, scraping up anything stuck to the bottom of the pan and slightly toasting the sauce.

While the stock and mushroom soaking liquid are cold, combine them, then whisk in the cornstarch. Stir this mixture into the pot with the seared meat and bring to a boil. Reduce the heat to a simmer and cook, covered, for 3 hours, stirring often to prevent sticking. Remove the cover and continue cooking over low heat until the meat is very tender and the liquid has reduced to a thick sauce, about 1 more hour. Taste and add soy sauce as desired.

Meanwhile, cook the noodles according to the directions on the package and strain. In a large mixing bowl, toss the noodles with with the meat sauce and the Cilantro-Mint Sauce. Serve on a platter (or in individual bowls), topping it off with the remaining meat sauce, followed by the scallions. Finish each bowl with the optional garnishes.

WUYUZI MIAN
Serves 4

WUYUZI IS CURED MULLET ROE, WHICH IS ENJOYED IN TAIWAN AS A SORT OF DELICACY, ESPECIALLY EATEN AROUND LUNAR NEW YEAR. We say sort of because it's a great example of *gu zao wei*, or old-fashioned Taiwanese flavor. Young people might not seek out wuyuzi. But when we were shopping at the markets in Tainan with Josh's mom, we stumbled onto a shop that sold only wuyuzi, and that started a conversation and the realization that Trigg has actually cooked with wuyuzi plenty of times before—only known by its Italian name, *bottarga*. (Bottarga is also typically drier than Taiwanese wuyuzi, which is more like the texture of dry salami.) In Taiwan, the cured mullet roe is typically sliced for serving on special occasions. It may not be hip in young Taiwanese circles nowadays, but it's right up there with our favorite ingredients, along with shiro dashi, pickled mustard greens, and chili oil. It's salty like seawater with a slightly fishy flavor that wraps into other ingredients so well. Find it in specialty food stores or online.

After our encounter with wuyuzi, the first thing that Trigg thought of was spaghetti con la bottarga, a Sicilian classic. This is a total bastardization of that—and the only recipe in this book where we'll instruct you to use Italian noodles—but we think it's an upgrade to the original. A spin on the original only works better in very few instances, we know! But, for example, "Atlantic City" by the Band is definitely better than Bruce Springsteen's original. So it happens.

In the Sicilian pasta con la bottarga, the noodles are loaded up with grated bottarga, garlic, olive oil, maybe some chile flakes, parsley, and lemon juice. We ran with sesame oil, chili oil, cilantro, and a splash of shiro dashi. We love garnishing it with a little gochugaru, Korean chile flakes, and sesame seeds, too. Go for Sichuan chile flakes if you like it spicier—or just use red pepper flakes or Calabrian chile if that's what you've got available. For this recipe, we suggest dried, thin pasta noodles like spaghettini, preferably from an Italian market. (We like the Setaro brand.) Trigg's wife, Patty Brown, used to work the noodle station for chef Justin Smillie at Upland when it was reviewed by the *New York Times*, and Pete Wells called him a "pasta savant," so you bet we listen to her wherever noodles are concerned. This is one of her favorite dishes at Win Son, and a real crowd favorite—among young people in Brooklyn, at least.

INGREDIENTS

Salt

1 pound (455 g) spaghettini or thin spaghetti

¼ cup (60 ml) plus 1 tablespoon toasted sesame oil

4 cloves garlic, grated

¼ cup (60 ml) plus 1 tablespoon shiro dashi

¼ cup (60 ml) House Chili Oil (page 258), or your favorite chili oil, such as Lao Gan Ma Spicy Chili Crisp

2 tablespoons chopped fresh cilantro, both stems and leaves

4 tablespoons (½ stick) unsalted butter, cut into small cubes

1 roe sack or 12 ounces (340 g) wuyuzi or bottarga, grated

½ bunch Thai basil leaves, sliced to wide ribbons

12 leaves shiso, sliced to wide ribbons

Red chile flakes, such as gochugaru or Sichuan chile flakes (optional)

Toasted white sesame seeds (optional)

Bring a pot of generously salted water to a boil. Cook the spaghettini until just under al dente, as the noodles will finish cooking in the sauce, and drain, reserving 2 cups (480 ml) cooking water.

In a large sauté pan, combine the 2 cups (480 ml) reserved water with the sesame oil, garlic, shiro dashi, chili oil, and cilantro. Heat to medium-low and swirl the pan occasionally for 1 minute, or until very fragrant. This is to "bloom" the ingredients and infuse the liquid with them. Do not let it come to a boil or start to smoke. Remove from the heat.

Add the slightly undercooked pasta, the butter cubes, and half the grated wuyuzi. Turn the heat back on to medium and toss with tongs to mix thoroughly. Cook for 1 to 2 minutes, stirring occasionally, until the noodles are cooked to al dente and the sauce has thickened and turned milky rather than translucent. Taste for seasoning and add salt, if desired.

Transfer the pasta to four serving dishes. Garnish each serving with handfuls of the basil and shiso, then top with the remaining grated wuyuzi. Finish with the chile flakes and/or sesame seeds, if using, and serve immediately.

SHIN RAMYUN, WIN SON STYLE
Serves 2

SHIN RAMYUN IS (THE) GOAT. This Korean brand of instant ramen is a must-have for any bachelor pad or college dorm. Trigg and his chef-mentor Pei Chang think it's a perfect food.

We know, so what are you doing reading this cookbook? Well, it's almost perfect in its conception per the instructions on the packet. As amazing as this culinary touchstone is, it takes on further dimensions and personality as a vehicle for some chili oil and fermented bean curd. Throw in some eggs, Italian sausage, and Stacy's Fire Roasted Jalapeño Pita Chips, and you've got a real party. Trust us and try this.

1 tablespoon neutral oil, such as soybean

1 pack (4 links) hot Italian sausage, casings removed

2 packs Shin Ramyun instant ramen

4 eggs

1 teaspoon jarred fermented bean curd with chili (aka dou fu ru)

1 (3-ounce/85 g) bag Stacy's Pita Chips, jalapeño flavor, crushed

½ bunch scallions, chopped

½ bunch fresh cilantro, both leaves and stems, chopped

1 small pack roasted seaweed snacks

1 tablespoon House Chili Oil (page 258) or your favorite chili oil, such as Lao Gan Ma Spicy Chili Crisp

In a medium to large saucepan, slick the bottom with a little oil and start browning the sausage while breaking it up with a fork.

Once it's fully cooked, bring 4 cups (960 ml) water to a boil. While your water is coming up to temperature, open the individual packs of dried veg and seasoning from the ramen packages and, when it's boiling, add to the water with the noodles.

Have two serving bowls at the ready. Over a small mixing bowl, crack the eggs in half one by one. Pass the egg yolk back and forth between the shells, separating the whites from the yolks. Let the whites fall into the mixing bowl, and place the raw yolks into the serving bowls. (Add 2 raw yolks per serving bowl.)

Give the noodles a stir to make sure they're fully submerged and cooking evenly, which should take about 3 minutes total. At this point, slowly pour in your egg whites while stirring, followed by a teaspoon of dou fu ru. Let cook for another minute.

Divide the noodles evenly between the two bowls with the yolks and then distribute the soup, thickened with egg whites and flecked with the now-hydrated vegetables.

Top with the crushed Stacy's Pita Chips, scallions, cilantro, seaweed snacks, and ½ tablespoon chili oil per bowl and serve.

YUN HAI SCALLION NOODLES
Serves 4

WE ONCE DID A POP-UP AT WIN SON WITH LISA CHENG SMITH OF YUN HAI. (See our conversation with her on page 32.) She made these scallion noodles, which were so incredible that she let us put them on the menu as a side dish. The star of the show is the scallion oil, which follows a simple technique but creates such a satisfyingly rich flavor. Paired with the incredible Taiwanese soy paste (see page 30) that Yun Hai sells, it's an amazing combo that adults and kids (like Juhee Brown, our model) love.

INGREDIENTS

2 bunches scallions

1 quart (950 ml) neutral oil, such as soybean, plus more to fry the eggs

1 cup Taiwanese soy paste

4 bundles Asian dried wheat noodles

4 eggs

1 tablespoon toasted white sesame seeds (optional)

1 teaspoon red chile flakes, such as gochugaru or Sichuan chile flakes (optional)

Fried shallots (optional)

NOTE: This recipe will make extra scallion oil, which you can save for another day. In addition to noodles, this flavorful oil can be drizzled on soups, stir-fries, or just rice.

Get a large pot of water boiling to cook the noodles.

Slice the scallions thinly on a hard bias but keep the white and green parts separate. Set a wire rack over a sheet pan and add four layers of paper towels.

In a medium saucepan, combine the neutral oil and the scallion whites. Bring the temperature of the oil up slowly to 325°F (165°C), when measured with a candy thermometer, and stir to keep the sliced scallion whites from clumping in the oil. This will help them fry evenly. When the oil is at temperature, add the scallion greens and continue stirring. Once the greens have stopped fizzing, carefully drain the fried scallions and transfer them to the paper towel–lined wire rack. Reserve the oil.

One by one, transfer the fried scallion bits from one layer of paper to the next layer underneath it, discarding the oil-soaked paper. By the final layer, you shouldn't have much oil saturating the paper, and the fried scallions can continue to cool down and dry.

When the oil is at room temperature, combine the soy paste with 1 cup (240 ml) of the scallion oil in a mixing bowl. The rest of the oil can be stored in an airtight container or jar for up to 2 weeks refrigerated.

Cook your noodles according to the directions on the package and drain. Add immediately to the soy paste and scallion oil mixture and mix thoroughly.

Meanwhile, heat a skillet with a couple tablespoons of neutral oil. Fry the eggs sunny-side up, working in batches as necessary. Arrange the noodles into four bowls. On top of each, place a crispy bottomed, sunny-side up fried egg, with a heavy dose of fried scallions, sesame seeds, chile flakes, and fried shallots, if using.

AUNTIE LEAH'S CORN SOUP

Makes 6 cups (1.4 L); serves 6 to 8

LEAH IS JOSH'S MOM, BUT SHE'S KNOWN TO MUCH OF HER EXTENDED FAMILY, INCLUDING THE WIN SON FAMILY, AS AUNTIE LEAH. Growing up, she would often make a large pot of this soup to carry Josh and his sister through a few days' worth of quick meals and snacks. Light yet filling, kid-tested, mom-approved.

If you're wondering why it resembles a typical American chicken and corn chowder, except for perhaps the egg drop, there's a bit of history to that. According to Katy Hui-wen Hung and Steven Crook's *A Culinary History of Taipei*, Green Giant made a big push in Taiwan in the nineties, encouraging home cooks to make corn soup. This type of soup has become so popular it's served in restaurants, especially Taiwanese steakhouses, as a side or appetizer.

INGREDIENTS

8 ounces (225 g) boneless chicken tenders or boneless breast, julienned against the grain into thin slivers 1 to 2 inches long

1 teaspoon rice wine, preferably Taiwanese, or use Shaoxing rice wine as a substitute

1 teaspoon cornstarch

1 teaspoon salt, plus more as needed

4 cups (960 ml) chicken stock

2 cups (290 g) freshly shucked corn kernels (about 2 ears)

1 (14¾-oz/420 g) can creamed corn, or 1½ cups (360 ml)

2 eggs, whisked

Ground white or cracked black pepper

4 scallions, sliced, for garnish (optional)

In a small bowl, combine the chicken, rice wine, cornstarch, and salt and mix gently by hand. Set aside for 20 minutes, or cover and chill in the refrigerator for up to overnight.

In a large pot, combine the chicken stock, fresh corn kernels, and, if using, the creamed corn. (If using homemade chilled corn soup instead of the can of creamed corn, do not add it yet.) Bring to a boil and then reduce the heat to a gentle simmer.

Slowly drop in the chicken one sliver at a time, stirring after each to ensure that the pieces don't stick together in the soup. Continue stirring in a circular pattern as you slowly pour in the eggs. If you are using chilled corn soup instead of the can of creamed corn, stir it into the mixture now.

Taste for seasoning, adding any extra salt and pepper as needed. Ladle into serving bowls and garnish with the sliced scallions to serve. The soup can be stored in the refrigerator in an airtight container for up to 5 days.

A Conversation with Auntie Leah

WHAT'S IN A TAIWANESE BUSINESS NAME?

JOSH'S MOM IS KNOWN AFFECTIONATELY AS AUNTIE LEAH TO THE REST OF THE WIN SON FAMILY. Based in Taiwan now, Auntie Leah has taken Josh, Trigg, and our pastry chef Danielle all over the island, showing them the best beef noodle shops, herb shops, fruit stands, and more. Her support and guidance have been paramount to the development of Win Son—and she also makes a great homestyle corn soup (page 124). We caught up with her on Zoom.

JOSH: Mom, so, remember when Trigg and I took our first trip to Taiwan? That was when you were living in Taiwan part time. As soon as we put our stuff down, we went out to Guohua Jie [Guohua Street in Tainan, famous for its food].

AUNTIE LEAH: Guohua Jie, for *o a jian* [oyster omelets, page 51]!

TRIGG: O a jian and the rice cakes.

JOSH: We went right away!

AUNTIE LEAH: I was very encouraged by you two doing the trip, you know? I had no idea why Joshua was starting a restaurant. I never thought of that, you know? I think it's because he found Trigg, I mean, a partner that he can work with. I really admire your patience.

TRIGG: Yeah, Josh has a lot of patience.

AUNTIE LEAH: And you have patience for cooking! So you need each other. In Chinese there's a word that says it—you cannot do anything apart from each other, you have to do it together, and it comes out a thousand times more successful. Uh, how do you say it? One person does one thing, another does another thing, and one plus one is two. But these two people work on one accord and it becomes—

JOSH: Three!

AUNTIE LEAH: No, three thousand! No, ten thousand. These two work in one accord and it's ten thousand times the power. So we apply that to your business, two people that work together in one accord, with the same mind, same purpose, same view—then you succeed.

But here I would like to say something about this: Don't make it too big. Because in your life, business is one part, but another thing is family life. Toward the end, family is everything. Your wife, your children, your parents . . . even your grandchildren. So, do not work too hard!

TRIGG: Heh.

AUNTIE LEAH: Get married, have children, Joshua!

TRIGG: Well, Josh is gonna be a good dad one day when he has kids. He's so sweet to my kids.

AUNTIE LEAH: Josh is gonna be a great daddy.

JOSH: Yea. Anyway! We were going to ask about Ah-Gong [grandfather] and how he started Winsome, his business.

AUNTIE LEAH: Yes, Grandpa started Winsome, what's the year? 1973 or '74. Winsome is the company he made from an investment from my uncles, and it was for the family.

JOSH: Growing up, I would always see little Winsome merchandise with the logo on it. We would always eat out of those rice bowls at Da Jojo's [uncle] house or Ah-Gong's house. I remember the letterhead and notepad that was made back then, with the logo and all the biz information on it—

AUNTIE LEAH: Address, phone number . . .

JOSH: Yes, and I asked if I could take a sheet from it, and I got one and I kept it. It was so cool. And, yeah, that kind of became the idea of the name of our restaurant. It still became the name in a different form.

AUNTIE LEAH: Even better, I like Win Son.

JOSH: Can you talk about what Winsome means? Why did Grandpa choose that name?

AUNTIE LEAH: *Ing* means profit, overflowing. Means you make a lot of money, simple. *Tsen* means success. Successfully make money.

JOSH: It's a little redundant!

AUNTIE LEAH: Who's the English major here?

JOSH: My mom was an English major!

TRIGG: But, *ing-son*—that's why Winsome is the English version, because of the sound, and the kind of similar meaning. Because there's a relationship between *ing* and *win*, right?

AUNTIE LEAH: Yeah, *ing* and *tsen* are both words that are, *win win win*!

JOSH: I see.

AUNTIE LEAH: I like Win Son better. All my sons.

CHAPTER 5
ENTRÉES

WHOLE ROASTED FISH with GARLIC-GINGER SAUCE

Serves about 8

ROASTING A WHOLE FISH IS AN EASY CROWD-PLEASER. There's nothing better than going to a re chao restaurant in Taiwan, where you can pick out the best-looking fish and seafood from tanks and watch the chef steam it. But roasting it at home is really good, too—and really easy. It results in crispy, delicious fish skin that keeps your fish nice and moist.

Look for responsibly farmed fish from a trusted fishmonger. Nowadays there are a lot of outfits that promise to match the number of fish they raise with an acreage of bivalve beds to help clean the oceans; the camera systems and automated feeders of farmed fish systems can also make for less wasteful feeding cycles. All this can help limit overfishing and ocean pollution. If your fishmonger has wild-caught whole fish, stick with something local, like striped bass, that's in season. Also, never forget the rule of thumb when buying fish, for freshness's sake: Pick fishies with clear, bright eyes and red gills.

INGREDIENTS

4 whole black bass fish (about 1 pound/ 455 g each), or other responsibly farmed or wild-caught whole fish

1 cup (240 ml) neutral oil, such as soybean, plus 2 tablespoons more if you don't have a rack insert

1 tablespoon salt

1 tablespoon cracked black pepper

1 cup (240 ml) Garlic-Ginger Sauce with Pickled Mustard Greens (page 257), or more as desired

2 lemons, halved

1 teaspoon chile flakes, 1 chopped scallion, 1 tablespoon pickled chiles (we like Sichuan chiles, which are salty and not very spicy), for garnish (optional)

Set your oven to 450°F (230°C).

Ask your fishmonger to snip off the dorsal and side fins. (These burn and become bitter.) Also ask for scaled and gutted fish. When you bring the fish home, rinse them well under cold water on their outside and inside the cavity.

Pat the fish dry with paper towels. Place each fish on a cutting board and, using a sharp knife, cut three deep slashes across their width, preferably on a bias, just until you hit bone.

Rub the fish down with the oil and season generously with the salt and pepper.

Set the fish on a wire rack set in a half-sheet pan, spacing the fish out so there's an inch (2.5 cm) or so of space in between each (see Note). (If you don't have a rack, grease the sheet pan with 2 additional tablespoons oil.) Roast for about 6 minutes, until the skin is golden brown. Remove the fish from the oven and reduce the oven's heat to 325°F (165°C). Spoon the garlic-ginger sauce with pickled mustard greens liberally over each fish, about 2 tablespoons per fish at least.

Return the fish to the oven to roast for another 8 minutes. When the fish comes out, serve each with a half lemon per fish for spritzing and any of the optional garnishes you prefer.

NOTE: We recommend roasting these on half-sheet pans with rack inserts. Go ahead and order some from webstaurantstore.com. This is the best way to get even air flow underneath whatever you're cooking. And the half-size pans fit in all ovens. They're the best for resting steaks out of the pan or roasting fish like this in the oven. They are good for veggies like potatoes, too. This is a restaurant kitchen game changer that every home cook should have, and they're like five bucks a piece. However, if you don't have the rack insert, just place the fish atop your sheet pan, but be sure to grease the bottom with some oil.

FRIED PORK CHOPS with BASIL
Serves 4

FRIED PORK CHOPS (*PAI GU*) ARE VERY POPULAR IN TAIWAN. Some are crispier, like *da ji pai* (big fried chicken), but some are glistening with caramelization. Some remind you of tonkatsu. The fried pork diversity in Taiwan is amazing.

Fried pork chops make us think of a Taiwanese chain called Formosa Chang. It's sort of fast food, but it's done well, and it's delicious. It's a place where you can get fried pork chops and blanched sweet potato leaves with a little Taiwanese soy paste and a side of Lu Rou Fan (page 151). This place and Bojangles are high on our fast-food restaurant favorites. It may not be the gold standard of fried pork chops, but it sets a great bar.

We could eat a whole plate of these fried pork chops alone easily, but they're great served over rice (*pai gu fan*) with some pickled mustard greens and a fried or boiled egg to round out a dinner.

FOR THE PORK CHOPS:
8 pork collar steaks or chops, sliced about ¼ inch (6 mm) thick (see Note)

3 tablespoons shio koji

1 tablespoon salt

2 teaspoons Chinese five-spice powder

2 tablespoons rice vinegar

2 teaspoons sugar

2 tablespoons light soy sauce

1 teaspoon toasted sesame oil

4-inch (10-cm) piece fresh ginger, peeled and minced

3 cloves garlic, minced

2 quarts (2 L) neutral oil, such as soybean

1 cup (130 g) sweet potato flour, for dredging (can be found in Asian markets)

1 bunch Thai basil leaves

FOR THE FINISHING SPICE:
1 tablespoon salt

1 teaspoon Chinese five-spice powder

1 teaspoon red chile flakes, such as gochugaru or Sichuan chile flakes

TO SERVE:
Steamed rice

Sunny-side up fried eggs

¼ teaspoon red chile flakes, such as gochugaru or Sichuan chile flakes (optional)

1 teaspoon toasted white sesame seeds

MAKE THE PORK CHOPS: One at a time, lay the pork steaks on a cutting board and pound them to an even thickness (about ½ inch / 12 mm) with a meat tenderizing hammer. For frying, you want the chops to cook evenly and quickly, so pounding them out is important.

In a bowl, combine the shio koji, salt, Chinese five-spice powder, rice vinegar, sugar, light soy sauce, toasted sesame oil, ginger, and garlic and coat the steaks with the marinade. Let sit covered in the fridge for 1 hour and up to 4 hours. (Too much longer and the vinegar will take over.)

In a pot at least double its quantity, so that it doesn't boil over, bring the neutral oil to 350°F (175°C), when measured with a candy thermometer.

In a dish, dredge your steaks thoroughly in the sweet potato flour. Make sure the flour gets in all the nooks and crannies, covering the topographical landscape of the pork.

Prepare a wire rack over a sheet pan for landing the pork chops out of the fryer.

Carefully drop the pork chops into the oil one by one, working in two batches of 4 chops per batch. Fry for 3 minutes. At 2½ minutes in, throw in a handful of basil. Remove the chops and fried basil at 3 minutes of frying. Repeat this step for the remaining 3 chops and basil.

Once you remove the chops from the fryer, place on the wire rack–lined tray. (If you let them rest out of the oil on a plate or a few paper towels, it will cause the bottoms to become soggy.)

MAKE THE FINISHING SPICE: Combine the salt, Chinese five-spice powder, gochugaru, and Sichuan chile flakes and sprinkle on each of the chops.

Serve the chops with steamed rice, fried eggs, and fried basil. Season the eggs with optional chile flakes and sesame seeds.

NOTE: We love to use pork collar, also known as CT Butt or coppa steaks. Look for it from butchers, but if you can't source it, ask your butcher to slice chops that are about ¾-inch (6-mm) thick.

STICKY RICE WITH SAUSAGE, SHRIMP, AND MUSHROOMS

Serves 6 to 8

STICKY RICE IS TRULY IRRESISTIBLE IN ALL ITS FORMS, AND IT COMES IN MANY OF THEM IN TAIWAN. Whether sweet or savory, or if it's stuffed inside pockets made of lotus leaves and steamed, you can't go wrong. We even stuff it inside a fried quail sometimes (page 140). At Win Son, we fold our shrimp cake (page 53) into our sticky rice. But since you probably don't have some shrimp cake left over in your fridge right now, we made this recipe using fresh shrimp, which is pretty great because you get plump morsels of shrimp along with juicy mushrooms throughout the seasoned rice.

INGREDIENTS

2 cups (400 g) glutinous rice (usually called *sweet rice* on packages)

2 tablespoons neutral oil, such as soybean

3 ounces (85 g) Taiwanese sausage or Cantonese sausage (aka *lapcheong*), diced (about 2 small links)

8 ounces (225 g) fresh shrimp, peeled, deveined, and chopped (8 to 10 large shrimp), or 8 ounces (225 g) leftover shrimp cake (page 53)

½ cup (43 g) chopped fresh oyster mushrooms

4 to 6 scallions, chopped

2 cloves garlic, minced

1½ cups (360 ml) Superior Broth (page 261) or chicken broth

½ cup (120 ml) rice wine, preferably Taiwanese, or use Shaoxing rice wine as a substitute

¼ teaspoon salt

1 tablespoon Shrimp Powder (page 260)

2 tablespoons soy sauce

Pinch MSG

Rinse and soak the rice. In a medium or large heavy-bottomed pot with a lid, such as a Dutch oven, heat the oil over medium-low heat. Add the diced sausage and cook, stirring occasionally, until the fat appears translucent, about 4 minutes.

Add the chopped shrimp, mushrooms, scallions, and garlic and cook, stirring frequently, for 1 to 2 minutes, until the scallions appear translucent and the shrimp are opaque. Strain the sticky rice, add to the pot, and increase the heat to medium-high. Stirring frequently, gently toast the rice grains afor 1 minute. Then add the broth, rice wine, salt, shrimp powder, soy sauce, and MSG and bring to a boil, stirring occasionally. Reduce the heat to a gentle simmer and cover. Cook covered for 10 minutes. Lift the cover and stir, scraping any bits that are sticking to the bottom. Return the cover and cook for another 10 to 15 minutes, until the liquid has fully evaporated and the rice is tender.

CLAMS WITH BASIL
Serves 4 to 6

RE CHAO MEANS "HOT STIR-FRY" AND ALSO REFERS TO A STYLE OF RESTAURANT IN TAIWAN. At some, patrons can select live fish, crabs, clams, and shrimp from tanks and fresh squid, chicken, vegetables, and more, all meticulously organized on ice. Stewed, fried, or stir-fried, it's all up to you, but meant to be shared in a group and washed down with Taiwan Beer. In Tainan, the re chao spots are huge and can spill out into the sidewalks along with good vibes perpetuated by people happily eating together. It's one of our favorite ways to eat in Taiwan. And one of the classic re chao dishes is clams with basil.

According to Katy Hui-wen Hung and Steven Crook in their book, *A Culinary History of Taipei*, in Taiwan's older days, one could easily collect freshwater clams while washing clothes in the river—ticking off two chores at the same time. Due to rapid population growth and industrialization post–World War II, clams aren't as abundant in the rivers today, although they're still teeming with shrimp. And various types of clams are still pervasive in the culinary landscape (around twenty!). Stir-frying clams with rice wine, garlic, and basil is a popular move. The type of basil used in Taiwan is distinct and fragrant; however, it's not indigenous. (It was likely brought by Hakka migrating from Fujian Province in the seventeenth century.) Use Thai basil, which is pretty similar and can be easily found in the US.

This dish is both delicious and educational in its representation of indigenous ingredients (originally, freshwater river clams) and layers of intertwined, immigrational influence—like the basil. We even invited some Taiwan Beer to the party in our clams. We don't change the method of steaming the clams open with rice wine (and beer) in the wok and stir-frying in garlic and fresh basil, but we do add a seasonal component at Win Son. Sometimes we integrate roasted red kabocha pumpkin into the sauce. In the spring we'll use a guacamole-textured puree of green garbanzo beans (see Note). The summer set is our favorite, though. We add wok-charred Sungold tomatoes and preserved lemon to complement the rice wine and basil.

And we always serve the clams with Scallion Pancakes (page 202) to sop up the sauce—sort of like one would with a piece of crusty bread in European cuisine. But you could always serve this with steamed rice, as part of a multicourse meal or alone.

INGREDIENTS

2 tablespoons grapeseed oil

4 cloves garlic, finely chopped

1½ cups (220 g) Sungold, grape, or cherry tomatoes, halved or kept whole if small

2 pounds (910 g) small clams, such as cockle, baby Manila, or littleneck, scrubbed and soaked in cold water for 20 minutes to purge (about 16 per pound)

½ cup (120 ml) Asian lager beer, such as Taiwan Beer

½ cup (120 ml) rice wine, preferably Taiwanese, or use Shaoxing rice wine as a substitute

¼ cup (60 ml) shiro dashi

1 tablespoon finely chopped preserved lemon peel

1 cup (20 g) fresh Thai basil leaves, plus more for garnish

2 tablespoons unsalted butter

1 teaspoon toasted white sesame seeds

½ teaspoon red chile flakes, such as gochugaru or Sichuan chile flakes (optional)

In a wok or large high-sided skillet, heat the oil over high heat. Add the garlic, tomatoes, and clams and shake the pan to mix them up a little—it's good to let the clams beat up and burst the tomatoes as they pop in the hot oil.

Reduce the heat to medium-low and add the beer, rice wine, shiro dashi, and preserved lemon; cover until the clams start to open, 3 or 4 minutes. Stir in most of the basil leaves (saving a few for garnish) and the butter as they start to open. Discard any clams that do not open after 5 minutes.

Transfer the clam mixture to a serving bowl. Sprinkle with sesame seeds and gochugaru, if using. Garnish with the extra fresh basil leaves and serve.

NOTE: Some of our favorite variations of this dish can be made by following the recipe as written, but not using the tomatoes or the preserved lemon. Add the purees described below, just as the clams are opening.

In the fall, preheat the oven to 325°F (160°C). Halve and seed 1 red kabocha squash. Dust with 1 teaspoon salt and 1 teaspoon Chinese five-spice and roast for 4 hours until soft. Put the roasted squash into a food processor and process until smooth.

In the spring, add 1 cup green garbanzo beans (200 g), 3 tablespoons olive oil, 2 teaspoons each of salt, pepper, and MSG into a food processor and process until smooth.

Any time of the year, add 1 cup (240 ml) of Charred Scallion Sauce (page 254).

STUFFED QUAIL WITH STICKY RICE AND KUMQUAT SALAD

Serves 4

STICKY RICE–STUFFED QUAIL MAKES A REALLY FUN ENTRÉE AS A SPECIAL TREAT. We were once invited to cook on a show hosted by our friends Ben and Brent from The Meat Hook, a whole-animal butcher shop nearby us in Brooklyn. We stuffed a whole, deboned chicken with sticky rice for their meat-centric show, *Prime Time*. That takes some doing, but with quail, you can buy them boneless. (*New York dressed* is the technical term for boneless quail; you might want to call ahead and ask your butcher to place a special order.) It's a great way to try cooking quail, as this preparation cooks quickly and evenly. This recipe utilizes our recipe for Sticky Rice with Sausage, Shrimp, and Mushrooms (page 136), which is also great on its own—as is the kumquat and herb salad that we love to pile on top of the whole thing.

FOR THE QUAIL CURE AND STUFFING:

4 boneless quail (aka New York–dressed quail)

3 tablespoons light soy sauce

3 tablespoons rice wine, preferably Taiwanese, or use Shaoxing rice wine as a substitute

1 tablespoon toasted sesame oil

⅓ recipe Sticky Rice with Sausage, Shrimp, and Mushrooms (page 136)

FOR FRYING:

6 cups (1.4 L) neutral oil, such as soybean

2 cups (260 g) cornstarch

1 cup (125 g) all-purpose flour

1 cup (130 g) coarse sweet potato starch

Salt

2 teaspoons "Chicken" Spice Mix (page 254)

FOR THE KUMQUAT SALAD:

4 cups (900 g) thinly sliced kumquats

1 tablespoon shiro dashi

1 tablespoon toasted sesame oil

Handful of fresh Thai basil leaves and cilantro leaves and sprigs

½ cup (55 g) thinly sliced scallions

Sprinkle of fried shallots and toasted white sesame seeds (optional)

¼ teaspoon red chile flakes, such as gochugaru or Sichuan chile flakes (optional)

CURE THE QUAIL: Place the quail in a large zip-top plastic bag and add the soy sauce, rice wine, and sesame oil. Squeeze out any air and seal shut. Refrigerate for 3 hours. Drain the cure, pat the quail dry, and place them on a wire rack fit atop a pan. Refrigerate overnight, or at least 12 hours, to dry.

Stuff each quail with a heaping tablespoon of sticky rice, cross the legs, and stick a toothpick through the legs to seal the cavity shut.

Temper the quail for 2 hours, letting it come to room temperature.

FRY THE QUAIL: After the quail has tempered, heat the oil in a large pot or deep-fryer. In a wide shallow bowl, combine the cornstarch and flour and stir in about 1 pint (480 ml) water, until the dredge matches the consistency of paint. Roll each quail in the wet dredge, then dust it with the sweet potato starch. Working in batches, fry each quail at 325°F (165°C) for 6 minutes.

Let them rest for 10 minutes. Season with salt and chicken spice.

MAKE THE SALAD: Roll the basil leaves and slice thinly to julienne. Toss together with the cilantro, kumquats, shiro dashi, sesame oil, and scallions.

Slice each fried quail in half lengthwise and transfer each stuffed quail to an to individual plate. Add equal portions of the salad to each plate. Garnish with the optional fried shallots, sesame seeds, chile flakes and serve.

ENTRÉES

STIR-FRIED CHICKEN AND WOOD EAR MUSHROOMS

Serves 4

THIS DISH IS A HOMEY STIR-FRY THAT TRIGG'S FRIEND JULIA SUNG INTRODUCED HIM TO. They met at a dog park when their dogs Mila and Ophy were puppies and he became great friends with her and her husband, Vinnie. Julia's family is from Taiwan and she grew up in Flushing, New York. Trigg was dropping something by their house one day while Vinnie and Julia were in the process of moving, and Julia gave him a container of stir-fried chicken and wood ear mushrooms her mom, Hui-Yun Sung, had whipped up for dinner. It was one of those incredibly delicious meals that's simple yet so satisfying. It made him feel so well-fed and taken care of after eating it, just like a good home-cooked meal made with love should.

2 pounds (910 g) boneless, skinless chicken thighs

2 teaspoons cornstarch

1 teaspoon salt

1 teaspoon MSG

3 tablespoons neutral oil, such as soybean

1 cup (240 ml) rice wine, preferably Taiwanese, or use Shaoxing rice wine as a substitute

2 ounces (55 g) dried wood ear mushrooms (aka black fungus; can be found in Asian markets)

¼ cup (60 ml) light soy sauce, plus more for seasoning the sauce (optional)

1 tablespoon toasted sesame oil

Taiwanese soy paste (optional)

1 bunch scallions, chopped (optional)

Steamed white rice, for serving

4 fried eggs (optional)

The night before you want to cook this, cut the chicken thighs into thirds so you have some nice fat chunks. In a medium bowl, toss the chicken with the cornstarch, salt, MSG, 2 tablespoons of the neutral oil, and ½ cup (120 ml) of the rice wine. Set in the fridge, covered, overnight.

Cover the wood ear mushrooms with 1 pint (480 ml) boiling hot water. Give the mushrooms an hour to hydrate in the hot water; you can do this the night before, while you marinate the chicken, and store the strained mushrooms in the refrigerator until needed. After they have hydrated, strain through a colander and discard the water.

Using a paring knife, cut off the root of each wood ear where the mushrooms clung to wherever they were growing. This end is tough and should be discarded.

When you're ready to cook, remove the chicken from the fridge and strain out the excess marinade.

Slick a wok, large sauté pan, or a Dutch oven with the remaining 1 tablespoon neutral oil over high heat. Once it's very hot, add the chicken and stir to spread the pieces around. Just when it starts to brown a little, add the mushrooms, the remaining ½ cup (120 ml) rice wine, the light soy sauce, and sesame oil. Let the liquids come up to a boil and reduce until there is a thick sauce. Season with extra soy sauce or the Taiwanese soy paste (see page 30), if desired. Remove from the heat and fold in the chopped scallions. Serve in individual shallow bowls with the rice and the fried egg on top, if using.

ENTRÉES

143

SAN BEI JI (THREE-CUP CHICKEN)

Serves 6

THE IDEA BEHIND THIS DISH IS THAT IT CONTAINS ONE CUP OF SESAME OIL, ONE CUP OF RICE WINE, AND ONE CUP OF SOY SAUCE—THREE CUPS, PLUS CHICKEN. Easy to remember. It's a very well-known dish in Taiwan that has Hakka roots—the Hakka are a minority originally from China that have a strong diaspora culture in Taiwan going back centuries. While we don't use exactly three equal portions of the key ingredients, our combination, braised with chicken, produces an amazingly salty, herbal, and fragrant dish, loaded with basil, garlic, and ginger. Traditionally, bite-size pieces of chicken leg cut straight through the bone with a cleaver are used. Since it might not be easy to find a butcher who will do that, we recommend getting some bone-in drumsticks, thighs, and wings to braise whole in our recipe.

INGREDIENTS

4 chicken legs, 4 thighs, and 4 wings (about 3½ pounds/1.6 kg total)

1 tablespoon sugar

1 tablespoon salt

1 tablespoon MSG

1 cup (240 ml) rice wine, preferably Taiwanese, or use Shaoxing rice wine as a substitute

¼ cup (60 ml) neutral oil, such as soybean

1 (2- to 3-inch / 5- to 7.5- cm) knob fresh ginger, peeled and thinly sliced

2 cloves garlic, grated

2 tablespoons toasted sesame oil

1 tablespoon cornstarch

½ cup (120 ml) Taiwanese soy paste

3 tablespoons dark soy sauce

1 bunch Thai basil

Steamed white rice, for serving

Red chile flakes, such as gochugaru or Sichuan chile flakes (optional)

Cut the legs and thighs in half and the wings in thirds by their joints. Use a heavy cleaver to chop them easily, but if you don't have a cleaver, just keep them whole. Cutting them in half creates more equal pieces and the marrow enriches the sauce.

Combine the chicken pieces with the sugar, salt, MSG, and ½ cup (120 ml) of the rice wine. Leave covered in the fridge overnight to marinate.

The next day, bring a large pot or Dutch oven filled with water to a boil. Carefully drop in the chicken pieces using a spider or a slotted spoon. The cold chicken will drop the temperature of the water. As the water comes back to a boil, protein will foam out of the chicken. This protein scum is easy to remove from the hot water with a spoon. Remove and discard it. Let the chicken cook in the water for about 2 minutes total. By the time the water comes back to a rolling boil, you should manage to skim most of the protein off. If you have a really strong burner, keep the heat set on medium so the water doesn't boil furiously. Strain the chicken and set aside in a bowl.

In the same pot or Dutch oven you were using, add the neutral oil and ginger slices and heat over medium-low heat. Sweat the thinly sliced ginger for about a minute. When it becomes aromatic and soft, add the garlic and sesame oil and stir for about 30 seconds.

Add the remaining ½ cup (120 ml) rice wine and bring to a boil by adjusting the heat to high. Mix the tablespoon of cornstarch with 1/2 cup of water in a small bowl, then whisk in the cornstarch slurry and bring the heat down to low.

Add the marinated chicken, Taiwanese soy paste, and dark soy sauce, then let the chicken lightly simmer for about an hour. You don't want to scorch the sauce, so stir frequently and check on the chicken once every 5 to 10 minutes. The dark meat pieces can be cooked more quickly, but they will become soft if you slowly cook them over the course of an hour. Be careful not to overcook. After 45 minutes, taste the chicken. It should be soft, but not falling apart. If you cook it too long, it will fall off the bone and you will have a stew of shredded chicken and bones. Ten minutes before it's ready, stir in almost all the basil, reserving a few leaves for garnish.

Serve in a large bowl, family style, or individually over rice, with the reserved fresh basil on top. Sprinkle with chile flakes, if using.

PEI'S WHITE MAPO TOFU
Serves 2 to 3

PEI CHANG IS A CHEF WHO TRIGG WORKED UNDER AT KESWICK HALL AND LATER TEN SUSHI IN CHARLOTTESVILLE, VIRGINIA, AND HE REMAINS ONE OF HIS MOST IMPORTANT CULINARY MENTORS. Pei grew up in Los Angeles, but his Chinese family is from Taiwan. He enlightened Trigg about the complicated political nuances of Taiwanese identity, even though the food they cooked together professionally was mostly Japanese. Pei later collaborated with Trigg on a Taiwanese pop-up dinner series before Win Son opened, trying out ideas that would help influence its menu and philosophy.

That said, this recipe is not representative of either Taiwanese or Japanese cuisine—it's just really good, and so easy. This was a family meal that Pei whipped up, using ingredients that were available as they were in regular rotation at Ten Sushi. The Sichuan classic Mapo Tofu has ground beef or pork, and a deeply umami fermented chili bean sauce called *doubanjiang*, along with Sichuan peppercorns to season the dish. Using the silken tofu that was on hand for miso soup, ground chicken for yakitori, and a few non-Sichuan seasonings, this pale-colored and no less delicious version was born. This recipe can easily be doubled if you are serving a crowd.

INGREDIENTS

¼ cup (60 ml) neutral oil, such as soybean

6 cloves garlic, minced

4 scallions, chopped, white and green parts separated

8 ounces (225 g) ground chicken

2 tablespoons oyster sauce or Taiwanese soy paste

¼ cup (60 ml) shiro dashi or ¼ cup (60 ml) water mixed with 2 teaspoons Hondashi brand stock (see page 30)

1 tablespoon sambal oelek, House Chili Oil (page 258), or your favorite chili oil, such as Lao Gan Ma Spicy Chili Crisp

½ cup (120 ml) cold water

2 teaspoons cornstarch

2 (12.3-ounce/349 g) packs firm silken tofu, cut into 1-inch cubes

In a wok, heat the oil over medium-high heat. Add the garlic and the white parts of the chopped scallions and stir for 2 minutes, or until fragrant. Add the ground chicken and break up with a wooden spatula into small pieces until they're cooked through, 2 to 3 minutes. Stir in the oyster sauce and shiro dashi. Stir in the sambal oelek or chili oil.

In a small bowl, mix together the cold water and cornstarch and pour the slurry into the wok. Bring to a boil and stir gently as the sauce thickens. Taste for seasoning, and if desired, add extra oyster sauce or chili sauce. Add the silken tofu cubes and give the wok a shake or two to incorporate the tofu into the sauce. Top with the green parts of the chopped scallions and serve.

A (Brief) Conversation with
PEI CHANG

TRIGG: We always say that Win Son came together because of a fortuitous confluence of different things—Josh found a space for the restaurant, I found an old stove. You're one of those things. So how did you start off cooking?

PEI: I don't have a good answer. I was raised by parents who ran restaurants. I didn't want to do it because I had to. I tried many different things, but eventually, I fell back on what I knew.

TRIGG: Wow, I thought you started cooking at a steakhouse in LA after culinary school. I didn't know you also worked at your parents' restaurants growing up. Did you do front of house, wash dishes, or prep work?

PEI: I did kitchen work—growing up as an Asian immigrant kid, they put you to work at a young age and there are laws against that, so you have to hide them in the kitchen.

TRIGG: Ha, did you like it?

PEI: I did up until high school, when I wanted to hang out with my friends.

TRIGG: Funny because I started working in restaurants in high school to escape my parents, and have some freedom. I could smoke cigarettes and hear funny shit from the chefs.

PEI: Yeah, I didn't get any of that because you can't smoke or tell dirty jokes to owners' kids.

TRIGG: At the Keswick, you had summer rolls and bulgogi on the menu, folding in these Asian references, and it was really new then, especially for Charlottesville. It was before Momofuku or Instagram, where people kind of woke up to tableside southeast Asian ingredients. Lao Gan Ma and Sriracha weren't widely known.

PEI: A lot of it came from me being from LA and moving to Virginia. I just couldn't get that stuff, so I made it.

TRIGG: Then you went next level at Ten Sushi.

PEI: Yes, no golf-window ketchup nozzle.

TRIGG: That experience working for you and getting Japanese culinary exposure . . . that helped me contextualize Taiwanese food later on. And your family meal was always so bomb.

PEI: Yeah, we just did what we wanted at family meal. It was what we wanted to eat and couldn't get otherwise.

LU ROU FAN

Serves 6 to 8

THIS CLASSIC TAIWANESE DISH IS SO SIMPLE THAT IT'S EASY FOR FOLKS TO MISS THE POINT. Traditionally, just a small ladle of this fatty, savory stew is served over steamed rice, almost like a seasoning. Think of the relatively small portion of a meaty ragù that your pasta clings to, soaking up its flavor. (This dish is sometimes even referred to as *Taiwanese* ragù in English.) At Win Son, we like to cut the richness with our Chile Vinaigrette (page 255), serve more than a small ladleful, and pair it with Fermented Chinese Broccoli, or just some gently cooked Chinese broccoli on the side. Garnishes can include Chile Vinaigrette, fresh chopped scallions, fried shallots, pickles, and chili oil. A six-minute Marinated Egg is fun to serve it with, too.

INGREDIENTS

2 pounds (910 g) boneless fresh pork belly, preferably skinless

6 dried shiitake mushrooms

2 cups (480 ml) boiling water

¼ cup (2 ounces/55 g) Chinese rock sugar, or if unavailable, demerara or light brown sugar

3 tablespoons neutral oil, such as soybean, or more if needed

3 bunches scallions, white and green parts, thinly sliced (about 15 scallions)

6 cloves garlic, chopped

1 teaspoon salt

1 teaspoon MSG

1 cup (240 ml) rice wine, preferably Taiwanese, or use Shaoxing rice wine as a substitute

½ cup (120 ml) light soy sauce

1 tablespoon dark soy sauce

1 tablespoon Taiwanese soy paste

1 (12-ounce/360 ml) can lager beer, preferably Taiwan Gold Medal brand

4 cinnamon sticks

8 star anise

6 curls orange peel removed using a vegetable peeler (optional)

1 pint (375 g) fried shallots (can be found in Asian markets)

Steamed white short- or medium-grain rice, for serving

OPTIONAL GARNISHES:
Chile Vinaigrette (page 255)

Chopped scallions or fresh cilantro

Fermented Chinese Broccoli (page 48), or any type of Asian pickle, such as yellow pickled daikon

Marinated Eggs (page 45)

Black sesame seeds

House Chili Oil (page 258) or your favorite chili oil, such as Lao Gan Ma Spicy Chili Crisp

Cut the pork belly into 2- to 3-inch-wide (5 to 7.5 cm) strips, set them on a rack over a sheet pan, and refrigerate overnight. This will help dry out the pork and make it easier to slice.

To rehydrate the dried shiitake mushrooms, find a mixing bowl that can fit a plate inside of it—almost like a lid that's just barely too small to fit over the bowl. Put the mushrooms in the bowl and soak with the boiling water. Place the plate on top of the mushrooms to weigh them down for 30 minutes, or until very soft. (Alternately, use a French press instead of the bowl and plate.) Use a slotted spoon to remove the mushrooms from the water and squeeze them dry with your hands. Save the soaking water. Snip the stems off with scissors and save them, too. Finely chop the mushrooms.

Bring a large pot of water to a boil. Thinly slice the pork strips against the grain into rough squares or rectangles with stripes of fat and meat along their length. Stack the square slices two or three high, and then slice into slivers with stripes of fat and meat along their length. Carefully drop the pork into the boiling water. Let it simmer for about 2 minutes. Pour the meat from the pot into a colander to drain.

In a large pot, heat the rock sugar with ¼ cup (60 ml) water over medium heat. As the water heats up, the sugar will begin to caramelize. Stir with a spoon to ensure that it caramelizes evenly. Once the sugar is liquid and bubbling, add the oil, which will slow the caramelization. Add the minced shiitakes. Stir for about 30 seconds, adding a little more oil if the caramel is getting too dark. Successively add the scallions and garlic and cook, stirring, for another 30 seconds to 1 minute, until they soften. Season with the salt and MSG. Add the pork belly and mix thoroughly. Pour in the rice wine and simmer until reduced by half, about 10 minutes.

Add the light and dark soy sauces, soy paste, the reserved mushroom water, and the beer. Finally, take the cinnamon, star anise, orange peels, and mushroom stems and wrap them in a double layer of cheesecloth tied tightly with a string. Drop this into the pot.

Simmer over low heat, uncovered, skimming off the fat that comes to the surface (you can save it for stir-frying) and stirring occasionally, for 1 hour. Then stir in the fried shallots and continue cooking for at least 1 more hour, until the meat is very tender and the liquid has cooked down to a loose, chunky consistency, sort of like chili that you're going to top a hot dog with. Add more water if the mixture is becoming too chunky or strong-tasting. Continue cooking uncovered to reduce if the mixture is too soupy. Discard the spice pouch.

Serve with the steamed rice and your choice of garnishes. Store refrigerated in an airtight container for up to 5 days, or freeze for up to 2 months.

DUCK LEGS CONFIT WITH ROCK SUGAR AND SPICES

Serves 6

WE CALL THIS DISH, SERVED ON A BED OF RICE AT WIN SON BAKERY, YA FAN ("DUCK RICE") AND IT'S A CUSTOMER FAVORITE. It's basically a slow-cooked duck leg confit, utilizing a thick caramel to impart a dark color. It is sort of inspired by the minced pork belly over rice, Lu Rou Fan (page 151), Taiwanese turkey rice, and all the delicious, simple Taiwanese dishes that highlight slow-cooked meat over rice. In these cases, it's all about the drippings from the meat seeping into the rice and covering each grain.

INGREDIENTS

FOR THE DUCK CURE:

1 cup (200 g) salt

½ cup (100 g) sugar

1 teaspoon ground cardamom

1 teaspoon ground Sichuan peppercorns

1 teaspoon ground coriander seeds

6 duck legs

FOR CONFITING:

2 quarts (2 L) duck fat

1 cup (7.5 ounces/200 g) Chinese rock sugar, or if unavailable, demerara or light brown sugar

1 pint (480 ml) rice wine, preferably Taiwanese, or use Shaoxing rice wine as a substitute

1 cup (240 ml) light soy sauce

3 cinnamon sticks

4 star anise

1 tablespoon coriander seeds

4 cardamom pods

FOR SERVING:

Steamed white rice

Marinated Eggs (page 45)

Scallions, both white and light green parts, chopped

Yellow pickled daikon (optional)

Thai basil leaves (optional)

CURE THE DUCK: Combine the salt, sugar, cardamom, peppercorns, and coriander seeds and massage the duck legs with it; you will have a lot of cure, so really bury the duck with it. Reserve 6 teaspoons of the cure to be used as a seasoning for serving. Arrange the legs in a container or casserole in a single layer, so they're not overlapping, and refrigerate overnight. The next day, rinse off the cure completely and pat the legs dry with paper towels.

CONFIT THE DUCK: Place the duck legs in an ovenproof dish, or another deep dish that will fit all the legs in a single layer—you could use two smaller ones, if need be. Preheat the oven to 265°F (130°C).

In a saucepan, melt the duck fat and get it hot. When bubbles start to fizz up, you're ready to go, but you don't want to boil the fat because it will start to burn.

In another saucepan, place the rock sugar with ½ cup (120 ml) water. Cook it over medium heat and, using a rubber spatula, press out the rocks until they melt into the water, which should take a couple minutes. Add the rice wine and let the mixture reduce. It will take on a caramel color pretty quickly. Reduce it to about half and then turn the heat to medium-low and stir frequently until the caramel has reduced by half again and thickened.

Pour the melted duck fat, the soy sauce, and rock sugar caramel over the duck legs, and add in the cinnamon, star anise, coriander seeds, and cardamom pods. Cover with parchment and cook in the oven for 4 hours. The duck should be ready when it starts to pull away from the bone by the leg, but verify this by pressing into the drum. It should give nicely to the touch.

TO SERVE: Put each duck leg in a bowl over rice with a marinated egg and some scallions. Garnish the rice with a teaspoon of the reserved duck cure and the pickled daikon and basil, if using.

154

BIG CHICKEN BUNS WITH FU RU MAYO, CILANTRO, AND SCALLIONS

Serves 4

WHEN JOSH WAS GROWING UP, HIS CHURCH HOSTED A POTLUCK ON THE FIRST SATURDAY OF THE MONTH, WHERE MEMBERS WOULD BRING HOMEMADE OR STORE-BOUGHT DISHES TO SHARE WITH EVERYONE FOR DINNER. One of the most popular dishes was a pineapple bun chicken sandwich from Carnation Bakery off Kissena Boulevard, which one of the "church aunties" would purchase by the dozens. The sweetness of the pineapple bun (aka *bolo bao*, page 199) really made it. Cradling a fried piece of chicken breast and mayo, it was one of those things that ran out fast.

Fast-forward to 2015, and fried chicken sandwiches were having a moment in New York City. Trigg was working at Craft and got into the habit of making fried chicken sandwiches for family meal. He'd sometimes take that energy into his backyard barbecues, too, and it was always a big crowd-pleaser. Fried chicken speaks to a lot of people. Taiwan has a great fried chicken street food culture, as evidenced by the popularity of Popcorn Chicken (page 165) and big fried chicken (*da ji pai*), which this dish is based on. Big fried chicken—as opposed to just a *ji pai*, or chicken cutlet—is a huge piece of fried boneless chicken breast seasoned with Chinese five-spice powder and cayenne.

This sandwich is inspired by that, and the pineapple bun sandwiches that Josh grew up with at church. We sourced the best bolo bao we could find from a neighborhood bakery run by Mr. Tu, but you could also make them from scratch, following our homemade Bolo Bao recipe. We also added a hint of funky fermented tofu (or *dou fu ru*) to the mayonnaise (Fu Ru Mayo), and shio koji (see page 29) to the chicken marinade, for sneaky depths of flavor. Last but not least, this chicken is coated in coarse sweet potato starch, as is done in Taiwan—it gives it an ultra-crisp exterior, although this starch may result in a paler-colored fried chicken.

A regular at Win Son says this sandwich reminds her of standing outside in the cold, waiting for the school bus, eating the warm, toasted, buttered pastry her mom packed for breakfast. This image warms our hearts, and we hope you'll feel the same way.

4 boneless skin-on chicken breasts, butterflied

FOR THE CHICKEN MARINADE:
1 pint (480 ml) shio koji

3-inch (7.5-cm) piece fresh ginger, peeled and grated or minced

6 cloves garlic

1 tablespoon cayenne pepper

1 tablespoon Chinese five-spice powder

FOR THE BATTER:
2 cups (260 g) cornstarch

1 cup (160 g) rice flour

2 cups (480 ml) water (can be carbonated water for a crispier, foaming breading)

1 cup (130 g) coarse sweet potato starch

FOR FRYING:
2 quarts (2 L) neutral oil for frying, such as soybean (or enough to submerge the chicken)

Ground white pepper

Cayenne pepper

Chinese five-spice powder

Salt

FOR ASSEMBLY:
4 Bolo Bao (page 199) or other soft, slightly sweet buns (see Note)

1 cup (240 ml) Fu Ru Mayo (page 256)

2 cups packed chopped fresh cilantro and scallions, for garnish

NOTE: Any Asian supermarket or Chinese bakery will sell a version of bolo bao; a concha from a Mexican bakery will work, too. Pretty much any sweet bun can be used as a substitute. Depending on your energy level, even a sweet potato roll or honey bun will do the trick (not as well, obviously). A doughnut would just be ridiculous and really good. We would really support that choice.

MARINATE THE CHICKEN: In a large bowl, combine the shio koji, ginger, garlic, cayenne, and Chinese five-spice powder. Dip the butterflied chicken into the marinade, rubbing it all over. Cover and chill for at least 4 hours or overnight.

BATTER THE CHICKEN: In a bowl, combine the cornstarch and rice flour, then slowly whisk in the water until the mixture is thinner than a paste, but not watery, similar to the consistency of wet paint. The batter should not be too gooey or too thick, or the chicken will be too crunchy to eat. Put the sweet potato starch in a separate shallow bowl.

Unfold the butterflied chicken pieces and thoroughly coat them in the batter, then dip into the sweet potato starch, shaking off any excess.

FRY THE CHICKEN: Meanwhile, bring your neutral oil up to 350°F (175°C), when measured with a candy thermometer. If doing this on a stovetop (rather than a deep-fryer), make sure you're frying in a large wide pot filled only halfway with oil (5 inches/12 cm oil is ideal), or else it could bubble over and not only cause a big mess, but burn you. You may also need to work in two batches to allow enough room for each piece of chicken to fry without sticking to one another. Set a wire rack over a sheet pan on the side for landing.

Lay the chicken pieces into the oil skin side down. It's sort of like landing a plane—as you hang the chicken from your grip and lay it into the pot, the hanging part hits the oil runway first toward the front of the pot and by the time you reach the middle, you're gently dropping the top end from your grip into the oil. It may sound corny and dramatic, but a graceful and careful motion like that makes the chicken land better in the oil, reduces hot splashing (and directs any errant splashes away from you), and results in a more even fry.

157

Let the chicken fry for about 8 minutes, turning over once halfway through. At a certain point the chicken will float, which indicates it's ready, but let it finish the full 8 minutes either way. Use tongs to transfer the chicken to the wire rack and let rest for 2 minutes. Season the fried chicken with a dash each of white pepper, cayenne pepper, and Chinese five-spice powder. Be sure to liberally season it with salt—it's a big piece of chicken and requires a proper dusting, like a sidewalk just before a snowstorm.

ASSEMBLE THE SANDWICHES: Cut the bolo bao in half with a serrated knife, smear a little of the mayonnaise on the cut sides, and toast in a skillet. Apply the mayo to the chicken pieces and use it as an adhesive for the cilantro and scallions. Set the seasoned pieces of fried chicken with mayo and herbs onto the buns. Cut the sandwiches in half, if you'd like, before serving.

FRIED CHICKEN WITH SESAME WAFFLES

Serves 8

CHICKEN AND WAFFLES ARE A CLASSIC OF THE AMERICAN SOUTH, BUT WE'VE GIVEN OUR TAKE A TAIWANESE TWIST WITH BLACK SESAME SEEDS IN THE WAFFLE BATTER AND FIVE-SPICE IN THE CHICKEN. We also serve ours with a simple gravy—like you might see with chicken fried steak. (The method for the fried chicken is the same as that of the piece of chicken in our Big Chicken Bun, page 155.) With a few fried basil leaves and a drizzle of maple syrup to top it off, it's a fun and messy, sticky, sweet, and savory platter of fun.

INGREDIENTS

FOR FRYING:
2 recipes Big Chicken (page 155; double the amount of fried chicken as described, without sandwich ingredients)

12 leaves fresh Thai basil (optional)

FOR THE GRAVY:
4 tablespoons butter

4 tablespoons all-purpose flour

2 cups (480 ml) milk

3 teaspoons salt

½ teaspoon Chinese five-spice powder, plus more for dusting

FOR THE WAFFLES
(makes about eight 7-inch Belgian or sixteen 3½-inch waffles):
2 cups (250 g) all-purpose flour

¼ cup (50 g) sugar

2 teaspoons baking powder

¼ cup (40 g) toasted and ground black sesame seeds

2 cups (480 ml) milk

4 eggs

½ cup (120 ml) Wadaman Golden Sesame paste or toasted white sesame paste

½ cup (120 ml) neutral oil, such as soybean

Butter or pan spray, as needed for greasing the waffle iron

Maple syrup, for serving (optional)

FRY THE BASIL: After frying and seasoning the chicken, as described on page 157, if using Thai basil, add the leaves to the hot oil and let them fry for about 5 seconds before transferring to a wire rack to drain.

MAKE THE GRAVY: In a small saucepan, melt the butter over medium heat. Add the flour and stir to incorporate. Let cook, stirring to toast gently, about 1 minute. (You should have a blonde, or light, roux.) Stir in half (1 cup) of the milk. Let it thicken as it comes to a bubble, stirring, then add the remaining 1 cup milk. Let it thicken and bubble, then stir in the salt and five-spice powder.

MAKE THE WAFFLES: In a large bowl, combine the flour, sugar, baking powder, and ground black sesame seeds. In a separate large bowl, combine the milk, eggs, sesame paste, and oil until smoothly incorporated. Slowly add the dry ingredients to the wet mixture, stirring, until fully incorporated.

Heat a waffle iron, and when ready, brush its surface with butter or use a pan spray. Follow your iron's directions to pour the appropriate amount of batter and to heat until cooked through. Repeat the process with the rest of the batter; you should yield about 8 large Belgian waffles or 16 smaller, 3½-inch (9 cm) waffles.

TO SERVE: arrange one Belgian waffle or two smaller waffles on each serving plate. Add a piece of fried chicken, and pour some of the gravy over the top. Arrange the fried basil leaves on each plate, if using, and dust each with an extra shake of five-spice powder. Serve with maple syrup at the table, if using.

FRIED CHICKEN WITH IMPERIAL SAUCE

Serves 6 to 8

IF YOU LOVE CHICKEN WINGS, ESPECIALLY SAUCY ONES, THEN THIS RECIPE IS FOR YOU. We like the five-spice marinade commonly used in Taiwanese fried chicken, but our marinade has a little bit of everything: buttermilk, cayenne, five-spice powder, dried ginger and garlic, mustard, even some curry powder. As for the chicken, at Win Son and Win Son Bakery, we get whole chickens and use the breasts for the Big Chicken Bun (page 155) and all the wings, legs, and thighs for our Big Chicken Box, which is the origin of this recipe, fried chicken tossed with a salty-sweet glaze that we call Imperial Sauce, plus fries, as shown here. Getting whole birds, which is cheaper, means that we can ensure that they're good, air-chilled chickens like Canadian Giannone, or Amish chickens from Pennsylvania, which are delicious. You also get the chicken backs out of the whole bird, which is great for making stock—like the Superior Broth (page 261). But of course, if you don't want to break down a chicken, or you prefer certain parts over others, you can make this recipe with parts—like all wings for a bowl of party snacks. And as an alternative to tossing this fried chicken with Imperial Sauce at the end, you could just season it once it comes out of the oil with a combination of Chinese five-spice powder, cayenne, salt, sugar, and Korean chile flakes for a version that won't get your hands too sticky with sauce (as fun as that is).

2 pounds (910 g) chicken thighs, drumsticks, wings, and/or breasts

FOR THE MARINADE:
1 cup (240 ml) buttermilk

½ cup (120 ml) Frank's RedHot sauce

1 tablespoon powdered ginger

1 tablespoon garlic powder

1 tablespoon Chinese five-spice powder

1 tablespoon cayenne pepper

1 tablespoon curry powder

2 teaspoons Chinese hot mustard powder

2 teaspoons smoked paprika

2 tablespoons cornstarch

1 tablespoon neutral cooking oil, such as soybean

1-inch (2.5-cm) piece fresh ginger, peeled and sliced

1 bunch scallions, roughly chopped

FOR THE DREDGE:
½ cup (65 g) cornstarch

½ cup (65 g) all-purpose flour

1 cup (130 g) coarse sweet potato starch

1 tablespoon salt

1 tablespoon MSG

FOR FRYING:
2 quarts (2 L) neutral oil for frying, such as soybean

FOR THE IMPERIAL SAUCE:
½ cup (120 ml) kecap manis

½ cup (120 ml) oyster sauce

2 tablespoons House Chili Oil (page 258) or your favorite chili oil, such as Lao Gan Ma Spicy Chili Crisp

1 tablespoon mirin

1 tablespoon light soy sauce

1 tablespoon Chinese black vinegar

2 tablespoons toasted sesame oil

TO SERVE:
1 tablespoon toasted white sesame seeds, for garnish

4 chopped scallions, for garnish (optional)

ENTRÉES

MARINATE THE CHICKEN: Combine all of the ingredients for the marinade in a blender and puree. In a large bowl, combine the chicken with the marinade and toss to coat evenly. Refrigerate for at least 4 hours or overnight.

DREDGE THE CHICKEN: In a large shallow bowl, combine all of the ingredients for the dredge. One by one, coat each piece of chicken thoroughly.

FRY THE CHICKEN: Meanwhile, in a heavy pot or Dutch oven, or a deep-fryer if available, heat the oil to 350°F (175°C), when measured with a candy thermometer. If doing this on a stovetop, make sure you're frying in a large wide pot filled only halfway with oil (5 inches/12 cm oil is ideal), or else it could bubble over and not only cause a big mess, but burn you. You may also need to work in batches to allow enough room for each piece of chicken to fry without sticking to one another. Set a wire rack over a sheet pan on the side for landing.

Lay each piece of battered chicken into the oil for 13 to 15 minutes, until golden brown. Turn them once halfway through. Transfer to the wire rack to drain.

MAKE THE SAUCE: In a large shallow bowl, combine the kecap manis, oyster sauce, chili oil, mirin, soy sauce, vinegar, and sesame oil. Toss the chicken pieces in the sauce to coat thoroughly.

TO SERVE: Sprinkle with the toasted sesame seeds and scallions, if using, and serve immediately.

POPCORN CHICKEN with BASIL
Serves 4

IN TAIWAN, YOU'LL FIND VENDORS SELLING PAPER BAGS OF THESE CRISP LITTLE MORSELS OF BONELESS FRIED CHICKEN AND TRANSLUCENT SHARDS OF DEEP-FRIED BASIL LEAVES, WHICH ARE TOSSED INTO THE OIL TOWARD THE END OF FRYING. Everything is dusted with white pepper, cayenne pepper, and Chinese five-spice powder, so it's incredibly fragrant and highly snackable. It's pretty hard to pass by a popcorn chicken vendor and not take them up on their offering.

We've used pretty much the same marinade and seasonings as in our Big Chicken Bun (page 155) for these boneless chicken pieces and went with thigh meat for better texture and flavor. (Dark meat is much preferred over white meat in Taiwan, too.) Popcorn chicken in Taiwan doesn't typically come with any sauce, but we don't see anything wrong with serving it with some Persimmon Red Hot Sauce (page 259), Fu Ru Mayo (page 256), or really any sauces you like. Maybe even blend up some Charred Fermented Scallions or Ramps (page 46) with the Fu Ru Mayo. It's fried chicken; enjoy it! Be cute and use toothpicks like they do in Taiwan. Try out this recipe with fresh squid or mushrooms to make popcorn squid or mushrooms, too. Just make sure to salt your mushrooms to release excess moisture in advance so they'll get crispy after frying.

One key ingredient to achieve the super-crunchy appeal of a classic Taiwanese popcorn chicken is the type of sweet potato starch used. We describe it as "course sweet potato starch," which has larger granules than fine sweet potato starch. Both types will work if you're trying to thicken a soup or sauce, but only coarse sweet potato starch will create that crisp, somewhat knobby shell on the surface of deep-fried foods when used for dredging.

FOR THE CHICKEN MARINADE:

8 boneless chicken thighs (can be skinless or skin-on)

1 pint (480 ml) shio koji

3-inch (7.5 cm) piece fresh ginger, peeled and grated or minced

6 cloves garlic, minced

1 tablespoon Chinese five-spice powder

FOR THE BATTER:

2 cups (260 g) cornstarch

1 cup (160 g) rice flour

2 cups (480 ml) water, or more as needed (can be carbonated water for a crispier, foamier breading)

1 tablespoon baking powder

1 cup (130 g) coarse sweet potato starch (see headnote on previous page)

FOR FRYING:

2 quarts (2 L) neutral oil for frying, such as soybean (or enough to submerge the chicken)

Handful fresh Thai basil leaves

FOR SERVING:

Ground white pepper

Cayenne pepper

Chinese five-spice powder

Salt

Kombu cha (powdered seaweed seasoning; optional)

Persimmon Red Hot Sauce (page 259), Fu Ru Mayo (page 256), and/or Ginger Deluxe Sauce (page 258), for dipping (optional)

MARINATE THE CHICKEN: Cut the boneless chicken thighs into 3 large pieces, about 2 square inches (13 sq cm) or so each. In a large bowl, combine the shio koji, ginger, garlic, and Chinese five-spice powder. Submerge the chicken pieces in the marinade. Cover and chill in the refrigerator for at least 4 hours or overnight.

BATTER THE CHICKEN: In a bowl, combine the cornstarch and rice flour, and slowly whisk in the water until the mixture is thinner than a paste, but not watery, similar to the consistency of wet paint. Add the baking powder and mix again. The batter should not be too gooey or too thick, or the chicken will be too crunchy to eat. Put the coarse sweet potato starch in a separate shallow bowl.

Thoroughly coat the chicken pieces in the batter, then roll each piece in the coarse sweet potato starch, shaking off any excess.

FRY THE CHICKEN: Meanwhile, bring your neutral oil up to 350°F (175°C), when measured with a candy thermometer. If doing this on a stovetop (rather than in a deep-fryer), make sure you're frying in a large wide pot filled only halfway with oil (5 inches/12 cm of oil is ideal), or else it could bubble over and not only cause a big mess, but burn you. You may also need to work in batches to allow enough room for each piece of chicken to fry without sticking to one another. Set a wire rack over a sheet pan on the side for landing.

Once the chicken is battered and not sticking together, carefully drop the chicken pieces into the hot oil. Don't be afraid to get close to the hot oil when dropping these bombs. The farther away from the oil, the bigger the splash.

Let the pieces fry for about 6 minutes. At a certain point the chicken will float, which indicates it's ready, but let it finish the full 6 minutes either way. At 5 minutes and 15 seconds, chuck in a handful of basil and step back. It will be louder than it will be messy, but it will spritz a little oil into the air above the pot, so don't be alarmed. Once it stops bubbling, use a spider to remove the chicken and basil onto the rack-lined sheet pan.

TO SERVE: Season the fried chicken with a dash each of white pepper, cayenne pepper, Chinese five-spice powder, salt, and seaweed seasoning. Serve alone or with one or more of the optional dipping sauces.

CHAPTER 6

DUMPLINGS AND SANDWICHES

PAN-GRIDDLED PORK BUNS

Makes about 6 dozen; serves 12

HOW WE ARRIVED AT SERVING THESE PAN-FRIED PORK BUNS CAN BE TRACED BACK TO THE DAYS BEFORE OPENING WIN SON. Trigg was trying to come up with the menu, feeling vastly unprepared. Josh was scrounging to get together the money to get us through the final stretch. We were wining and dining investors that never came through, washing dishes with hot water heated up in the woks, and skating by in almost every sense.

One of the best pieces of advice that a mentor of Trigg's, chef James Tracey, gave him, was to not try to compete with artisans that have been honing their craft for generations. Don't bake bread if you're next door to an amazing bakery, essentially. We're in New York and we were confident we could find some kind of dumpling or bun we'd be proud to serve. We looked long and hard for the right type. And we wanted to work with a smaller shop, not buy from a large corporate brand.

One weekend Trigg found a bag of *xiao long bao* ("little juicy buns," commonly known as soup dumplings in English) in his freezer that Josh had left there. Being hungry and having to do things like sell his watch to pay rent, it wasn't long before Trigg cooked them up on a skillet, browning the bottoms and adding water to the pan and covering it while they steamed through. They were amazing. The next day, we met with Yula from Li Chuen, the small Brooklyn shop where Josh had gotten them, and worked out a deal to buy her frozen buns for the restaurant. She ships frozen buns all over the country and locally to grocery stores and restaurants, has a ton of experience doing all this, and we loved working with her. She is a tough lady whose children had to beg her to reduce her work schedule from seven to six days per week. On our first pickup, we noticed that her business made scallion pancakes, too. So we were thrilled when she agreed to sell them to us, as well. Win Son would never be what it has become without Yula, her company, and her hard work.

During the pandemic, prices went up and we could no longer afford to buy from her. Being the true badass that she is, Yula didn't flinch at losing our business after nearly four years of working together. But while losing that business relationship was sad, it may have been one of the best things that's happened to us. We were able to give work to some of our team members who were desperate for it during the pandemic as we worked out our own pork buns and scallion pancakes. We took pork buns off the menu for the first time in years while we practiced twisting their tops over and over again. Finally, we got to a point we were comfortable with and started selling them again. We also started making our own Scallion Pancakes (page 202). By the time people returned to the city and business started to pick up again, our homemade pork bun and pancake production was hitting its stride.

This recipe is easier if you start a few days before you want to serve these dumplings, or you won't have enough time to let the gelatin set and the dumpling filling to gel. No pun intended. We recommend you:

Make the pork stock and the gelatin on day 1. Mix the meat on day 2. Make dough and fold the dumplings on day 3.

Monitoring and maintaining the temperature of the meat is important, and letting it sit in the fridge after you mix it will help make sure this happens without any angst. You don't want to be staring at the fridge waiting for the meat to hit a temperature goal. Letting it set overnight helps you stay organized and gives you time on day 3 to focus on making the dough.

Cooking is all about mise en place, which may be a cliche to say, but it is as true as ever. Your things need to be in place and ready to roll to maintain organization and efficiency— sure, for aesthetic pleasure and organizational preference, but more importantly, for food safety, cleanliness, and product quality. Treat your home kitchen like a pro kitchen.

This recipe might look complicated, but we hope you'll try it out with friends and family as a fun project, and freeze some of the pork buns for a rainy day. Find them in your freezer one night, and whip up a delicious and convenient meal.

INGREDIENTS

FOR THE PORK STOCK:

1 pork trotter

1 cup (240 ml) rice wine, preferably Taiwanese, or use Shaoxing rice wine as a substitute

1 tablespoon ground white peppercorns

FOR THE GELATIN MIXTURE:

¼ cup (60 ml) unflavored gelatin

½ cup (120 ml) cold water

1 quart (950 ml) boiling hot water

FOR THE FILLING:

2 pounds (910 g) ground pork

1 tablespoon plus 1 teaspoon pork lard (optional)

1 tablespoon plus 1 teaspoon dark soy sauce, preferably mushroom flavored

2 tablespoons light soy sauce

1 tablespoon plus 1 teaspoon neutral oil, such as soybean

2 teaspoons toasted sesame oil

3-inch (7.5-cm) piece fresh ginger, peeled and minced

1 bunch scallions, chopped

1 teaspoon salt

2 teaspoons MSG

1 tablespoon plus 1 teaspoon sugar

FOR THE DOUGH:

8 cups (1 kg) all-purpose flour

1 cup (120 g) high-gluten flour

2 tablespoons salt

FOR FRYING:

1 cup (240 ml) neutral oil, such as soybean

FOR SERVING:

House Chili Oil (page 258), Chile Vinaigrette (page 255), Sweet Soy Dipping Sauce (page 261), Garlic-Cilantro-Chili Dipping Sauce (page 257), or just Chinese black vinegar and soy sauce

DAY 1

MAKE THE STOCK: Put the trotter in a large Dutch oven and cover with water. Bring it up to a boil. Skim the foam from the top and discard as the water boils for 2 to 3 minutes, until no more foam is rising. Remove the trotter, set aside, and discard the water.

In the clean Dutch oven, combine the trotter, rice wine, 2 quarts (2 L) water (or enough to cover the trotter), and the ground white peppercorns.

Cook on the stovetop at a simmer until the meat is tender to the touch, about 4 hours. After the trotter is cooked, remove from the liquid and let it come down to room temperature on a tray. Peel the skin off the trotter, chop it up, and put it back into the stock.

Let the stock cool down and set aside the amount you need for this recipe—1 cup (240 ml). Store the extra, which can be used to make more batches of buns or soup stock, in a sealed container and freeze for up to a month.

MAKE THE GELATIN: Prepare 1 quart (960 ml) of boiling-hot water. Bloom the gelatin in the ½ cup (120 ml) cold water for about 2 minutes, then whisk in the boiling water and let it sit out until it reaches room temperature. Then leave it in the fridge in an airtight container overnight. The gelatin needs to fully cool down and set.

DAY 2

The next day, remove the gelatin from the container and cut it into cubes. Grind it like the meat so it's the same texture and consistency. If you don't have a meat grinder, use a French mill or pulse in a food processor.

MAKE THE FILLING: Prepare your ingredients. Keep the cold ground pork in one bowl. Combine the ¼ cup pork stock and the pork lard (if using) and keep it hot in a separate bowl. In another bowl, combine the dark soy sauce, light soy sauce, neutral oil, and sesame oil. In a third bowl, combine the ginger and scallions. And in another bowl, mix together the salt, MSG, and sugar.

After you have the ingredients prepped, you are ready to mix. First, in a stand mixer on low speed, mix the ground pork with 2 tablespoons plus 1 teaspoon water. Second, mix in the ground gelatin and mix at low speed. Third, with the mixer on low speed, slowly pour in the hot stock and pork fat. It's important to keep your mixer on so that the hot fat and stock mixture emulsifies with the gelatin and the meat evenly. The cold meat will crash the temperature of the stock and the fat and the gelatin will carry the flavor through the filling, distributing it all evenly.

Mix the ginger and scallions into the meat, followed by the dark soy sauce, light soy sauce, sesame oil and neutral oil mixture, and the salt, MSG, and sugar mixture until well-combined. Store your meat filling in a container and set inside the fridge to cool. This will also allow the flavors to marry.

DAY 3
MAKE THE DOUGH: Combine the all-purpose and high-gluten flours. Mix 1 quart (960 ml) of tepid water slowly into the flours. When the dough comes together and just stops sticking to your hand, but is still as wet as possible, it's ready.

Portion it out into 4 manageable pieces, wrap each of them up in plastic wrap, and let them set in the fridge for 30 minutes.

Take the dough out and, working with one piece at a time, roll it out with a rolling pin. Using a ring cutter, cut out roughly 2-inch (5 cm) disks. Each dough circle should weigh about ½ ounce (14 g).

Remove the meat from the fridge and transfer to a metal bowl. Place that bowl into a container with ice to keep it cold while you're working. Each bun should hold about ½ ounce (14 g) meat. Weigh out a portion of meat to see what ½ ounce looks like visually, then eyeball the rest. The scoops of meat filling don't have to be the exact same weight, but they do need to be consistent in size.

FOLD THE BUNS: If you're right-handed, hold the dough portion in your left hand and, using a spoon in your right hand, scoop about a ½-ounce (14 g) portion of meat and place it in the center

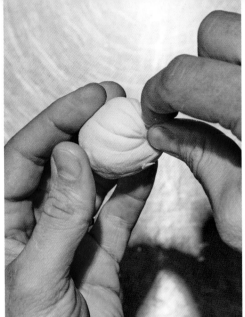

of the dough. Look at the dough as a clock. Start at six o'clock. Use your right thumb to hold the dough from the flap underneath at six o'clock. Using your index finger, take a five-o'clock flap to your thumb at six o'clock and twist these flaps counterclockwise as you pinch them together. It's important to keep your thumb where it is, continuing to bring new folds to your thumb with your index finger, from four o'clock and three o'clock and so on, each time locking the fold in by twisting counterclockwise until the bun is entirely sealed at the top. You can do this, but you need to make a few ugly buns first, and you need to try. If you can make agnolotti, ravioli, or gnocchi, you can make this, too. This dough is much more forgiving than fresh pasta dough. It's stretchy from the high-gluten flour and soft from the hydration. Keep folding, about twelve times, and keep practicing. Check out YouTube videos on how to fold soup dumplings, or xiao long bao.

Set each finished bun down on a floured tray and get them ready to cook or freeze. Once they're frozen, you can bundle them together in a sealed container in the freezer and keep for a month.

PAN-FRY THE BUNS: Add the neutral oil to a nonstick pan and set a batch of the buns onto the surface with ½ inch (12 mm) space in between each one. They will grow a little as they cook.

Add cold water until the buns are halfway submerged. Place the lid on the pan, cook on high for 5 minutes if frozen or about 2 minutes if fresh, then medium-low for 4 minutes. Cook until the water has evaporated and the buns are golden brown.

TO SERVE: Top with House Chili Oil, Chile Vinaigrette, Sweet Soy Dipping Sauce, Garlic-Cilantro-Chili Dipping Sauce, or just Chinese black vinegar and soy sauce to serve.

PAN-FRIED CHIVE POCKETS
Makes 12

JOSH'S PATERNAL GRANDMOTHER MADE INCREDIBLE *JIUCAI HEZI* (CHIVE POCKETS OR BUNS). THIS TAIWANESE STREET FOOD SEEMS SIMPLE GIVEN ITS FILLING OF MOSTLY FLAT CHIVES (SEE PAGE 31), OR *JUICAI*, BUT IT IS SO SATISFYING. The filling is augmented with slippery glass noodles and scrambled eggs; sometimes cooks might add some minced shiitakes, dry tofu, or dried baby shrimp inside, too. But it's all about the bright green, juicy chives. We often indulged in a couple orders of these along with steamer baskets of soup dumplings, platters of stir-fried rice cakes, cold pig ear salad, and marinated cucumbers at Nan Xiang Xiao Long Bao, one of our favorite places in Flushing. When our pastry chef Danielle started working with us, we figured we could finally get these things on the menu. Our version is totally vegetarian, but with crispy bottoms and juicy centers, it's one of those things that everyone is going to love.

FOR THE DOUGH:
2½ cups (315 g) all-purpose flour

1 cup boiling water

FOR THE FILLING:
½ pound (225 g) thin, clear mung bean starch noodles (aka bean thread, glass noodles, or vermicelli)

Neutral oil, such as soybean, as needed

6 eggs, beaten

¼ pound (115 g) Chinese flat chives, finely chopped (about 1 large bunch)

½ teaspoon salt

½ teaspoon MSG

½ teaspoon white pepper

MAKE THE DOUGH: Put the flour in a heatproof bowl, then add the hot water (should be used just after being boiled), stirring with a fork until the flour resembles a shaggy mass. On a lightly floured surface, knead the dough until it's a soft, smooth ball. You may need to wait until it cools down slightly to handle.

Rest the kneaded dough in an oiled bowl, covered, for 30 minutes.

MAKE THE FILLING: Soak the noodles in boiling hot water for 5 minutes. Rinse in cold water and then chop the noodles into small pieces. Heat 2 tablespoons of neutral oil in a pan and cook the beaten eggs, stirring to scramble them. You don't want to undercook or overcook the eggs.

In a bowl, combine the noodles, scrambled eggs, chives, salt, MSG, and white pepper.

Divide the dough into 12 equal portions. Roll each portion out onto a lightly floured surface into a round disk around 7 inches (17 cm) in diameter. Take 2 tablespoons of the filling, place in the center of each disk, and fold in half to form a semicircle, similar to a hand pie. You can seal the pockets in a few different ways—pinch the edges between your fingers or to use a fork and press the edges down.

In your pan, warm enough neutral oil to cover the bottom over medium heat. Add the pockets to the oil. Work in batches if needed, allowing at least 1 inch (2.5 cm) of space in between the pockets. Cover with a lid and cook for about 5 minutes. Remove the lid, flip the pockets over, and fry on the other side for about 3 minutes, or until golden brown. Transfer to paper towels or a wire rack to drain, and repeat with the remaining pockets. Serve immediately.

LAMB WONTONS

Makes about 35; serves 4 to 6

ONE TIME TRIGG'S FRIEND JULIA SUNG WAS IN THE KITCHEN AT WIN SON AND SHE SHARED THIS GAME HER FAMILY PLAYS EVERY LUNAR NEW YEAR. They make wontons and stash a whole peanut inside one wonton. The person who finds the wonton with the peanut gets an extra fat *hongbao*, or red envelope stuffed with money. The catch? If you accidentally eat the peanut, you get nothing.

We once held this contest in our restaurant where we put a peanut in one of our wontons and would buy the dinner for the winning customer. It's tricky, though, since people have peanut allergies, so we had to warn everyone who ordered wontons and anyone with the allergy was obviously disqualified. We forget who won, but it was hilarious.

Though wontons are most commonly filled with pork, or a combo of pork and shrimp, these are made with an unconventional lamb filling, which is spiced up with cumin and coriander. It's served on a bed of labneh and you can add chili oil at your own discretion. This makes for a fun twist on a familiar dish that never gets old.

INGREDIENTS

1 pound (455 g) ground lamb

1 tablespoon grated fresh ginger

1 tablespoon grated garlic

2 teaspoons red chile flakes, such as gochugaru or Sichuan chile flakes

½ teaspoon salt

1 teaspoon toasted white sesame seeds

1 teaspoon toasted sesame oil

1 tablespoon light soy sauce

2 teaspoons rice wine, preferably Taiwanese, or use Shaoxing rice wine as a substitute

1 heaping cup (45 g) packed flat chives or 4 large scallions, chopped

1 pack square yellow wonton wrappers (about 50)

2 teaspoons cumin seeds, for dusting (optional)

1 cup (240 ml) labneh

1 cup (240 ml) Sweet Soy Dipping Sauce (page 261)

House Chili Oil (page 258) or your favorite chili oil, such as Lao Gan Ma Spicy Chili Crisp (optional)

1 cup (16 g) chopped fresh cilantro leaves and tender stems (optional)

2 teaspoons "Lamb" Spice Mix (page 259)

Fold together the lamb, ginger, garlic, chile flakes, salt, sesame seeds, sesame oil, soy sauce, rice wine, and chives (do not overmix). Marinate in the refrigerator overnight, or for up to 2 days.

To make a wonton, place a wrapper in a diamond shape on your palm. Place about 1 teaspoon of the filling horizontally along the lower half of a wrapper. Dip your finger in water and trace the sides of the wrapper to wet it; wet a line just above the center of the wrapper. Fold the bottom edge over the filling and seal along the sides, and at the top, leaving about ½ inch (12 mm) of the wrapper at the top edge. Be sure to seal the edges securely shut, and try to squeeze out any air pockets. Wet the corners of both bottom edges of the wrapper, and twist them backward to meet. Pinch where they meet to seal the wrapper there. Repeat with the rest of the filling and wrappers.

As you fold the wontons, place them on a lightly floured surface such as a sheet pan. Freeze if not using immediately; the wontons can be boiled from frozen without thawing.

Bring a large pot of water to a boil. Drop in the wontons in batches (according to however many you're serving) so as not to overcrowd the pot. Cook for about 6 minutes, until they float and the skins are translucent. Carefully remove the wontons with a slotted spoon or spider and transfer to a bowl.

Using the back of a spoon, spread the labneh on a platter to serve family-style. Arrange the boiled wontons on top. Sprinkle with the cumin seeds, Sweet Soy Dipping Sauce, and the chili oil, if using, and finish with the chopped cilantro and "Lamb" Spice Mix.

PURPLE SWEET POTATO GRILLED CHEESE DUMPLINGS

Makes 6

SAVORY AND SWEET, THIS FUN TAKE ON A GRILLED CHEESE CAME ABOUT FROM TRIGG'S EXPERIMENTS WITH MAKING A DOUGH FROM RICE FLOUR AND SWEET POTATOES. When using purple sweet potatoes, the dough becomes neon-orchid. Wrap this over a chunk of fontina cheese and then crisp it for a comforting snack that happens to be gluten-free.

INGREDIENTS

6 medium (about 2 pounds/ 910 g) purple sweet potatoes

2 egg yolks

2 tablespoons neutral oil, such as soybean

2 teaspoons salt

½ cup (60 g) rice flour, plus more for dusting

1 pound (455 g) fontina cheese

Preheat the oven to 325°F (165°C). Stab the sweet potatoes with a fork three times on each of the potatoes' four "sides." Place on a sheet pan and bake for 1 hour. Check in on them; they need to be soft to the touch, so that when you squeeze with your fingers, you could push through the potato. Then it's done. Leave the oven on.

While they're still hot, slice open the potatoes with a paring knife and spoon out the cooked sweet potato into a bowl. Pass the potatoes through a ricer or French mill.

Whip up the two egg yolks and a tablespoon of the oil, and fold them into the milled sweet potato, then add the salt.

Add the rice flour a small handful at a time, using a fork to gently fold the rice flour into the potato mixture. After the dough has come together, flour the counter and press out the dough with your hands. Dust the dough again with flour and shape into a rectangle. Press and repeat twice. You want to work the dough until it comes together and feels slightly pliant without falling apart, but you don't want to add too much rice flour or it will become tough and dry.

Using a rolling pin, roll out the purple dough rectangle to about ¼ inch (6 mm) thick and then cut out 6 squares with a knife, about 3 by 3 inches (7.5 by 7.5 cm). Place a 2½-ounce (70 g) or ¼-cup (25 g) chunk of fontina cheese in the center of each square, and fold the bottom of the square over it. Fold the top flap of the square over that, and each side over that to form a smaller square. Seal it shut by gently pressing down.

Slick an oven-safe pan with the remaining tablespoon of oil and sear the cakes until golden brown. Flip the sandwiches and then throw the pan into the oven at 325°F (165°C) for about 7 minutes, until golden brown all over. Let cool for a few minutes. Cut each sandwich in half on a diagonal (the cheese will be oozing) and serve immediately.

NUTRITIOUS SANDWICHES
Makes 6

IN KEELUNG, THE FAMOUS PORT CITY NORTH OF TAIPEI (NEAR JUIFEN), THERE'S A NIGHT MARKET STALL THAT SELLS "NUTRITIOUS SANDWICHES" (IN MANDARIN, *YING YANG SAN MING ZHI*), WHICH HAVE BECOME A SENSATION IN TAIWAN. Creative food concepts can take off quickly in Taiwanese night markets, and once one dish is poppin', it will reappear in a different night market. Oftentimes stall owners have multiple locations in multiple markets, but they also inspire imitators. We're not sure if we sampled the original "nutritious sandwich" or a riff, but whatever it was, it was absolutely delicious. It's a crispy, deep-fried, oblong bun that's split across the top and stuffed with ham, cucumber, tomato, and sweet mayo. Behind the countertop, a hawker cook was basting and turning the bread loaves like doughnuts in a wok fryer, fresh to order.

For our version at Win Son, we fry our milk dough (page 197) and stuff it with a seared slab of homemade shrimp cake, pickled pineapple slices, jalapeños, cilantro leaves, and a slice of fried mortadella. Our initial version just had ham and no shrimp cake, and wasn't a big seller; also we had a lot of pork on the menu. So we switched to a shrimp patty to make it pescatarian. During the pandemic, we took the Nutritious Sandwich off the menu because it's really great as a piping-hot sandwich, but we didn't think it'd work well for takeout. When we reopened in 2021, we decided to reunite the two versions—with a twist, and use a slice of crispy mortadella instead of ham. Trigg was thinking fried speck so big props to chefs Isak Buan and Brian Girouard for the mortadella move. The sandwich now has a loyal following and the mortadella addition makes it really special.

Of course, you can skip the mortadella or shrimp cakes, depending on what you have on hand.

INGREDIENTS

½ cup (120 ml) mirin

½ cup (120 ml) rice vinegar

6 half-ring slices fresh pineapple

2 fresh jalapeños, thinly sliced

3 tablespoons neutral oil, such as soybean

6 Shrimp Cakes (page 53)

½ recipe Milk Buns (page 197, but don't bake, complete the steps up until the 6 buns are proofed)

6 (¼-inch/6 mm) thick slices mortadella or ham

6 tablespoons (90 ml) Fu Ru Mayo (page 256)

1 cup (16 g) loosely packed fresh cilantro leaves and small sprigs

In a bowl or liquid measuring cup, mix the mirin and rice vinegar. Divide the liquid between two small bowls, and place the pineapple slices in one and the jalapeño slices in the other. Let them quick-pickle for at least 30 minutes, or up to 2 days.

Prepare the milk buns: You can just bake the buns as described on page 198, if preferred, but frying them is recommended. After the buns have proofed for 3 hours, or until doubled in size, in a 6-quart (5.7 L) pot, heat the oil up to 325°F (165°C) when measured with a candy thermometer.

Carefully place the buns in the oil and, using a spoon, flip them over every 30 seconds until they are golden brown. We like to baste the top while the bottom fries to promote even cooking. After about 5 minutes of frying, remove the buns with a slotted spoon and let them rest and drain.

Preheat the oven to 350°F (175°C). Heat a large skillet or cast-iron pan over medium-high and pour in 2 tablespoons of the neutral oil. Working in batches if need be to allow space in between, place the shrimp patties down to sear each side, like hamburgers. Once the color is nicely developed on both sides, place the pan in the oven to bake the patties for 10 minutes. Transfer the shrimp patties to a wire rack set over a sheet pan.

Turn the oven off, but place the milk buns in the oven so that they warm with the residual heat.

After you remove the shrimp patties, you can sear the mortadella in the same pan. Add the remaining tablespoon of neutral oil and then the mortadella slices, working in batches if need be to allow space in between. Get good color on both sides, like you would with Spam. Cook for 1 to 2 minutes per side on medium-low heat, and then let drain next to the shrimp cakes.

Remove the warmed buns from the oven and slice them carefully with a serrated knife. Slather each with a tablespoon of the mayo, and arrange a shrimp patty, mortadella slice, slice of pickled pineapple, a few slices pickled jalapeño, and a few cilantro leaves and sprigs in each one. Serve immediately.

FRIED SOFT-SHELL CRAB SANDWICHES

Makes 6

FOR TRIGG, WHO'S FROM THE MID-ATLANTIC REGION, THERE'S NO BETTER SEASON THAN SOFT-SHELL CRAB SEASON. They're the best fried and there's no real two ways about it. We've made this recipe using our Milk Buns (page 197), deep-fried instead of baked (like in the recipe for the Nutritious Sandwich, page 182). But if you're in a hurry, go ahead and just use Martin's Potato Rolls instead. The mayo in this version is studded with our Fermented Chinese Broccoli, for a chunky sort of rémoulade, and the sandwich is showered with fresh, whole Thai basil leaves for a fragrant finish.

INGREDIENTS

½ recipe Milk Buns (page 197, but don't bake, complete the steps until the 6 buns are proofed)

½ cup (112 g) Fermented Chinese Broccoli (page 48), including both broccoli and the juices

½ cup (120 ml) Fu Ru Mayo (page 256)

2 quarts (2 L) neutral oil for frying, such as soybean

6 soft-shell crabs

2 cups (260 g) coarse sweet potato starch (see headnote in Popcorn Chicken, page 165)

2 tablespoons salt, plus more for dusting

1 cup (130 g) cornstarch

1 cup (160 g) rice flour

1 teaspoon red chile flakes, such as gochugaru or Sichuan chile flakes, plus more for serving

½ teaspoon Shrimp Powder (page 260; optional)

1 bunch Thai basil leaves

Complete the steps for the Milk Buns on page 197 up until letting them proof for 3 hours until they double in size.

To make the sauce, chop the fermented broccoli finely, by hand or in a food processor, and mix with the fermented bean curd mayo. Set aside.

In a 6-quart (5.7 L) pot, heat the oil up to 325°F (165°C), when measured with a candy thermometer. Carefully place the buns in the oil and, using a spoon, flip them over every 30 seconds until they are golden brown. We like to baste the top while the bottom fries to promote even cooking. After about 5 minutes of frying, remove the buns with a slotted spoon and let them rest and drain on a rack placed in a sheet pan.

Using kitchen scissors, cut the eyes/mouths off the soft-shell crabs. Pull back the tail piece and cut that off as well. Lift up the wings and slide your sheers under the gills, then snip those off. Place the prepared crabs on a rimmed baking tray. Set a shallow bowl holding the sweet potato starch and 1 tablespoon of the salt, combined, next to this.

Bring the oil up to 350°F (175°C). Mix the cornstarch, rice flour, and remaining tablespoon of salt with 2 cups (480 ml) water to make a slurry, and pour over the crabs. Remove the crabs from the slurry mixture, making sure they have an even coating of slurry covering them. Dredge them in the sweet potato starch and carefully lay them into the hot oil. Step away; they will pop and splatter. Let them fry for 3 minutes total, flipping them at 1½ minutes.

Remove and set onto a rack inside a sheet pan to drain, and dust with a pinch each of gochugaru flakes, shrimp powder, and salt.

To assemble the sandwiches, slice the buns in half carefully with a serrated blade; they should still be pretty warm. Place each crab on a bun and douse it with a heavy tablespoon of the mayo. Top with a few basil leaves and serve with extra sauce and chile flakes, if using, on the side.

BEEF ROLLS
Makes 8

BEEF ROLLS ARE SORT OF AN LA THING. Trigg's old chef mentor Pei Chang first got him hip to these delicious pancake-beef sandwiches and it's something we've always had on the menu at Win Son. With sliced braised beef shanks, they're almost like a stuffed pita or gyro, a beautiful mess of sauces fresh herbs, and incredible sliced meat, spilling out from a crispy, flaky scallion pancake. Ours are loosely inspired by a late-night meal Trigg once had with chefs Jon Yao of Kato restaurant and Mei Lin at 101 Noodle Express in LA, though we stuff ours with a fried egg that oozes as you try to stuff it all in your face.

INGREDIENTS

1 recipe Braised Beef Shanks (page 102)

2 cucumbers, peeled, thinly sliced, and julienned

½ cup Chile Vinaigrette (page 255)

Neutral oil, such as soybean, as needed

8 eggs

Salt

8 Scallion Pancakes (page 202)

½ cup (120 ml) Kewpie mayonnaise

8 tablespoons (120 ml) Taiwanese soy paste

1 bunch fresh cilantro, both leaves and stems, coarsely chopped

1 bunch scallions, chopped

FOR SERVING:
Garlic-Ginger Sauce (page 257; optional)

Win Son Romesco (page 262; optional)

In a saucepan, gently heat up the beef shanks in the braising liquid.

Toss the julienned cucumbers with the Chile Vinaigrette and set aside.

Heat a pan with 2 tablespoons oil and, working in batches, fry the eggs sunny-side up. Season each one with a pinch of salt as they cook.

When you're ready to assemble the rolls, remove the beef shanks from the braising liquid and let them cool on a cutting board. Thinly slice along their length.

On a cutting board, lay out your scallion pancakes. Spread 1 tablespoon Kewpie mayo and 1 tablespoon soy paste on each pancake. Then on each pancake, add some cilantro, scallions, marinated cucumbers, beef slices, and a fried egg. Roll up the pancakes and cut into slices (or simply fold the pancakes in half and cut across the center). If desired, drizzle the top with a little more soy paste and fresh herbs and serve with garlic-ginger sauce or Win Son romesco.

SLOPPY BAO
Makes 12; serves 6

WE DIDN'T REALLY WANT TO TOUCH BAO WHEN WE FIRST OPENED WIN SON BECAUSE WE THOUGHT IT WAS THE ONLY THING ANYONE REALLY KNEW ABOUT TAIWANESE FOOD. Eddie Huang and David Chang were slinging bao, and we didn't want to jump on that train. We get it—fluffy steamed white bread clutching juicy nuggets of fillings is delicious. But we wanted to approach the cuisine seriously, introduce new dishes, and avoid looking like imitators. Besides, our culinary inspirations are largely from Tainan, where Josh's family is from, whereas bao is more of a northern Taiwanese thing. Or it used to be, before it was everywhere.

In the end, this was silly and hypersensitive on our part. So we circled back to our Lu Rou Fan (page 151), a classic Taiwanese braised meat sauce, thinking that it would be great to stuff into a bao, sort of like a sloppy Joe. This makes Trigg think of the lunch lady played by Chris Farley in the song by Adam Sandler on *SNL*. Whatever sloppy Joe reminds you of, good or bad, this is bound to be better.

INGREDIENTS

12 store-bought bao buns, or mantou

¾ cup (180 ml)
Lu Rou Fan (page 151)

1 bunch scallions, thinly sliced

½ cup (120 ml) Chile Vinaigrette (page 255)

12 teaspoons (60 ml) kecap manis or Taiwanese soy paste

12 teaspoons (115 g) Butter-Fried Peanuts (page 40)

In a steamer lined with parchment paper, arrange the buns and close the lid. Steam the buns for about 6 minutes, until fully softened.

In a saucepot, warm up the lu rou fan, stirring so it doesn't scorch.

Combine the sliced scallions with Chile Vinaigrette and set aside.

Set the buns in the dish you're going to serve them on, such as a large shallow bowl or a dish with a lip so they can lean against the edge. Using a large spoon in one hand, open the buns with your other and spoon the stewed minced pork into each bun.

Top with a spoonful of the quick-marinated scallions, a drizzle of kecap manis, and some of the butter-fried peanuts. Repeat with the remaining ingredients for 12 bao.

CHAPTER 7

BREADS AND BREAKFAST

Bao, Milk Breads, Bings
TAIWANESE AMERICAN BREAKFAST AND PASTRIES

TAIWAN HAS AN AMAZING BREAKFAST FOOD CULTURE, AND BREAKFAST IS ALWAYS ONE OF OUR FAVORITE MEALS WHEN WE'RE THERE. The typical breakfast street food stalls or small shops serve up *shaobing* (a sesame seed–studded, oblong bun) and *youtiao* (a twisted, deep-fried pastry) along with fresh soy milk, or *doujiang*. So they're often called shaobing youtiao joints by default. The interesting thing is that both shaobing and youtiao—and many of the other pastries at these breakfast shops—are made with wheat, associating them with the period after Chiang Kai-shek's Nationalist Army retreated to Taiwan, bringing 2 million mainland Chinese along in the late 1940s. But breakfast culture in Taiwan was around before then, of course—and older Taiwanese staples from before that period include *fan tuan*, a sticky rice roll that's one of our favorite foods on the planet.

While these cuisines have melded into the "Taiwanese breakfast food" that we know today, we have taken this genre in a decidedly New York direction at Win Son Bakery, which we opened in 2019. It's a place where homemade milk bread or a scallion pancake mingles with bacon, egg, and cheese. In the morning, fan tuan and fresh sweet or savory soy milk can start you off. And by night, you can tuck into a griddled burger or fried chicken box. We had been serving some Taiwanese breakfast dishes for weekend brunch since 2016, but being able to do so on a day-to-day basis with Win Son Bakery allowed us to really push the envelope.

The concept took the typical New York City coffee shop or breakfast deli experience, and the Taiwanese shaobing youtiao or breakfast stall experience, and rolled them up like a fried egg tucked inside a scallion pancake. There are homemade milk buns, scallion pancakes, pineapple buns, freshly fried mochi doughnuts, and a slew of unique pastries that cleverly incorporate Taiwanese ingredients and inspiration. And our heroine for all that is our very talented pastry chef, Danielle Spencer.

Danielle was formerly a pastry chef at Craft, where she worked alongside Trigg on morning shifts. She was also roommates with Trigg and his wife Patty when we were opening Win Son, so she's been around since the beginning. When we decided we were going to open a bakery that would serve many Chinese and Taiwanese-style pastries and breads, she was the first person we thought of. No, she's not Taiwanese American. But having lived close to Chinese bakeries when she first moved to New York had given Danielle a deep affinity for all the baos, bings, egg tarts, and other sweet and

LEFT: Danielle Spencer, Win Son Bakery pastry chef. RIGHT: Danielle and sous chef Gabrielle Cambronero tossing donuts.

savory pastries that they served. After honing her skills in European pastry, Danielle traveled to Taiwan with us—and Auntie Leah, Josh's mom, of course—to learn about and explore Taiwanese pastries, its bakeries, and breakfast food culture.

Of course, we couldn't bring Taiwanese breakfast culture to Brooklyn and transplant it here in its exact form. Through the recipes in this section, many of which Danielle created, you'll see how we forged connections between European traditions and techniques and those of Taiwan and China. Sometimes, it's not so obvious. A Blueberry Mochi Muffin (page 234) with a chewy crumb was inspired by *nian gao*, a sticky rice cake. Sometimes the original Taiwanese treat took a very different direction when it was debuted at the bakery, like the Sun Cookie (page 247), which has a sticky brown butter glaze instead of

filling. With other recipes, we worked to really nail down our technique for a classic version, like with our Scallion Pancakes (page 202)—but serve it in ways we'd never seen before.

For our Bolo Bao (page 199), we make a version with chocolate. It reminds us of chocolate babka, a savory-sweet Russian bread marbled with chocolate, which you can find loaves of in most bagel shops and Jewish delis throughout New York City. It's just another example of how we're always nodding to the typical bakery lineup in New York City. And of how we're using the best of our skills, passion, and knowledge of Taiwanese cuisine to turn it on its head.

MILK BREAD AND BUNS
Makes one 13 by 4-inch (33 by 10 cm) loaf or 12 buns

IN ADDITION TO CLASSIC TAIWANESE BREAKFAST FOODS LIKE FAN TUAN (PAGE 215), SWEET AND SAVORY SOY MILK (PAGES 219 AND 220), AND DAN BING (PAGE 206), WE WANTED TO MAKE A LOT OF THE THINGS YOU'D FIND IN A CHINESE BAKERY IN-HOUSE WHEN WE WERE OPENING WIN SON BAKERY. So we set out to create a rich milk bread (a rich, Japanese-style bread that shares similarities with brioche). It's typically baked in a neat loaf and sliced thinly to be used to make sandwiches in Chinese bakeries. These simple sandwiches are delicious, and that's all about having really tasty, fresh bread. Danielle and our team developed a milk bread dough that hits all the right notes for us. Use a loaf pan with this recipe to make a loaf for sandwiches. Or make buns that you can slice open and stuff with fillings, like our Bacon, Egg, and Cheese (page 209).

197

INGREDIENTS

3¾ cups (900 ml) whole milk

2 teaspoons active dry yeast

1 tablespoon plus 1 teaspoon salt

8 cups (1.1 kg) bread flour

½ cup (100 g) sugar

1 pound (455 g) butter, softened to room temperature, plus more to butter the pan

In a saucepan, heat the milk over low heat. Stirring frequently, bring the milk up to 75 to 80°F (24 to 27°C), with a candy thermometer inserted into the liquid, but not against the pan. Remove from the heat.

Pour the warm milk into the bowl of a stand mixer set with the dough hook and add the yeast, salt, flour, and sugar. Mix on the lowest speed just until all the ingredients have come together, about 4 minutes. Increase the speed to the second-lowest setting and add the softened butter. Mix until thoroughly combined, 8 to 10 minutes, until the dough is strong enough for you to grab a small piece of it and stretch it out until it appears almost translucent (aka the windowpane test).

Transfer the dough to a large bowl and cover tightly with plastic wrap. Chill in the refrigerator for at least 6 hours, or up to 2 days.

When you are ready to bake, preheat the oven to 350°F (175°C).

To make a loaf, coat the inside of a 13 by 4-inch (33 by 10 cm) Pullman loaf pan with butter. Turn the dough into the loaf pan and cover loosely with plastic wrap or a flour-dusted cloth or towel and let sit at room temperature until it has nearly doubled in size, about 1 hour. Bake for 35 to 40 minutes, until golden brown.

To make buns, slick your work surface with a little oil or spray. Cut and portion the dough into 12 even portions. Roll the dough portions into balls, making a circular motion with your palms.

Set the buns at least 4 inches (10 cm) apart on a greased sheet of parchment paper on a sheet pan. Cover loosely with plastic wrap or a flour-dusted cloth or towel and let sit at room temperature until they have doubled in size, about 1 hour. Bake for 12 minutes and check the buns; if golden brown on top and if a toothpick inserted into the center of one comes out clean, remove from the oven. If they need more time, keep a close watch and check in again every 5 minutes.

Remove from the oven and let cool on a rack for several minutes before serving.

Milk bread is best enjoyed the day it is baked, but can be stored covered for up to a week.

BOLO BAO
(PINEAPPLE BUNS)

Makes 12

BOLO BAO (OR PINEAPPLE BUNS) ARE CLASSIC CHINESE BUNS THAT ARE BAKED WITH A CRACKLY EGG WASH ACROSS THE TOP, SO THEY SORT OF RESEMBLE THE EXTERIOR OF A PINEAPPLE, WHICH IS HOW THEY GET THEIR NAME. We've been sourcing excellent bolo bao from a local bakery run by Mr. Tu for our our Big Chicken Bun (page 155) since Win Son opened.

But as we were developing recipes for Win Son Bakery, we decided to make our own version, working with a milk bread dough, a rich, Japanese-style bread similar to brioche (page 197). We ended up making bolo bao that utilized our milk dough base, but with a technique that enabled its center to resemble the layers found in a kouign-amann pastry, or a croissant. We've also added a chocolate bolo bao variation, with cocoa powder in the crust. Here's the secret formula.

FOR THE BUN DOUGH:

3¾ cups (900 ml) whole milk

2 teaspoons active dry yeast

1 tablespoon plus 1 teaspoon salt

8 cups (1.1 kg) bread flour

½ cup (100 g) sugar

1 pound (455 g) butter, softened to room temperature

FOR THE COOKIE CRUST:

½ cup (1 stick) butter, softened

1 cup (200 g) sugar

2 egg yolks

1⅓ cups (165 g) all-purpose flour

½ teaspoon baking powder

1 tablespoon cocoa powder (optional, for a chocolate variation)

1 egg, lightly beaten

MAKE THE DOUGH: In a saucepan, heat the milk over low heat. Stirring frequently, bring the milk up to 75 to 80°F (24 to 27°C), with a candy thermometer inserted into the liquid, but not against the pan. Remove from the heat.

Pour the warm milk into the bowl of a stand mixer set with the dough hook and add the yeast, salt, flour, and sugar. Mix on the lowest speed just until all the ingredients have come together, about 4 minutes. Increase the speed to the second-lowest setting and add the softened butter. Mix until thoroughly combined, 8 to 10 minutes, or until the dough is strong enough for you to grab a small piece of it and stretch it out until it appears almost translucent (aka the windowpane test).

Transfer the dough to a large bowl and cover tightly with plastic wrap. Chill in the refrigerator for at least 6 hours, or up to 2 days.

PREPARE THE COOKIE CRUST: In the bowl of a stand mixer, lightly cream the butter and sugar. Scrape down the sides with a spatula and add the yolks; mix until just combined. Add the flour, baking powder, and cocoa powder (if making the chocolate variation) and mix until just combined. The dough can be used right away or refrigerated for up to 2 days.

When you're ready to bake, slick your work surface with a little oil or spray. Cut and portion the bun dough into 12 even portions. Roll the dough portions into balls, making a circular motion with your palms. Dust with flour to prevent sticking. Set the buns at least 4 inches apart on a greased sheet of parchment paper on a sheet pan.

Take about 1½ tablespoons of the cookie crust dough and flatten it into a disk with your hands, dusting your surface with flour if it's sticking. The disk should be large enough to place over a bun and cover the entire top. Repeat and top all the buns with a disk of the cookie crust.

Cover the pan of buns loosely with plastic wrap or a flour-dusted cloth or towel and let sit at room temperature until they have doubled in size, about 1 hour. Meanwhile, preheat the oven to 350°F (175°C). Combine the beaten egg with ¼ cup (60 ml) water and brush the tops of each of the buns with the egg wash.

Bake for 20 to 25 minutes. You're looking for the buns to be golden brown on the bottom and the cookie on top a little on the lighter side. If it needs more time, keep a close watch and check in again every 3 minutes.

Remove from the oven and let cool on a rack for several minutes before serving. It's best enjoyed the day it is baked but can be kept in a breadbox for up to a few days.

SCALLION PANCAKES

Makes about 8

BEFORE WE OPENED WIN SON, WE HAD EVERY INTENTION OF MAKING OUR OWN SCALLION PANCAKES. These crispy, flaky, savory snacks are a real favorite of ours, and we think a good scallion pancake is a marker of a good restaurant. It was a lot of work, but homemade was the only option we figured would be good. (Since then, however, we've found some really good frozen brands of scallion pancakes, so we take that back!) However, soon after we opened, Trigg made a trip to pick up the pork buns we were sourcing from a small business in the area, Li Chuen, and saw that they also made wholesale scallion pancakes. Yula, the owner, sent him off with a pack to try, and they were perfect. It ended up saving a lot of time on daily prep. Removing it from our to-do list was a lifesaver.

When the COVID-19 pandemic hit, Yula didn't have the workforce to make the pancakes for us at an affordable rate, so we went back to doing it all in-house. Thanks to her generosity, we picked up a few tips on pancake-making as well. We learned how important it is not to overwork the dough. You want soft, flaky layers swirled in each pancake, studded with scallions, not a tough and too-chewy cardboard. Hydrate the dough enough so that when it rests, it sweats a little and stays soft before shaping it. It's all handwork, and no rolling pins are even needed for this method.

INGREDIENTS

4 cups (500 g) all-purpose flour, plus more for brushing

1½ cups (360 ml) tepid water (105 to 110°F/40.5 to 43°C)

Neutral oil, such as soybean, for greasing and pan-frying

2 teaspoons salt

1 teaspoon MSG

4 tablespoons (60 ml) melted pork lard, vegetable shortening (such as Crisco), or melted butter, or more as needed

1 bunch scallions, thinly sliced

Sweet Soy Dipping Sauce (page 261), for dipping

In the bowl of a stand mixer, mix the flour and tepid water on low speed until the dough comes together and is smooth. It should feel moist to the touch, but not stick to your finger. If the dough looks shaggy or too dry, add more water a tablespoonful at a time.

Place the dough on a lightly oiled prep surface. Roll the dough into a long snake and divide into 8 evenly sized pieces. Roll the pieces into balls (see photo 1). Let rest for 20 minutes on an oiled tray or sheet pan covered with parchment paper or plastic wrap. Once fully rested for 20 minutes, the dough will be slightly deflated (photos 2 and 3).

On another sheet pan, place 2 cups (250 g) flour. Place a dough ball into the middle of the flour and cover the top with flour. Just press the dough ball lightly with your four fingers spread so that you can flatten it enough to add on the next dough ball and repeat to create a stack. Proceed like this until all four dough balls are stacked. Make sure there's plenty of flour covering the dough. Press lightly with the heel of your hand so that the dough balls flatten together into personal pizza–style disks, about 6 inches (15 cm) wide. Press twice with your hand so that you don't overwork the dough. Overworking the dough yields a hard pancake.

Pick up the stack and gently shake the disks as you turn the stack in your hands, kind of like you're shaking sand off a beach towel. The weight of the dough and gravity will do most of the stretching work. When you separate the disks onto the prep surface, they should be 7- or 8-inch (17 or 20 cm) disks (photo 4).

Next, sprinkle a pinch each of salt and MSG on each pancake, then 2 tablespoons thinly sliced scallions (photo 5), and finally a tablespoon of melted shortening or pork lard onto each pancake.

Roll up each disk (photo 6), and stretch the rope gently (photo 7) so it elongates to 10 to 12 inches (25 to 30.5 cm). As you stretch the snake as long as you can, try not to tear it. If the dough starts to break, that's an indication that it didn't

rest long enough, that it has been overworked, or that it is too dry.

Curl up each side of the ropes until the opposing coils meet, then slide one side under the other (photos 8–10). Set each coil onto an oiled tray, covered with parchment or plastic wrap, and let rest for 30 minutes.

On an oiled prep surface, press the pancakes into disks using your four fingers (photo 11)—no rolling pin is needed. You simply (and gently) smash the coils with your four fingers. The dough is soft so it compresses very easily into a flat disk, similar to the way they were pressed into disks earlier on in the recipe; however, now there's a lot more fat in the dough so as long as the surface of the table is oiled, the coils won't stick as you press them into flat pancakes. Be careful to press them evenly so they cook evenly.

Put the pancakes onto oiled layers of parchment and take them right to the stove if cooking immediately. Or fold them into layers of plastic wrap in order to keep them separate and freeze them (photo 12). If you're going the freeze way, this is another opportunity to let gravity help with the shape. Freezing them together sets them into even disks and locks in their shape.

When you're ready to cook them, you can start off with a fresh or frozen scallion pancake. In a skillet, heat 3 to 4 tablespoons of neutral oil over medium-high heat and once hot, place a pancake down in the center. Reduce the heat to medium and let it cook until nicely browned and bubbly on the bottom, reducing the heat to medium-low if it's starting to brown too dark in spots. Flip over and let the other side cook until the pancake is golden brown and air bubbles arise. In total, each scallion pancake will take 4 to 6 minutes. Remove from the pan and cut each pancake into quarters for serving. These are great served with Sweet Soy Dipping Sauce (page 261).

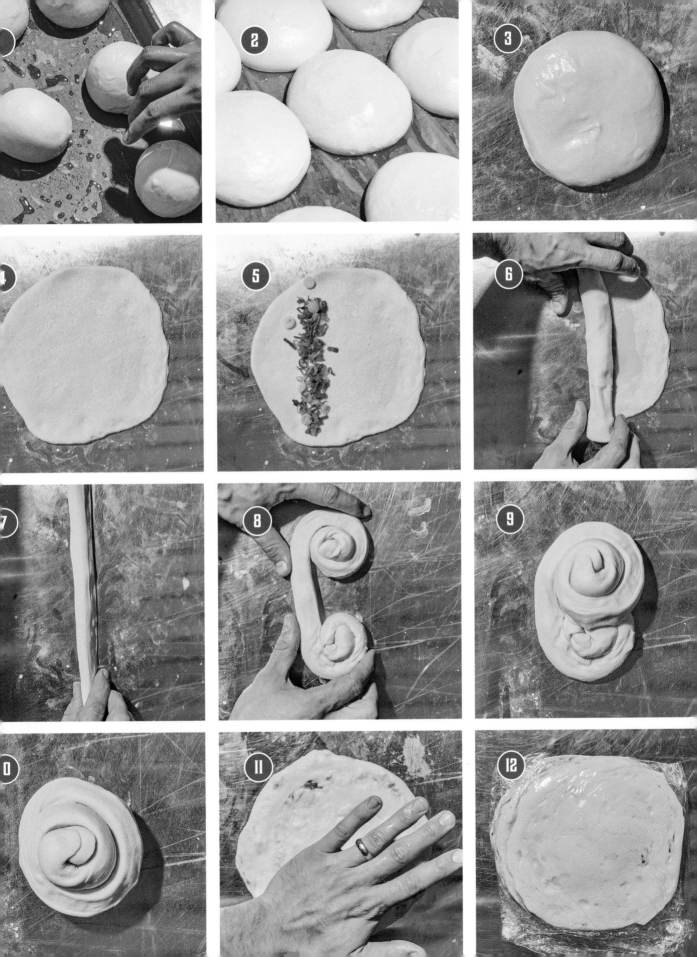

DAN BING

Serves 6

JOSH'S COUSIN ERIC ACCOMPANIED US ON MANY OF OUR TRAVELS IN TAIWAN, AND OUR FONDEST MEMORIES WITH HIM INVOLVE THE BREAKFASTS WE'D ORDER IN TO WHEREVER WE WERE STAYING. In Hualien, we'd get dan bing from a local shop with a side of turnip cake (like ours on page 54). There's really no better way to start the day.

Dan bing is a pretty simple egg crepe that's rolled up and cut into bite-size pieces that you dip into sauce. Here's a classic way to enjoy it, with a flourish of fresh Thai basil that gets cooked into the eggy bliss. We love the carb-on-carb energy of so many Taiwanese breakfast treats, like *shaobing youtiao* (a sesame-crusted wheat bun stuffed with a long fried Chinese pastry), so one move you could do if you're really craving a double-dose of Taiwanese breakfast snacks is to pile a scallion pancake (page 202) on your dan bing. Smack a slice of American cheese in between them if you want to get really crazy. It's insanely good.

FOR THE CREPES:
8 eggs

1¾ cups (420 ml) whole milk

6 ounces (170 g) all-purpose flour

2 tablespoons glutinous rice flour

1 teaspoon salt

3 tablespoons melted butter

FOR THE EGG FILLING:
8 tablespoons (120 ml) neutral oil, such as soybean, plus more as needed

6 eggs

3 tablespoons shiro dashi

1 tablespoon toasted sesame oil

20 fresh Thai basil leaves, roughly chopped

OPTIONAL SAUCES, FOR SERVING:
Taiwanese soy paste

Ginger Deluxe Sauce (page 258)

Sweet Soy Dipping Sauce (page 261)

Sea Mountain Sauce (page 260)

MAKE THE CREPES: In a bowl, whisk together the eggs, milk, all-purpose flour, glutinous rice flour, salt, and melted butter. Chill for 1 hour.

Heat a nonstick 8-inch (20 cm) skillet over medium. Add 1 tablespoon neutral oil. Ladle about ½ cup (120 ml) of the crepe batter into the skillet, and tilt it until the batter runs evenly across the bottom of the skillet. Allow the batter to set and pull away from the edges of the skillet a bit. Flip the crepe to continue cooking on the other side. The crepe should be pretty pale and yellow at this point and be done in a couple minutes. (It will get browned further later.) Remove and set aside; repeat with the remaining batter until you have at least 6 crepes.

MAKE THE EGG FILLING: In a medium bowl, whisk the 6 eggs with the shiro dashi and toasted sesame oil. Add a few Thai basil leaves.

Heat the nonstick skillet over medium and add another tablespoon of neutral oil. Pour half of the scrambled egg mixture and basil into the center of the skillet. Immediately place a cooked crepe on top. Wait 45 seconds for the eggs to set and flip the whole thing over. Quickly fold the edges of the pancake inward, like a C-fold, and flip it again so the seam of the folded crepe is facing down. (Cooking the seam side first will lock the crepe closed, with the egg and herb mixture cooking into the seam and acting as an adhesive.) Flip and cook for another 2 minutes, or until the pancake is golden brown (reduce the heat if it's getting too dark). Repeat with the remaining eggs and crepes.

TO SERVE: Let cool a few moments before cutting into inch-long slices. Serve with any of the sauces you choose.

BACON, EGG, AND CHEESE MILK BUN OR SCALLION PANCAKE
Serves 4

AT WIN SON BAKERY, WE WANTED TO SERVE TAIWANESE BREAKFAST STAPLES LIKE SOY MILK, FAN TUAN, AND OUR MILK BUNS WITH EGG, BUT WE ALSO REALLY WANTED TO FIGURE OUT A WAY TO SERVE AN AMERICAN-STYLE BACON, EGG, AND CHEESE IN A UNIQUELY WIN SON, OR TAIWANESE AMERICAN, WAY. So Trigg went back to his family meal vault for this one, recalling a time when some leftover dan bing were griddled with melted cheese and bacon. It reminded us of street-cart scallion pancakes served with fried eggs in Taiwan. We ultimately decided to fold bacon and cheese into that street-cart speciality to keep it simple for our Taiwanese American BEC. And as another option, we serve our BEC on a milk bun at the bakery, too.

We source our bacon and much of our meats through Heritage Foods, a nearby distributor of heritage meat founded by Patrick Martins, a good friend of ours. His wife, Anne Saxelby, founded Saxelby Cheesemongers, and Anne personally chose a cheese to tie this sandwich together. She introduced us to Reading Raclette from Spring Brook Farm, an Alpine-style semi-firm raw cow's milk cheese inspired with a sublime melt. We were going for the melti-ness of American cheese—but with a more nuanced flavor that you immediately knew was way better. And we love being able to support craft cheesemakers in our region, too. Look for it—or search for a nice, melty Swiss style from your local cheesemonger.

INGREDIENTS

8 eggs

2 teaspoons salt

4 tablespoons (60 ml) neutral oil, such as soybean

4 slices Raclette cheese (or another melty, Swiss-style cheese)

12 slices cooked crispy bacon

4 Scallion Pancakes (page 202) or Milk Buns (page 197)

2 teaspoons salt

2 teaspoons MSG

Butter, if using Milk Buns (page 197)

Ginger Deluxe Sauce (page 258), for serving

In a large mixing bowl, whip the eggs with the salt and oil and transfer to a small pitcher so you can pour from it. It's important to really whip the eggs and emulsify them. If you have a handheld immersion blender or a regular blender, use that. (This is a great trick for making scrambled eggs fluffy or omelets super smooth.)

Heat a skillet over medium-high heat and add 1 tablespoon of oil. Pour about 2 ounces (60 ml) of the beaten egg in the pitcher into the center of the pan and reduce the heat to low. Immediately place a slice of Raclette cheese and 3 slices of bacon on the egg.

If serving on a scallion pancake: Working quickly, lay the scallion pancake over the eggs, bacon, and cheese, and season with ½ teaspoon each of the salt and MSG, then flip the whole thing over.

Still working quickly, fold the edges of the pancake inward, like a C-fold, and flip it again so the seam is facing down. Cooking the seam in the pan will lock the pancake closed. Flip and cook for another 2 minutes, or until the pancake is golden brown. Repeat with the remaining eggs, cheese, bacon, pancakes, salt, and MSG.

Let cool for a few moments before cutting the pancakes into bite-size slices, or in half like a sandwich. Serve with ginger deluxe sauce on the side.

If serving on a milk bun: Slice each bun in half and butter the cut sides. Toast them in a skillet on the buttered sides until golden brown. Pour about 2 ounces (60 ml) of the beaten egg in the pitcher into the center of the pan and turn the heat to low. Move the eggs to the center of the pan, then tilt the pan all around to spread the eggs again. Place a slice of Raclette cheese in the center, season with ½ teaspoon each of the salt and MSG, and fold up the eggs to create an omelet. Repeat with the remaining eggs, cheese, salt, and MSG so you have four omelets. Slide the omelets on the bottom buns and top each with three slices of bacon. Top each sandwich with a dollop of ginger deluxe sauce or serve it on the side.

ZHU JIAO, EGG, AND CHEESE MILK BUN

Serves 6; makes one 6-inch (15 cm) torchon

TROTTERS AND KNUCKLES ARE NOT ONLY ENJOYED IN TAIWAN, WHERE THEY'RE ESSENTIAL FOR STOCK-MAKING, OR ARE SOMETIMES RED-BRAISED UNTIL GLISTENING AND FALLING OFF THE BONE. You can get pickled pork feet in gas stations where Trigg grew up in Virginia. On a bus ride from Santiago, Chile, to Cuzco, Peru, he bought braised pork knuckle for 10 cents. One of the French preparations for pork trotters that Trigg picked up from his time at Craft involved picking the braised trotter meat and reducing the braising liquid to a thick glue that binds the pieces in a neat torchon, a technique that will come in handy for this recipe. We thought about all these associations with this essential cut of pork when we created this dish, which features an incredibly juicy, rich pork cutlet. Served with either a scallion pancake or milk bun with an egg, some melty Raclette cheese, and our Russian dressing–inspired Ginger Deluxe Sauce for a wild fusion of flavors, this breakfast sandwich will really wake you up (or maybe put you to bed). This pork is also great when used in place of bacon in our BEC (page 209).

While this dish is part of Win Son Bakery's breakfast sandwich lineup, you can use the first part of this recipe to make braised pork knuckle, or *zhu jiao* (aka trotter, or pork shanks with the feet attached), along with a really delicious, collagen-rich broth. Season the broth with some light soy sauce or shiro dashi and sesame oil, maybe some herbs, and use it for a noodle soup. Top the soup with pieces of the tender pork knuckle and you have a falling-apart meat component to slurp up with your noodles.

⬡ INGREDIENTS ⬡

FOR THE BRAISED PORK:
4 pork trotters

1 pint (480 ml) rice wine, preferably Taiwanese, or use Shaoxing rice wine as a substitute

1 quart (950 ml) chicken stock (It's OK if this is water with chicken bouillon powder.)

1 head garlic, halved

4-inch (10-cm) piece fresh ginger, peeled and sliced

1 bunch scallions

1 tablespoon white peppercorns

2 tablespoons Chinese black vinegar

FOR FRYING THE PORK:
1 cup (125 g) all-purpose flour

2 eggs, beaten

1 cup (45 g) fresh breadcrumbs, ground in a food processor or blender

Neutral oil, such as soybean, as needed

FOR THE SANDWICH:
8 Scallion Pancakes (page 202) or Milk Buns (page 197)

Butter, as needed

6 eggs

6 slices Raclette cheese (or another melty Swiss-style cheese)

½ cup (120 ml) Ginger Deluxe Sauce (page 258)

BRAISE THE PORK: Put the trotters in a large Dutch oven and cover with water (about 4 quarts/3.8 L). Bring it up to a boil. Skim the foam from the top and discard it as the water boils, for 2 to 3 minutes, or until no more foam is rising. Remove the trotters from the water and set aside. Clean the Dutch oven.

In the clean Dutch oven, add the rice wine and chicken stock. Carefully place the trotters into the liquid with the garlic, ginger, scallions, and white peppercorns.

Preheat your oven to 315°F (155°C) and place the Dutch oven in the center rack. Braise until the meat is tender to the touch, about 4 hours. After they're cooked, remove the trotters from the liquid and let them come down to room temperature on a tray.

Strain the broth through a fine-mesh strainer and discard the solids. Let the broth settle and skim the fat off the top of the liquid. Discard the fat and return the braising liquid to the pot. (Note: This braising liquid is absolutely delicious. There's a little funk to it, but season it up and it makes a perfect soup. Stop cooking the broth

at this step if you want to make a soup. For this recipe though, we are going to turn the heat on high and reduce the liquid.)

Let the braising liquid simmer uncovered for 2 to 3 hours, until very thick and gluey in consistency, stirring occasionally to prevent scorching. Skim the fat while it's reducing. To test if it's thick enough, add a drop of the hot liquid to a plate. Tilt the plate on its side; if the liquid runs very slowly, you're there.

Meanwhile, when the pork trotters are cool enough to handle, remove the skins and set aside. Gently scrape the fat off with the back of a paring knife, but try to keep from tearing the skin. The bigger the skin pieces, the better, because this will be the outer layer of the torchon.

After the skins are all cleaned up, pick the meat from the feet. There are a lot of bones in the feet, so take your time. The shank section of the trotter will yield the most meat. (If you see a dark line tracking along some of the meat, it's a blood vessel, which you can wipe off.) Set aside the picked meat and fatty bits, and discard the bones.

Add the picked meat and fatty bits to the pot with the thickened stock and stir it carefully so you don't break up all the meat, but you do cover it completely. Add the black vinegar and let the mixture come down to room temperature.

Set out a 2-foot-long (60 cm) rectangular piece of plastic wrap on a countertop. Arrange the skins into a foot-long by about 4-inch-wide (30.5 cm by 10 cm) rectangle and place the glazed pork meat mixture on top.

Using the plastic wrap, fold the meat in the skin over itself and roll it up tightly. Poke holes in the torchon before rolling it too tightly, using a cake tester or unfolded paper clip, then apply another layer of plastic wrap in the same method and repeat the process three times.

If your torchon looks like a football, you're not doing it right. Each time you roll the meat in the plastic wrap, use your hands to form an even tubular shape and don't go so tight that all the meat bunches in the middle. After the third round of shaping, roll the pork tube in aluminum foil and twist the ends carefully. Place into an ice bath and let sit for 1 hour. Once cold, you can remove the torchon and slice it into 6 hockey-puck-sized patties.

FRY THE PORK: Place the flour in a shallow bowl and set it beside a shallow bowl of the beaten eggs. Next to that, in another shallow bowl, place the finely ground breadcrumbs. Dredge the pucks in the flour, then dunk them in the beaten eggs, and then dredge them in the finely ground breadcrumbs.

Cook in a well-oiled pan to golden brown and you have an incredible, gooey pork cutlet. (If not using immediately, you can individually wrap each puck in plastic and freeze for up to 2 months; they can be pan-fried straight from the freezer.)

ASSEMBLE THE SANDWICHES: Cut the milk buns in half, if using. Toast the buns or the scallion pancakes in a pan until golden brown.

Meanwhile, slick a nonstick skillet with a little butter and fry an egg sunny-side up for each sandwich. (Alternately, you can beat the eggs and pour them into the pan to create small omelets; scrape the eggs toward the center of the pan a few times until they are gently set. Divide into six portions.)

For each sandwich, add a fried pork puck onto a scallion pancake or the toasted bun bottom, layer a slice of the fried egg or omelet and a slice of cheese on top, and drizzle with the ginger sauce. If using a scallion pancake, fold it in half and cut into wedges. If using a milk bun, top it with the remaining half. Serve immediately.

FAN TUAN

Makes 8

A ROLL OF STICKY RICE STUFFED WITH *YOUTIAOU* (A LONG DEEP-FRIED CHINESE PASTRY), PORK FLOSS, PICKLES, AND SAUCES—FAN TUAN ARE A GO-TO TAIWANESE BREAKFAST CHOICE, AND THEY'RE ONE OF OUR FAVORITE FOODS PERIOD. While it's hugely popular in Taiwan, it's actually Shanghainese in origin. We've been making them at Win Son Bakery since it opened, and it's great to see folks who'd never encountered anything like it fall in love with it, too.

We did a lot of trial and error getting these just right. After several more travels to Taiwan, and as we prepared to open Win Son Bakery, we had a breakthrough. And it came by way of none other than Eddie Huang. We met Eddie when he was in NYC around 2018, after being written about along with him in a few stories about Taiwanese food. He was someone who always seemed to be ahead of his time when it came to trends—like with opening Baohaus and celebrating Taiwanese steamed bun culture. He definitely paved the way for Taiwanese food in popular culture in the US.

Trigg told Eddie he didn't like where he was at with fan tuan, especially the rice part. So on a Friday night, Eddie came by the restaurant and gave Trigg some pointers. He approved of the Koda Farms glutinous rice we were using, but told us to get the rice hot in a dry wok first, then massage in 1 tablespoon oil per 1 cup (200 g) rice. This way, the grains stay lubed up and separate while they cook, but still stick together. You can see that in a cross-section of the finished roll now.

We then honed in on our fan tuan: Plenty of fan tuan places include fried eggs in them, but we decided to cook our fried eggs a little on the soft and creamy-yolked side, so that they stay jammy even when cooled down. We make sure to fry the youtiao stick hard and crunchy for contrasting textures as you bite. We also make a vegetarian fan tuan without the pork floss but with smoked tofu.

But without the techniques we picked up from Eddie, we might not have been confident enough to put fan tuan on the menu.

2 cups (400 g) dried sweet or glutinous rice

2 tablespoons plus ½ cup (120 ml) neutral oil, such as soybean, plus more for frying

2 cups (480 ml) cold water

8 large eggs

Kosher salt and ground white pepper

2 large *youtiao* (aka Chinese cruller), cut into 1- by 4-inch (2.5 by 10 cm) batons; see Note

½ cup (70 g) *rousung* (aka pork floss; see Note)

8 teaspoons pickled mustard greens, chopped; see Note

8 scallions, thinly sliced

8 teaspoons kecap manis or Taiwanese soy paste

In a pan, toast the sticky rice dry over medium heat, stirring constantly until hot, about 4 minutes. Transfer to a metal mixing bowl and massage in 2 tablespoons of the oil.

Transfer to a rice cooker with the cold water. Cook according to instructions and keep warm. Makes about 4 cups (840 g), so you'll have some left over. Alternatively, if cooking rice on a stovetop, just bring to a boil covered and reduce heat to medium-low, so that it's steadily bubbling gently, for about 20 minutes, until the rice is tender and the water is fully absorbed.

In a large skillet, heat 2 tablespoons of the oil over medium-high heat. Crack in 2 eggs and season with salt and pepper. Cook until almost sunny-side up, about 2½ minutes. Flip to lightly set the yolk, taking care to keep it runny. Set the eggs aside. Repeat with the remaining eggs.

In a large skillet, heat oil 1 inch (2.5 cm) deep over medium-high heat. Add the youtiao and cook, turning as needed, until very golden all over, about 2 minutes. Transfer to a paper towel–lined plate.

Spritz a clean work surface with some water from a spray bottle or wipe with a damp towel. Lay a sheet of plastic wrap on the wet area and spread ½ cup (105 g) of the rice out into an even layer, about a 6- by 5-inch (15 by 12 cm) oval. Top the rice with 1 cooked egg and a piece of youtiao. Add 1 tablespoon rousung, 1 teaspoon pickled mustard greens or radish, and some scallions, and drizzle with 1 teaspoon kecap manis. Roll it up tight and halve it crosswise. Repeat the process until you have 8 rolls. Keep wrapped in the plastic for serving, so that the eater can squeeze it out as they eat it.

NOTE: *Rousung and pickled mustard greens can be found in Asian markets or online. Youtiao can be found in Asian markets or bakeries. Alternatively, you could use brioche or a different bread of your choice.*

DOUJIANG (FRESH SOY MILK)

Makes about 2 quarts; serves 6 to 8

YOU CAN MAKE YOUR OWN FRESH, HOMEMADE SOY MILK. It's a little difficult and requires some patience, but freshly made soy milk is well worth it. This rich soy milk is unflavored and can be refreshing on a hot day when served cold, and it's so soothing piping hot. Go on to season it with signature salty components for Xian Doujiang (page 220), or sweeteners for Tian Doujiang (page 219). You will need to have a nut milk bag in order to make this recipe, but they are cheap and can be used to make other nut milks.

INGREDIENTS

1 pound (455 g) dried yellow soybeans, preferably organic

In a large container, soak the beans with 4 quarts (3.8 L) water overnight. They will soak up the water and grow, so make sure you provide space for that or they will burst out of the container as they expand.

The following day, drain the water and blend the soaked soybeans with 3 quarts (2.8 L) fresh water; you may need to work in two to three batches so you'll be blending about 1 pint (375 g) soybeans with 3 pints (1.4 L) cold water each time until smooth. Pour the raw soy milk into a large pot. Your Dutch oven will work, or a tall pasta or stockpot, too.

At this point the raw soy milk tastes starchy. We really like to cook it with the pulp, which adds a level of creaminess as the water slowly cooks out of the milk and the soy milk becomes

ever so slightly more concentrated. We're not reducing it by much, maybe an inch total from the original level in the pot.

Set the pot on the lowest heat possible on your stove and don't let it simmer. It should steam lightly for 3 to 4 hours, depending on your stovetop. You don't have to stir it if you keep it below a simmer. Simmering or boiling will cause the soy milk to scorch, and if this happens you need to discard the milk and start over.

After the milk is ready, strain through a chinois or fine-mesh strainer, slowly and carefully. It's best to let the temperature come down for 30 minutes, then strain it so it's still hot, but won't burn you with a vengeance. It passes through the chinois more easily while it's hot.

Then you'll need to pass it through a nut milk bag in order to remove all of the pulp. Once the straining is complete, cool down the milk and store in an airtight container for up to two days in the fridge.

TIAN DOUJIANG (SWEET SOY MILK)

Serves 2 to 4

INGREDIENTS

2 tablespoons demerara sugar

2 tablespoons hot water

4 cups (960 ml) Fresh Soy Milk (page 218)

GENTLY SWEETENED FRESH SOY MILK IS A REAL TREAT. You can serve it hot or cold. Our version is sweetened with simple syrup made with the slightly unrefined demerara sugar for a slight hint of molasses. But you can use other types of sugar, or even maple syrup or honey, instead of making simple syrup. A *youtiao* (savory donut stick) is a quintessential pairing with soy milk.

In a small bowl, stir the sugar into the hot water until it dissolves to make a simple syrup. Add to the soy milk, making it as sweet as you like. If serving your soy milk hot, heat it up first, then stir in the syrup. Pour into individual mugs for serving.

XIAN DOUJIANG (SAVORY SOY MILK)

Serves 2

IF YOU ARE HUNGOVER, OR IF YOU'RE A FLAVOR JUNKIE OR TEXTURE FIEND, THEN THIS WILL REALLY APPEAL TO YOU. Salty (*xian*) soy milk is one of the most delicious things you can slurp up with a spoon. It starts with fresh soy milk that gets seasoned with some soy sauce and black vinegar, which slightly curdles it in the coolest way. Then it's topped with crunchy, tasty things like a crisp *youtiao* (a Chinese deep-fried long pastry), *rousung* (or pork floss), salted radish, pickles, scallions, cilantro, chili oil, sesame seeds, and fried shallots. Our secret ingredient here, per usual, is shiro dashi (see page 30).

One of the driving visions behind our bakery concept was seeing people walking out of the bakery on the way to work with a coffee cup that could easily be a cappuccino or a latte, but instead it was filled with curdled soy milk—the perfect blend of American coffee culture and Taiwanese breakfast culture.

INGREDIENTS

2 cups (480 ml) Fresh Soy Milk (page 218)

2 teaspoons Chinese black vinegar

2 tablespoons shiro dashi

2 teaspoons House Chili Oil (page 258) or your favorite chili oil, such as Lao Gan Ma Spicy Chili Crisp

1 teaspoon sliced scallions

1 teaspoon chopped fresh cilantro

1 tablespoon rousung (aka pork floss)

1 teaspoon fried shallots

1 teaspoon toasted white sesame seeds

1 *youtiao* (Chinese fried long pastry), cut to 1-inch (2.5 cm) sections resembling big, puffy croutons

In a saucepan, bring the soy milk up to a boil. Divide the black vinegar and shiro dashi between two small bowls or mugs. Pour a cup of piping hot fresh soy milk into each.

Garnish each bowl or mug with a teaspoon of chili oil and a scattering of the scallions, cilantro, rousung, fried shallots, toasted sesame seeds, and youtiao croutons and enjoy immediately.

A Conversation with Katy Hui-Wen Hung

WHAT IS TAIWANESE FOOD HISTORY?

IN 2018, KATY HUI-WEN HUNG AND STEVEN CROOK COWROTE THE BOOK *A CULINARY HISTORY OF TAIPEI: BEYOND PORK AND PONLAI*, FILLED WITH FASCINATING INSIGHTS INTO REGIONAL FOODS THROUGHOUT TAIWAN. We met Katy during her travels to the US later that year and have been friends ever since. Her personal blog continues to be a source of rich inspiration and aha moments for us. Trigg and Cathy got together on a Zoom call for this chat, as Katy is based in Taiwan, and they told her about how we were working on this book.

TRIGG: It is sad that travel has paused because Josh and I were going to Taiwan once or twice a year before the pandemic hit. We think how helpful it would have been to get coffee and do this meeting in person.

KATY: At the end of 2020, we were saying that by summer we'd travel, but that changed. It's been two years now.

TRIGG: I don't want to be misconstrued as trying to be an authority on Taiwan.

KATY: First of all, you are not Taiwanese. So, if you say something that even an average Taiwanese person doesn't understand, they probably feel a little bit, ugh . . . but talking with you and meeting with you, and having regular conversations, I do feel very good about you two. Cathy, I think we owe it to you because your book really opened the door. It at least put Taiwan on the map. So that's a big contribution for Taiwanese cuisine. And Trigg, you are very keen on history.

TRIGG: Definitely.

KATY: I feel like all your enthusiasm to learn about Taiwanese history and all the questions you ask are quite touching, actually. Because I don't find that interest here with Taiwanese chefs. So that's quite special. Maybe because if you are Taiwanese, people think they should already know Taiwanese history. But because you are an outsider, you're humbler. I don't find that humbleness in Taiwanese chefs. They might say, "I'm just a cook; I just cook and eat. So I don't need to learn about Taiwanese history."

CATHY: Thanks for mentioning my book, but I feel like it was inevitable, like someone was going to do it. Do you get that feeling? That Taiwanese food was just on the verge of greater appreciation? Certainly you were researching it.

KATY: No, you definitely put it on the map. It was the first time that people said,

"Wow, there's something called Taiwanese food." When was that published?

CATHY: 2015.

TRIGG: As someone who was learning about Taiwanese cuisine, it was extremely exciting to have talked to both of you and to have read your books beforehand.

KATY: I'm sure what you learned from the book and from Taiwan's history, it will come out in your work.

TRIGG: In conversation, I often cite your article on *bian dang* [Taiwanese bento boxes] and how they were a relic of the Japanese colonial rule, and there's a nostalgia for that in Taiwan.

KATY: Do you have a bian dang recipe in your book?

CATHY: There's the fried pork chops, which are common in bian dangs.

TRIGG: Well, my takeaway from your article was that during martial law in Taiwan, Chiang Kai-shek was trying to superimpose classical Chinese culture onto Taiwan, and Japanese culture was being stamped out. However, the local folks that had been in Taiwan for some time, as we've learned in books and in conversations, thought that the Japanese time wasn't so bad as it was in other colonies of imperial Japan. So whether it's flavor nuances or the usage of certain Japanese seasonings or the physical presentation of lunch in bento, that culinary nostalgia lingers, and people craved it.

KATY: You know the pickled radish you eat with a bian dang? That is a Japanese tradition. You would find it in basically every old-time Taiwanese bian dang.

Basically, yes, Chiang Kai-shek wanted to create a small China for himself—he only intended to stay temporarily. But the interesting thing about food is even though the Chinese soldiers who came with him discriminated and tried to remove every Japanese element from the culture, architecturally and with things like road signs, when it comes to Japanese food, nobody argued and people are still eating it.

TRIGG: I think that's a big thesis of our restaurant—that good food can bring us together no matter its origins. When Josh and I were opening Win Son, we didn't know what to call ourselves. We thought, *We just want to make people happy eating food, and maybe if they learn something about Taiwan, that's a plus.*

KATY: I think your book will be different than others; you want to present Taiwan without borders and invite people to enjoy and have conversation.

CHAPTER 8

DESSERTS AND PASTRIES

FRIED MILK DOUGH SUNDAES wITH PEANUTS AND CILANTRO-MINT SAUCE

Serves 6

PEANUTS AND CILANTRO ARE A SIGNATURE COMBO IN TAIWANESE CUISINE—YOU'LL FIND CHOPPED CILANTRO AND CRUSHED PEANUT POWDER GRAZING ALL KINDS OF DISHES, FROM SOUPS TO STEAMED BUNS. Then there's also a popular Taiwan night market dessert of ice cream rolled up into a crepe with fresh cilantro and shaved peanut brittle. It's fresh and herbal, salty, sweet, and crunchy. At Win Son, we make a sundae out of this idea, only it's with hot fried dough (using the same batter as our Milk Buns, page 197). (At home, you could consider replacing with a store-bought doughnut instead.) In addition to the chopped cilantro, we drizzle it with emerald-green Cilantro-Mint Sauce (page 255) along with creamy sweetened condensed milk, and we top it all with our Butter-Fried Peanuts (page 40). Flaky Maldon salt makes the finishing touch.

INGREDIENTS

½ recipe Milk Buns
(page 197), but don't bake,
complete the steps until
the 6 buns are proofed.
(Alternately, you can
substitute this with 6
store-bought doughnuts.)

4½ cups (1 L) neutral oil
for frying, such as soybean
(skip if using store-bought
doughnuts)

3 pints (1.4 L) vanilla ice
cream

1 cup (240 ml) Cilantro-
Mint Sauce (page 255)

1½ cup (360 ml) sweetened
condensed milk, plus more
as desired

½ cup (70 g) Butter-Fried
Peanuts (page 40)

2 tablespoons chopped
fresh cilantro

2 teaspoons Maldon salt

Complete the steps for the Milk Buns on page 197 up until letting them proof for 3 hours, until they double in size.

In a 6-quart (5.7 L) pot, heat the oil up to 325°F (165°C) when measured with a candy thermometer.

Carefully place the buns in the oil and, using a spoon, flip them over every 30 seconds, until they are golden brown. We like to baste the top while the bottom fries to promote even cooking.

After about 5 minutes of frying, remove the buns with a slotted spoon and let them rest and drain for about 5 minutes.

Gently slice the buns in half using a serrated knife and put each bottom portion into six separate medium bowls, because this dessert gets a little messy.

If possible, remove the ice cream from its container in a whole rectangle and cut it into a half-pint (240 ml) block per bun; alternately, you can just scoop about half a pint (240 ml) per bun. (It's a big portion and you can go smaller if you want.) Place the ice cream on top of the bottom half of each bun. Top each with 1 tablespoon cilantro-mint sauce and put the top bun on.

Cover the top bun with some sweetened condensed milk, about 2 tablespoons for each dessert.

Next, add about 1 tablespoon butter-fried peanuts to each dish, finish with a pinch of cilantro leaves and some Maldon salt, and serve immediately.

RED DATE CAKES

Makes 12 to 16

DURING ONE OF OUR LAST DAYS IN TAIWAN WHEN WE WERE RESEARCHING FOR WIN SON BAKERY, JOSH'S MOM TOOK US TO A CHINESE HERBAL MEDICINE SHOP IN TAINAN, WHERE HER FAMILY HAS GONE FOR DECADES. There was a big pile of Chinese red dates, also known as jujubes, and Josh's mom mentioned that they were a good price to Danielle Spencer, our pastry chef. So that's how Danielle wound up with a huge bag of red dates on her flight home, since she was down to the last of her Taiwan currency and didn't want to lose the exchange fee.

She ended up creating this luscious pastry from them. The idea is borrowed from English sticky toffee pudding, which typically incorporates ground dates for a round sweetness. But instead of using Turkish Medjool dates like you often do for the English pastries, the Chinese red dates or jujubes are ground up to give it that signature honey-like sweetness—and maybe medicinal effect? We'll leave you to judge.

FOR THE CAKE BATTER:

1½ cups (190 g) pitted
Chinese red dates
(aka jujubes)

1 teaspoon baking soda

1 cup (225 g) butter

2 cups (400 g) sugar

2 teaspoons vanilla extract

4 eggs

2¼ cups (280 g)
all-purpose flour

2 teaspoons baking powder

1 teaspoon salt

FOR THE TOFFEE SAUCE:

½ cup (120 ml) heavy cream

1 cup (225 g) butter

1 pound (455 g) dark brown
sugar

2 tablespoons salt

Preheat the oven to 325°F (165°C). Check the dates to make sure all the pits are removed. Finely chop them or pulse them a few times in a food processor, stopping to scrape down the sides.

MAKE THE BATTER: In a tall pot, bring 2 cups (480 ml) water to a boil. Add the pulsed dates and baking soda, turn the heat down to low, and cook until the water has almost evaporated, stirring occasionally, for about 4 minutes, which should cook the raw baking soda flavor out. Let it cool down completely.

Use a stand mixer set with the paddle attachment to cream the butter and sugar together. Scrape down and add in the vanilla and eggs. Then, add in the flour, baking powder, salt, and the cooled date mixture. Mix until just combined.

Prepare twelve muffin tins with muffin liners (if not available, then grease the muffin tins with butter). Pour in the batter divided equally among the muffin tins. Bake for 14 to 18 minutes, until a toothpick inserted into the center just comes out clean. Remove from the muffin tins and let cool.

MEANWHILE, MAKE THE SAUCE: First, in a tall pot over medium-low heat, pour in the cream and then add the butter, sugar, and salt. Melt everything together, then cook for 6 minutes, or until golden brown. Be sure there aren't any dry sugar spots in the pot, which could scorch while everything else is melting.

To assemble, pour the toffee sauce over each cake liberally as soon as they're out of the oven. Let the cakes topped with toffee sauce cool for at least 30 minutes to settle before serving. Cakes can be stored for up to a week covered and refrigerated, although they're best enjoyed freshly baked.

DESSERTS AND PASTRIES

CUSTARD TOAST

Makes 6

WE LOVED THE CUSTARD TOAST WE'D SAMPLED WHILE TRAVELING AROUND ON THE SUBWAYS IN TAIWAN. We knew we had to resurrect the memory of this sweet bread, toasted, with a light layer of custard applied to the top, when we opened Win Son Bakery. Our toast starts out as something that resembles bread pudding or French toast, then it gets slathered with a simple custard. At the bakery, we torch the tops with a blowtorch for a crispy, brûléed effect, but here we suggest simply sliding your toast back into the oven to let it bubble until it gets golden brown, in case you don't have a torch.

INGREDIENTS

FOR THE BREAD PUDDING BASE:

2 cups (480 ml) whole milk

½ cup (100 g) sugar

1 teaspoon salt

1 teaspoon vanilla extract

8 eggs

2 cups (480 ml) cold heavy cream

FOR THE CUSTARD:

2 cups (450 g) butter, softened

2 cups (400 g) sugar

4 egg yolks

1 tablespoon plus 1 teaspoon salt

1 cup (125 g) nonfat milk powder

FOR ASSEMBLY:

6 (1 to 1½-inch/2.5 to 4 cm) thick slices Milk Bread (page 197) or brioche

MAKE THE BREAD PUDDING BASE: In a medium saucepan, bring the milk, sugar, salt, and vanilla just to a boil. Remove from the heat. In a separate mixing bowl, beat the eggs. Slowly pour in a very small scoop of the hot milk mixture while beating the eggs to temper them. Continue beating and pour in a little more. Continue until you've incorporated all the hot milk mixture.

Pour in the cold heavy cream. Strain and use immediately or refrigerate if using later.

MAKE THE CUSTARD: In the bowl of a stand mixer, cream the butter and sugar using the paddle attachment. Scrape down the sides and add the yolks. Mix until just combined. Add the salt and milk powder and mix.

Preheat the oven to 325°F (165°C).

ASSEMBLE THE TOAST: Lay the slices of bread on a sheet pan and toast them until golden brown, about 6 minutes or so. Do not turn off the oven.

Pour the bread pudding base into a pan or large-enough vessel for a piece of bread to fit inside. Soak one side of the toasted slice. Remove the soaked slice then smooth a light, even layer of custard spread (around 3 tablespoons) over the top with an offset spatula (or butter knife). Return the slice to the sheet pan, custard spread side up, and repeat with the remaining slices.

Place the pieces of bread back into the oven, until the custard is bubbly or light brown, about 6 minutes. Serve immediately.

BLUEBERRY MOCHI MUFFINS

Makes 12

WE LOVE ADDING A NEW PASTRY FOR SPECIAL OCCASIONS THAT HAPPEN THROUGHOUT THE YEAR. For Chinese New Year, we wanted to offer *nian gao*, a smooth cake made from sweetened sticky rice flour. It holds a special place for Josh, since his mom used to make her version of it every year. While recipe testing, we began to apply the same thought process that we did with the Mochi Doughnuts (page 237), to end up with a perfect amount of Q texture in a dessert (Q texture might be translated as "bouncy" or "springy" and it's a real obsession in Taiwan). So we used millet flour along with sticky rice flour, like with the Mochi Doughnut, to create a soft yet pleasantly chewy crumb—which also happens to make the pastry gluten-free.

While testing this nian gao batter, Trigg baked a batch inside some muffin molds that were around at the time. The resulting mochi muffin poofed at the top just like, well, a muffin, and then it occurred to us that we didn't have anything muffin-like on our bakery menu. So we went for that theme—next adding blueberries to the batter. This batter can take on any ground spice you want to add, or fruit that's in season. It's super fun to make seasonal variations of this muffin throughout the year.

INGREDIENTS

1 cup (225 g) plus
2 tablespoons unsalted
butter, plus more for greasing

4 eggs

1⅓ cups (315 ml) whole milk

1 cup (240 ml) plus
2 tablespoons neutral oil,
such as soybean

1 cup (200 g) sugar

2 tablespoons baking powder

1 teaspoon salt

1⅓ cups (145 g) millet flour

5 cups (800 g) glutinous
rice flour

2 cups (290 g) fresh or
frozen blueberries

Preheat the oven to 350°F (175°C). In a small saucepan, melt the butter until fluid but not bubbling. Immediately remove from heat.

In a large mixing bowl, whisk together the eggs, milk, and oil in a medium bowl. Stir in the sugar, baking powder, salt, millet flour, and glutinous rice flour. Whisk until there aren't any lumps. Stir in the melted butter. Gently stir in the blueberries.

Prepare a muffin tin by either greasing with butter or lining with muffin liners. Fill each tin halfway with the batter. Bake for 12 to 14 minutes, until golden brown on top. Serve immediately.

235

MOCHI DOUGHNUTS
Makes about 12

TAIWAN IS FAMOUS FOR Q OR QQ TEXTURES, WHICH MAY BE BEST TRANSLATED AS "BOUNCY" OR "SPRINGY." Think boba, gummy bears, and mochi, a sticky rice treat popular throughout East Asia. These doughnuts are made with sticky rice flour for a chewy bite that stretches in a very Q way. Mochi doughnuts are definitely a thing in Taiwan, and Danielle really gravitated to the ones she sampled throughout Taiwan, having made many fried doughnuts fresh to order in her time at Craft, working under doughnut and overall pastry legend Karen DeMasco.

In Tainan, we also sampled mochi doughnuts made with millet flour in addition to sticky rice flour, and Danielle was eager to start recipe-testing as soon as she returned. She landed on this formula that's satisfyingly QQ, delicious, and also completely gluten-free. Once they're out of the fryer, they can be coated with sugar and your choice of additional seasonings—at Win Son Bakery, we love a classic sugar and cinnamon topping, but you can add to yours some toasted and ground black sesame seeds, ground black cardamom, ground ginger, and any other spices you love. Or just toss them with sugar—sometimes that's all you need.

INGREDIENTS

FOR THE BATTER:

5 cups (800 g) glutinous rice flour

1½ cups (165 g) millet flour

1⅔ cups (335 g) sugar

⅓ cup (65 g) baking powder

3 tablespoons salt

3 cups (720 ml) whole milk

1 cup (225 g) unsalted butter, melted and cooled

6 eggs

FOR SHAPING AND FRYING:

2 quarts (2 L) neutral oil for frying, such as soybean

¼ cup (40 g) glutinous rice flour, plus more for cutting out the donuts

TO FINISH:

1 cup (200 g) sugar

2 tablespoons ground cinnamon (optional)

MAKE THE BATTER: In the bowl of a stand mixer, combine all of the ingredients for the batter and mix with the paddle attachment until a smooth dough forms. Wrap the dough in plastic wrap and refrigerate for 3 hours or overnight.

SHAPE AND FRY THE DOUGH: In a fryer or Dutch oven, preheat the oil to 325°F (165°C), when measured with a candy thermometer.

Sprinkle ¼ cup (40 g) rice flour on a flat surface and on top of the dough and roll it out until it's about ½ inch (12 mm) thick. Cut doughnuts about 3 inches (7.5 cm) in diameter using a doughnut cutter, concentric cookie cutters, or a drinking glass and a shot glass, flouring the cutters to avoid sticking. Combine the leftover pieces and roll out the dough again into a ½-inch-thick (12 mm) layer as many times as possible, to create as many doughnuts as you can.

Work in batches so as not to overcrowd the fryer. Once the oil is up to temperature, gently place as many doughnuts as will comfortably fit into the oil and allow to fry for 3 minutes before carefully turning them over. Fry the other side for 3 minutes and drain on a cooling rack with something underneath to catch any excess oil.

To finish, on a plate, mix the sugar and cinnamon, if using. Toss the doughnuts with the mixture and serve immediately.

BANANA CARAMEL TART

Makes one 8-inch (20-cm) tart; serves 6 to 8

DANIELLE CREATED A MINIATURE VERSION OF THIS TART FOR TRIGG'S WEDDING. She made a variety of miniature tarts for dessert, and knowing Trigg and Patty love banana cream, created a banana version. She did this even though she hates bananas and can't even stand the smell of them, so you know this was made with love. With a layering of fresh bananas and a dark banana caramel, and a vanilla pastry cream topped with unsweetened whipped cream inside a super-flaky, melt-in-your-mouth puff pastry base, it really stole the show, and it was the one dessert that everyone spoke of and would bring up months after the wedding. Danielle gets requests for it for special events, and when we serve it as a special at Win Son, it sells out every time.

This tart is an accumulation of a few recipes that need to be made prior to assembling. It's a bit of a labor of love, but we think it pays off with its deliciousness.

FOR THE TART SHELL:
3 cups (375 g) all-purpose flour

1½ teaspoons sugar

1 teaspoon salt

¾ cup (170 g) cold unsalted butter, cut into small cubes

1 egg

1 egg white

1½ tablespoons cold water

FOR THE PASTRY CREAM:
1 cup (120 ml) whole milk

¼ cup (50 g) sugar

½ teaspoon salt

½ teaspoon vanilla extract

2 tablespoons cornstarch

3 egg yolks

FOR THE BANANA CARAMEL:
2 cups (400 g) sugar

4 cups (960 ml) pureed bananas

1 teaspoon salt

FOR ASSEMBLY:
2 fresh bananas

1 cup (240 ml) whipped cream (or ½ cup/120 ml heavy cream, whipped)

MAKE THE TART SHELL: In the bowl of a food processor or stand mixer with a paddle attachment, mix the flour, sugar, salt, and cubed butter just until the butter pieces are pea-sized. Add the egg, egg white, and water and mix until a shaggy dough forms. Ball up the dough, wrap in plastic, and refrigerate for an hour at least. When the dough has chilled, roll out to a roughly 9-inch (23 cm) diameter circle, so there's excess to trim from the 8-inch (20 cm) tart pan. (Alternately, if you have miniature tart pans, this dough can be rolled out into smaller pieces to fit each of those.)

Tuck the dough into the tart pan and pat down gently. Trim the edges neatly with scissors. Refrigerate the lined pan for 30 minutes or freeze for 15 minutes. Preheat the oven to 350°F (175°C) and bake the tart shell for 25 minutes, or until golden brown. (This may take less time if using miniature tart pans.) Let cool completely before filling.

MAKE THE PASTRY CREAM: In a medium saucepan, heat the milk, sugar, salt, and vanilla to a boil. In a separate bowl, mix together the cornstarch and egg yolks until smooth.

When the milk mixture just starts to bubble a tiny bit, remove from the heat. Take a small ladle or scoop of this hot milk mixture and slowly pour it into the egg yolk mixture while stirring it rapidly to temper the eggs. Repeat with another ladle or scoop, while stirring, until all of the milk is incorporated.

Return the combined mixture to the saucepan and heat it over low heat. Stir constantly until the mixture has thickened enough to coat the back of a spoon and "burps" whenever it bubbles (meaning it's thick enough to make a burping sound when a bubble pops to the surface). Strain the mixture through a fine-mesh sieve and let cool completely.

MAKE THE BANANA CARAMEL: Place the sugar in a tall pot and add just enough water to make it look like wet sand (about ⅓ cup /80 g). Heat over medium until the sugar has turned a medium caramel color; don't stir the sugar while it's caramelizing, as it may cause it to crystallize. Remove from the heat. Slowly incorporate the banana puree and salt into the hot caramel.

ASSEMBLE THE TART: Slice the fresh bananas and line the bottom of the tart with a single layer of slices. Spoon and smooth banana caramel over the banana slices until you can barely see them.

Layer the pastry cream on top of that and smooth out to the edges of the tart shell. Gently scoop the whipped cream on top of the pastry cream and serve.

ALMOND MILK YULU

Serves 4

IT WAS A REALLY HOT SUMMER DAY IN TAINAN WHEN AUNTIE LEAH TOOK US TO A LITTLE SHOP NEAR JOSH'S GRANDFATHER'S HOUSE FOR ALMOND MILK YULU. With soft tofu, barley, and red beans, this cold dessert or snack is lightly sweet and so refreshing. All the textures play against one another in a really fun way (a real hallmark of Taiwanese cuisine) and it's subtly rich and filling, too. It's one of our favorite beverages or sweets, especially when you are looking for a good way to cool off in the summer, so we had to try making it, too. We went with Marcona almonds from Spain, which have a lot of olive oil absorbed in them for a great flavor and snap. But you could opt for regular roasted almonds.

INGREDIENTS

1 pint (375 g) Marcona almonds, roasted and salted

1 cup (200 g) sugar

1 cup (195 g) red adzuki beans

1 cup (200 g) pearl barley

1 taro root

1 block silken tofu (any size)

Soak the roasted, salted Marcona almonds in 1½ quarts (1.4 L) of water overnight. Puree in a food processor the next day until you have a nice almond milk. (We don't think it's necessary to strain the pulp out of this one through a nut milk bag.)

Make a simple syrup: Combine the sugar and 1 cup (240 ml) of water and bring to a boil, stirring to dissolve. Let cool.

Soak the adzuki beans overnight in enough water to cover by 3 inches (7.5 cm). The next day, strain, and cover with water again in a saucepan. Bring to a boil, then reduce the heat to a gentle simmer and cook until tender, 30 minutes to 1 hour. Drain and transfer to a mixing bowl. Gently fold in half the simple syrup. Let sit for at least 2 hours or up to 2 days. (Alternately, you could get a can of cooked, sweet red beans from an Asian market.)

Bring a pot of 2 quarts (2 L) water up to a boil. Add the pearl barley and, when it's tender, after about 12 minutes, strain through a colander. Transfer to a mixing bowl and stir in half of the remaining simple syrup.

Cut the taro into 2-inch (5 cm) chunks and boil in water until soft. Mash in a mixing bowl with a fork, and stir in the remaining simple syrup.

Cut the silken tofu into small squares.

In four cereal bowls, place a fat tablespoon of mashed taro, a tablespoon of red beans, a tablespoon of barely, and a generous amount of silken tofu squares in each. Pour in the cold, slightly salty Marcona almond milk until everything is covered like cereal.

WIN SON
CHOCOLATE CHIP COOKIES
Makes 12 to 18

IN THE SPRING OF 2020, AFTER REOPENING FOR TAKEOUT AND DELIVERY ONLY DUE TO COVID-19, WE HAD TO TEMPORARILY SCRAP A LOT OF MENU ITEMS FROM WIN SON BAKERY. We cut some of the pastries and the laminated bolo baos were on hold. This was in part due to the fact that our incredible pastry chef, Danielle, couldn't work because she has asthma and it would be too risky for her health. Trigg was managing the bakery kitchen in the morning and the restuarant in the evening, so we pared down. He always had wanted to add chocolate chip cookies to the menu, so he shot his shot. One time, Josh's girlfriend, Emily, brought chocolate chip cookies to a party and we crushed them. They had a coffee flavor, so he added some finely ground espresso and brown butter to our recipe. We also feel that the cookie dough benefits from rest, so let it chill at least 24 hours in advance of baking it. Plan ahead to bake it on the day after you mix the dough. It's pretty simple, not that difficult, but a perfect cookie—and comfort—to us.

INGREDIENTS

3 cups (675 g) unsalted butter

4¾ cups (575 g) bread flour

3 cups (375 g) all-purpose flour

2 teaspoons baking soda

3 tablespoons salt

1¾ cups (350 g) sugar

3 cups (660 g) packed dark brown sugar

¼ cup (25 g) espresso grounds or finely ground coffee beans

2 teaspoons vanilla extract

4 eggs

3 egg yolks

2 cups (340 g) dark chocolate chunks, coarsely chopped from a chilled bar

3 cups (525 g) semisweet chocolate chips

In a medium-large saucepan, melt the butter over medium heat. Let it bubble and continue cooking until it turns medium brown in color and smells very nutty. Remove from the heat and pour into a heatproof 2-cup (480 ml) measuring cup. Once the foam has receded, it should be about ¾ cup (180 ml). Add enough water to bring the amount up to 1 cup (240 ml) in total. Set aside.

Sift together the bread flour, all-purpose flour, baking soda, and salt; do not skip this step.

The brown butter should be semi–room temperature before mixing begins. In the bowl of a stand mixer using the whip attachment (not the paddle), cream together the brown butter, sugar, dark brown sugar, espresso grounds, and vanilla extract. Or, just cream them by hand using a whisk, or with an electric eggbeater. You want to make sure the mixture has been creamed very well, for at least 6 to 8 minutes. When creamed well, the mixture will be the color of light brown sugar and not look greasy at all, like it did in the beginning.

Slowly mix in the eggs and egg yolks, scraping down the dough from the sides of the bowl. Next, slowly incorporate the sifted dry ingredients. Fold in the chocolate chunks and chips. Using an ice cream scoop, scoop the dough into 12 to 18 balls. Wrap each with plastic wrap and refrigerate for at least 1 day in advance of use. (The dough balls can also be frozen for up to 5 days.)

Thaw the dough overnight if it has been frozen. Preheat the oven to 375°F (190°C). Line a sheet pan with parchment and arrange the cookie dough scoops with at least 3 inches (7.5 cm) of space in between. Bake for 12 to 15 minutes, depending on their size, or until crisp and browned at the edges. Transfer to a wire rack to cool several minutes before serving.

SUN COOKIES
Makes about 16

THE SUN COOKIES THAT WE SERVE AT WIN SON BAKERY CAME A LONG WAY FROM THEIR INSPIRATION—*TAI YANG BING*, OR SUN CAKE, IN TAIWAN. Sun Cakes are delicious, flaky pastries with a lot of buttery layers thanks to being rolled up and smashed (sort of like scallion pancakes), and they're also filled with a caramel-like filling of sticky maltose syrup. We were enamored with these in Taiwan, but we didn't want to do an exact replica. Danielle ended up taking the idea of these layers and transposing them into a visual swirl like a Swiss roll, with a pastry similar to puff pastry. And instead of hiding the syrup inside the cookie, she created a brown-butter pine nut filling that gets rolled up into the pastry. In the end, this pinwheel-shaped tribute to the original is more like a cookie than a cake.

<< INGREDIENTS >>

FOR THE TOP PORTION OF DOUGH:

2 sticks cold unsalted butter, cut into small cubes

2 cups (250 g) all-purpose flour

1 tablespoon salt

1 tablespoon sugar

FOR THE BOTTOM PORTION OF DOUGH:

2 cups (250 g) all-purpose flour

4 tablespoons (½ stick) cold unsalted butter, cut into small cubes

1 tablespoon sugar

1 tablespoon salt

FOR THE PINE NUT FILLING:

1 cup (2 sticks) unsalted butter

1 cup (135 g) pine nuts

2 cups (440 g) packed dark brown sugar

1 teaspoon salt

NOTE: *You could substitute the top and bottom portion of dough with premade puff pastry sheets, which won't have quite the same effect as this recipe but will make a great cookie nonetheless.*

MAKE THE TOP PORTION OF THE DOUGH:
In the bowl of a stand mixer using the paddle attachment, mix the butter, flour, salt, and sugar together until just combined. Cut a piece of parchment paper to 6 by 9 inches (15 by 23 cm) and press the mixture onto the paper evenly; cover with plastic and refrigerate overnight.

MAKE THE BOTTOM PORTION OF THE DOUGH:
In the bowl of a stand mixer using the paddle attachment, combine the flour, butter, sugar, and salt. Start mixing on the lowest speed. Continue mixing until the butter pieces have become pea-sized, and start drizzling in 1 cup (240 ml) water until it becomes a shaggy-looking mass. If you see a lot of dry bits, mix for 1 to 2 minutes longer. Press into a rough square about 5 inches (12 cm) that is relatively flat. Cover with plastic and refrigerate overnight.

MAKE THE PINE NUT FILLING: In a medium saucepan, melt the butter over medium heat. Once it has melted completely, add the pine nuts. Stirring often, cook the pine nuts in the butter until the butter has become golden brown and nutty. It's important to stir to prevent the nuts from sticking to the bottom of the pan and burning as they toast. Remove from the heat.

Add the dark brown sugar and salt. Stir until the sugar and pine nuts are well combined. Cool in a heatproof vessel. The filling can be used when completely cool or can be refrigerated for up to 3 months. Freezing is not necessary.

Prior to the assembly, pull out the top portion from the fridge and let it temper, warming until it becomes malleable. (The bottom portion doesn't need to temper.)

On a well-floured surface, dust the bottom portion with flour and roll it out until it is larger than the top portion. You want to still try to keep it in a rectangular shape.

Place the top portion on the bottom portion and fully enclose the top portion. You don't want to see any of the top portion sticking out, so it's important to roll out the bottom piece to be large enough. If you need to stretch the bottom portion to cover any openings, that's OK.

Roll out the square of the combined top and bottom pieces lengthwise until it has reached 18 inches (46 cm) or so. It's important to reach this size, because if you roll the dough out smaller, it will be thicker once folded, and it is difficult to roll out a very fat block.

It does not matter in this next step if you start left or right; all that matters is that you're consistent throughout the process.

Take the left side of the dough and fold it over into the middle. Take the right side of the dough and fold it over the left side, creating a letter fold. If the right side of the dough doesn't fully fit over the left side, adjust the left to make sure the right can go over it completely.

Wrap the dough in plastic wrap and refrigerate for 30 to 45 minutes. Repeat this rolling out and folding process 2 more times, continuing to wrap and refrigerate in between.

When the dough has reached its final fold, wrap and refrigerate for at least 1 hour.

To assemble the cookies, roll your refrigerated puff pastry out to a rectangle 24 inches in length by 12 inches in width (61 by 30.5 cm). Spread your cooled pine nut filling across the dough. You want the filling to be evenly spread and not too thick.

From the bottom to the top, start rolling the dough up like a cinnamon roll until you have a spiraled log. Refrigerate the log on a sheet pan until firm enough to cut, about 2 hours. Cut into 1-inch-thick (2.5 cm) cookies.

Preheat the oven to 350°F (175°C) and place the cookies 2 inches (5 cm) apart on a sheet pan lined with parchment paper. Bake until golden brown, 12 to 14 minutes. The cookies will be fragile while hot, so allow to fully cool on the sheet pan before removing them.

STRAWBERRY MARGARITA AIYU JELLY

Serves 6 to 8

AIYU JELLY IS A FASCINATING DESSERT ENJOYED IN TAIWAN THAT'S MADE FROM THE SEEDS OF A CREEPING FIG PLANT. When rubbed together, the seeds create a gel that thickens liquid. Legend in Taiwan is that it was invented when someone was taking a sip of water in a creek and noticed that a patch of the water had jellied, spontaneously by nature. The jelly is now a popular summer treat—similar to grass jelly, another dessert common in Taiwan, China, and Southeast Asia.

When we were in Taiwan with Josh's mom and Danielle, our pastry chef, we went to a place that served aiyu jelly with slices of lemon, lime, and pineapple on top, which was so refreshing. We made a version of this cold dessert with strawberry juice, lime, and a bit of tequila, which is totally optional, but reminds us of a strawberry margarita, another summer refresher.

For this recipe, we've followed the instructions for making aiyu jelly from Yun Hai, which imports these seeds from Taiwan and sells them online. It's one of the only places, we're pretty sure, you can get this ingredient in the States.

INGREDIENTS

FOR THE JELLY:
1 pack Alishan Aiyu seeds (order online from Yun Hai)

FOR THE STRAWBERRY MARGARITA:
4 cups (480 ml) fresh strawberries, ends trimmed

¼ cup (60 ml) fresh lime juice

2 tablespoons simple syrup (see page 219)

¼ cup (60 ml) tequila

MAKE THE AIYU JELLY: Follow the directions on the package. Divide into four small bowls or wide margarita glasses. Break up a little into chunks and keep chilled until you're ready to pour the margarita on top.

MAKE THE STRAWBERRY MARGARITA: Blend the strawberries in a blender until smooth; you should have about 2 cups (475 ml) of strawberry puree. (Straining it next is optional based on your preference.) Stir the puree together with the lime juice, simple syrup, and tequila and ice to chill. Strain out the ice, then pour the chilled liquid over the broken-up jelly. Serve cold.

CHAPTER 9

SAUCES, SPICES, AND RECIPE BUILDERS

CHARRED SCALLION SAUCE
Makes 1 pint (480 ml)

CHARRING SCALLIONS OR ANY TYPE OF ONIONS DRAMAT-ICALLY INCREASES THE DEPTH OF FLAVOR FOR STOCKS AND SAUCES, OR JUST AS A SIDE DISH FOR DINNER. Trigg loves to char scallions or ramps when in season (see Fermented Scallions or Ramps, page 46). His mentor Pei Chang used to make a charred scallion ranch dressing for wings and it was fire. For this sauce, we puree the charred scallions and add a lot of oil to emulsify and shine it out. You can easily do this at home on a cast-iron pan as described in this recipe. But if you have a barbe-cue going, you also can grill the scallions—just be sure to toss them in oil and salt first.

As a variation, you can simply add fresh basil leaves. This makes a bright green sauce that we serve with our oyster omelet (page 51), but it could go with just about any of the appetizers or snacks.

3 bunches scallions

1 cup (240 ml) neutral oil, such as soybean

Salt

MSG

FOR THE BASIL-SCALLION SAUCE VARIATION:
1 cup (20 g) fresh basil leaves, loosely packed

DIRECTIONS: Cut the scallions more or less in half lengthwise so you have white and light green parts and very green parts of the scallions in each piece. Heat a pot of lightly salted water, enough to submerge the very green scallion parts, and bring to a boil. Meanwhile, prepare a large bowl filled with ice water on the side. Drop the greens into the boiling water and keep them there for 5 seconds. Remove with tongs (or strain) and plunge immediately into the ice bath. Let cool thoroughly, then drain and pat dry.

Heat a heavy-bottomed skillet or cast-iron pan with a couple tablespoons of the soybean oil. Once the oil is sizzling-hot, add the scallion whites and light green pieces and don't move them for several seconds, so that they each char on the bottom. (You may want to work in batches to ensure that you're not overcrowding the pan and preventing them from charring.) Sprinkle them with a generous pinch of both salt and MSG. After the bottoms are nicely charred, stir and continue cooking until they char a bit more all over and are tender, about 2 minutes.

Transfer the blanched scallion greens and charred scallions to a blender (preferably a high-speed blender like a Vitamix). If making the basil-scallion sauce variation, add the fresh basil leaves now. Blend, stopping to scrape down the sides, until the scallions are well chopped. Then gradually pour in the neutral oil, while blending, until incorporated. Keep blending until the mixture is smooth. Add more salt and MSG to taste. Keep refrigerated in a jar or airtight container for up to 1 week.

"CHICKEN" SPICE MIX
Makes 1 pint (375 g)

THERE ARE A LOT OF FRIED CHICKEN RECIPES IN THIS COOK-BOOK, AND A LOT OF LOVE FOR FRIED CHICKEN IN TAIWAN. What makes Taiwan's fried chicken so special, we think, is not only the super-crispy starch crust, but also the amazing aroma of the cayenne pepper and Chinese five-spice powder, which are sprinkled liberally all over the chicken once it's out of the fryer. This scent will be nostalgic for anyone who's walked through a night mar-ket in Taiwan, melding with the scent-memories of the stinky tofu vendor, the *lu wei* (braised food) stand, and more classic night market finds.

In the recipes throughout the book, we experiment with variations on this scent or seasoning blend, dialing in the perfect flavor for the application at hand. But this particular spice mix recipe is a reliable go-to for any fried chicken you might make. And it can be reapplied to countless other dishes in your home kitchen. We think it's a great all-purpose spice for chicken and poultry, like quail (page 140). Use it for fresh squid that you deep-fry or grill, or for some chicken thighs that you throw on the grill. Or just eggs and maybe fried rice. Whatever you're cooking, adding this spice mix will tingle your nostrils with classic Taiwanese scents.

2 tablespoons cayenne pepper

2 teaspoons Chinese five-spice powder

2 teaspoons kombu cha (powdered seaweed seasoning)

1 teaspoon ground white pepper

DIRECTIONS: In a bowl, combine all of the ingredients and store in a jar or airtight container. It can be stored for months but is best enjoyed within 1 month.

CHILE VINAIGRETTE
Makes 1 pint (480 ml)

WHEN EATING DUMPLINGS, THINK OF BLACK VINEGAR, SOY SAUCE, AND CHILI OIL AS YOUR BUILDING BLOCKS FOR A GREAT DIPPING SAUCE. These are some of the things you'd typically find on the table at a dumpling shop in Taiwan. If it's *xiao long bao* (aka Shanghainese soup dumpling), you'll also find young ginger, slivered in crunchy threads, swimming in black vinegar as your sauce. Our chile vinaigrette is meant to reflect all these elements, balanced out with sweetness. This vinaigrette is also great to use as a marinade or topping for grilled meats.

½ cup (120 ml) House Chili Oil (page 258) or your favorite chili oil, such as Lao Gan Ma Spicy Chili Crisp

¼ cup (60 ml) mirin

¼ cup (60 ml) soy sauce

¼ cup (60 ml) Chinese black vinegar

½ cup (120 ml) neutral oil, such as soybean

DIRECTIONS: In a blender, combine the chili oil with the mirin, soy sauce, and black vinegar. Blend until smooth. Add in the neutral cooking oil and blend until emulsified. This sauce can be stored in an airtight jar or container in the refrigerator for up to one year.

CILANTRO-MINT SAUCE
Makes about 1 pint (480 ml)

THIS SILKEN, EMERALD-GREEN PUREE IS ONE OF THE MOST VERSATILE SAUCES. It's in our take on the classic Taiwanese ice cream crepe with crushed peanuts and cilantro (page 227)—a truly amazing combination of flavors that we associate so strongly with Taiwan. Then, it's in our take on *zhajiangmian* (page 115), a northern Chinese noodle dish that's well-loved in Taiwan. And we also sneak it into our Guohua Street Salad (page 80) for a touch of sweet, herbaceous flavor. It's really a very simple sauce—a liquefied blend of cilantro, mint, and sugar—that you can drizzle onto anything, sweet or savory.

½ cup (100 g) sugar

1 bunch fresh cilantro

1 bunch fresh mint

½ cup (120 ml) light corn syrup

DIRECTIONS: In a small saucepan, make a simple syrup by bringing ½ cup (120 ml) water to a boil. Remove from the heat and stir in the sugar until dissolved. Set aside and cool for several minutes.

Bring a large pot of water to a boil and prepare two large bowls with ice water. Submerge the cilantro bunch in the boiling water for no more than 10 seconds, then immediately transfer to an ice bath to cool down. Repeat the process with the mint bunch, in the other ice bath. Once the herbs are cool, rinse and shake out the water well. Remove the leaves from just the mint bunches, discarding the stems for another use; the cilantro stems can stay. In a blender or food processor, working in two or more batches, depending on their size, process half the herbs and half the simple syrup and corn syrup (or ⅓ of everything if working in three batches), until the leaves are very finely processed. Stop and scrape down the sides with a spatula if necessary. The resulting sauce should be thin enough to drizzle, so if you need any extra liquid, go ahead and mix in a small splash of water at a time. Store in an airtight container in the refrigerator for up to a few days or in the freezer for a month.

DASHI
Makes 6 cups (1.4 L)

THIS IS A BUILDING BLOCK FOR A LOT OF SOUPS AND STIR-FRIES. At Win Son, we usually use a bottle of shiro dashi (page 30), which is a more concentrated dashi mixed with white soy sauce, for an instant hit of flavor. But dashi itself can be made separately and used with shiro instead. And if you don't want to go through the trouble of making dashi, instant dashi powder (see page 30) can make your life a lot easier. No shame in that shortcut, either.

20 square inches (130 sq cm) kombu

6 cups (1.4 L) cold water

¼ cup (3 g) packed bonito flakes

DIRECTIONS: Submerge the kombu in the cold water and let soak for 30 minutes or overnight. Pour the mixture into a saucepan over medium heat and slowly bring just to a boil. Remove from the heat and add the bonito flakes. Let steep for 3 to 4 minutes, until the flakes begin to sink. Strain the solids from the liquid and return the broth to the pot. Reserve the kombu and save it in the refrigerator for making dashi at another time (up to 1 month).

FU RU MAYO
Makes 1 pint (480 ml)

THIS RECIPE IS JUST ABOUT AS SIMPLE AS IT GETS, BUT THE FLAVORS ARE PRETTY COMPLEX. It starts with *dou fu ru* (see page 26, sometimes called *fu ru* for short), fermented tofu cubes that are jarred in their own brine. (Find them in an Asian supermarket or online.) Shelf-stable and super concentrated, this tofu is a great vegan umami flavor booster. Although we use this mayo on our fried chicken sandwich, the Big Chicken Bun (page 155), you could slather it on your next BLT, steamed bun, or anything that can use a little more savory depth.

¼ cup (60 ml) jarred fermented bean curd with chili (aka dou fu ru)

1½ cups (360 ml) Kewpie mayonnaise

DIRECTIONS: In a small bowl, gently mash the fu ru with a spatula or fork. Transfer to a blender or food processor along with the mayo and puree until smooth. Keep refrigerated in a jar or airtight container for up to 1 week.

GARLIC CONFIT
Makes about 1 pint (480 ml)

STREET VENDORS IN TAIWAN SELLING GRILLED SAUSAGES ON A STICK WILL GIVE YOU A WHOLE GARLIC CLOVE. Or you might get a paper bag filled with mini sausages and a few garlic cloves. Either way, the idea is to eat bites of the raw clove in between bites of sausage. This was counterintuitive to Trigg's training as a chef but at the same time exciting, as he's always had a penchant for garlic. In fact, he'd been scolded for adding too much garlic to family meal that it caused servers' breaths to stink.

We put plenty of raw garlic in dishes at Win Son, but we also mess around with this garlic that is roasted slow and low, swimming in oil—garlic confit. We get its color pretty deep golden brown but not black; you don't want the garlic to become bitter. It's one of those stealthy flavor builders for sauces and dishes, like the Black Sesame Noodles with Mushrooms (page 112). The garlic cloves can then be pureed and added to sauces or served whole, and the oil can be drizzled over dishes for a rich garlicky finish.

1 cup (145 g) garlic cloves, peeled

Soybean, avocado, or grapeseed oil to cover

DIRECTIONS: Preheat the oven to 275°F (135°C). Place the garlic cloves in a small casserole or oven-safe dish and cover with just enough of the oil to submerge them. Cut a sheet of parchment paper to fit across the top of the garlic, and snip out a small hole in the center to allow steam to escape. Confit (meaning to cook in fat or oil) for 1 hour.

Let cool completely. Store the whole cloves in the oil in an airtight container in the refrigerator for up to a month.

GARLIC-CILANTRO-CHILI DIPPING SAUCE
Makes 1 pint (480 ml)

NOTICEABLY SWEET, TANGY, AND HERBAL, AND ACCENTED WITH FRESH CILANTRO, THIS SAUCE IS WHAT WE USE FOR BOILED *JIAOZI* (DUMPLINGS) AND SILKY WONTONS, BECAUSE THEIR SOFTER SKINS REALLY ABSORB THIS LOOSE SAUCE WELL. We can't help ourselves from adding chili oil to all dipping sauces, but this recipe works without it just as well, so leave it out if you prefer.

1 head garlic, smashed and peeled

1 bunch fresh cilantro, both leaves and stems, coarsely chopped

4 scallions, coarsely chopped

¼ cup (60 ml) House Chili Oil (page 258) or your favorite chili oil, such as Lao Gan Ma Spicy Chili Crisp (optional)

¼ cup (60 ml) rice vinegar

1 tablespoon black rice vinegar

½ cup (120 ml) light soy sauce

2 tablespoons sugar

¼ teaspoon ground white pepper

1 teaspoon toasted sesame oil

DIRECTIONS: In a food processor, pulse the garlic several times, stopping to scrape down the sides, until finely chopped or minced. Add the coarsely chopped cilantro and scallions and pulse several more times, stopping to scrape down the sides. Alternately, you could also chop everything by hand. Transfer the chopped herbs and garlic to a bowl. Add the rice vinegar, black rice vinegar, soy sauce, sugar, white pepper, and sesame oil and stir well to dissolve the sugar. Add more of anything else to taste.

GARLIC-GINGER SAUCE WITH PICKLED MUSTARD GREENS
Makes 1 quart (950 ml)

THIS IS SIMILAR TO A CLASSIC GINGER-SCALLION SAUCE, WHERE HOT OIL IS POURED OVER THE HERBS TO GENTLY FRY THEM. Only we've added cilantro, garlic, and pickled mustard greens for a chunky, pungent green condiment. This sauce is great to use as a marinade for grilled shrimp (page 95). Or puree it up and combine with Kewpie mayo and lemon juice to add to your Beef Roll (page 188). Or serve it with roast chicken.

Need another idea? Season black bass fillets with this sauce, add a little shiro dashi (see page 30), and steam it—it's insanely good. (One tip we picked up from the chef Damon Wise, a good friend, is that black bass, particularly those local to New York waters, gets a wonderfully supple texture when you steam it.) The texture and flavor of this condiment thinned out with a little shiro dashi is irresistible. Just put it on everything, and submit to having garlic breath for life.

1 tablespoon pickled mustard greens (aka *suen cai*; can be found in Asian markets)

1 bunch scallions, chopped

4-inch (10-cm) piece fresh ginger, peeled and julienned

4 cloves garlic, minced

1 bunch fresh cilantro, leaves and stems, chopped

1 cup (240 ml) soybean oil

Salt

Sugar

MSG

DIRECTIONS: Drain the pickled mustard greens from the liquid in their packaging and submerge in ice water for 30 minutes. Drain and squeeze out thoroughly. Roughly chop. Transfer to a food processor and process until evenly minced.

In a deep heat-safe bowl, place the scallions, ginger, and garlic. In a separate pan, heat the oil over high heat until smoking-hot, about 3 minutes. Carefully pour the hot oil all over the aromatic mixture, standing away as it sizzles for 5 seconds. Then stir the mixture to ensure all the pieces cook in the hot oil, which will get rid of the raw flavor of the aromatics. Let the mixture cool for 10 minutes before folding in the minced pickled mustard greens. Add the salt, sugar, and MSG to taste. The sauce can be stored in the fridge in an airtight container for up to a week.

GINGER DELUXE SAUCE
Makes about 1 pint (480 ml)

WE ORIGINALLY CREATED THIS SAUCE JUST FOR THE FRIED CHICKEN AT WIN SON BAKERY, BUT IT'S PRETTY TASTY AND NOW COMES ON OUR BURGER AND ALONGSIDE, IF NOT ON, ALL THE BREAKFAST SANDWICHES. In the summer, we make a version of this sauce (which is sort of inspired by Russian dressing) incorporating blistered Sungold tomatoes, and the umami from those combined with the fermented bean curd, or *dou fu ru*, makes it super savory and funky. The best time to use Sungolds is the first two weeks in August, but this sauce is delicious without them, all year round. Ginger Deluxe has become a staple condiment at Win Son Bakery and we're sure there are plenty more uses for it we're yet to discover. If you are lucky enough to have Sungolds on hand, just blister them in the broiler for a few minutes until they burst and start to take some color and fold them into the mayo.

3-inch (7.5 cm) piece fresh ginger, peeled and cut into thin coins

4 scallions, roughly chopped

1 clove garlic, peeled

1 cup (240 ml) Kewpie mayonnaise

½ cup (120 ml) ketchup

½ teaspoon cracked black pepper

¼ teaspoon smoked paprika

¼ teaspoon mustard powder

¼ teaspoon garlic salt

1 tablespoon jarred fermented bean curd with chili (aka *dou fu ru*; see page 27)

1½ teaspoons Worcestershire sauce

Salt and/or MSG (optional)

DIRECTIONS: In the bowl of a food processor, place the ginger, scallions, and garlic and pulse several times, stopping to scrape down the sides, until the mixture is very finely chopped. Add the mayonnaise, ketchup, pepper, paprika, mustard powder, garlic salt, fermented bean curd, Worcestershire, and salt and/or MSG (if using) and blend. Taste for seasoning, adding extra salt and MSG, if desired. Store the sauce covered in the refrigerator for up to 1 week.

HOUSE CHILI OIL
Makes about 1 quart (950 ml)

AS MUCH AS WE LOVE LAO GAN MA SPICY CHILI CRISP (SEE OUR RANT ON CHILI OIL, PAGE 26), WE JUST HAD TO FASHION OUR OWN CHILI OIL TO INFUSE THE PERFECT BLEND OF SPICES. When making this recipe, it's important to respect the order of operations so you don't burn the spices and so that the oil becomes infused with loads of flavor. Start by making garlic and shallot oil. Go low and slow throughout the whole infusion process or else you will ruin all these harmonious flavors that enhance the aromatics. The black cardamom lends a smoky, savory flavor that we think is really key so don't skip that ingredient even if it's a little hard to find. At Win Son, we air-dry kumquats and infuse them along with the spices, but in this recipe, since you probably will not want to go to all that trouble, just drop in a couple orange peels. The citrus and Sichuan peppercorns play an important part in giving this oil a depth of personality.

1 quart (950 ml) peanut oil

1 head garlic, skin-on, lightly smashed with the heel of your hand

1 fat finger fresh ginger, skin-on, lightly smashed with the heel of your hand

3 shallots, skin-on, lightly smashed with the heel of your hand

4 to 6 cinnamon sticks, broken

1 bay leaf

4 star anise cloves

2 to 3 black cardamom pods, shells removed

2 teaspoons whole Sichuan peppercorns

6 to 8 strips orange zest, peeled with a vegetable peeler

1 cup (150 g) dried Sichuan chile peppers, such as erjingtiao, stems removed and coarsely crushed in a mortar and pestle or spice grinder

1 cup (96 g) gochugaru (aka Korean chile flakes)

½ cup (72 g) fennel seeds, crushed with a mortar and pestle or spice grinder

2 teaspoons green Sichuan peppercorns, crushed with a mortar and pestle or spice grinder

½ cup (75 g) toasted white sesame seeds, crushed with a mortar and pestle or spice grinder

2 teaspoons salt

2 teaspoons MSG

1 tablespoon sugar

2 teaspoons dried ginger powder

1 tablespoon fennel pollen

DIRECTIONS: Place the oil in a 4-quart (3.8 L) saucepot with the lightly smashed head of garlic and the ginger, shallots, cinnamon, bay leaf, star anise, black cardamom, whole Sichuan peppercorns, and orange zest. Steep the oil with these aromatics for 3 hours at 225°F (110°C), measured using a candy thermometer. Or, transfer to a 225°F (110°C) oven for 4 hours.

Place the Sichuan chile peppers and gochugaru into a pot large enough to hold the infused oil after it's strained. Arrange a chinois or fine-mesh sieve on top of the pot. Carefully strain the alliums and aromatics from the oil into the ground chile mixture. After you have safely transferred the strained, hot oil into a pot with the chile flakes, stir to make sure the oil infuses and incorporates evenly with the chiles. Then, immediately stir in the crushed sesame seeds, fennel seeds, and crushed Sichuan peppercorns. Finally, season with the salt, MSG, sugar, dried ginger powder, and fennel pollen.

Allow the chili oil to come down to room temperature in a safe place and let it sit overnight to settle, un-refrigerated. Keep in a jar in the refrigerator for up to a year.

"LAMB" SPICE MIX
Makes about ¾ cup (25 g)

SPICES ARE OFTEN A TOUGH PRODUCT TO HARVEST OR PROCESS, WHICH IS WHY THEY'VE CAUSED PEOPLE TO TRAVEL LONG DISTANCES AND DANGEROUSLY AROUND THE WORLD AND TO START WARS WITH ONE ANOTHER OVER THE CENTURIES. Nowadays, the global spice market is incredibly opaque, and the people who grow your spices are exploited while countless middlemen rake in profits. We encourage you to explore companies like Burlap & Barrel, SOS Chefs, and many more distributors of single-origin spices that you can order online. Plus, you might find something new and crazy that you fall in love with. We love the fermented lime powder from Burlap & Barrel. Its deep, heady, tangy aroma pairs well here with bold spices like cumin and Sichuan peppercorns.

This is a spice mix that we use a lot for lamb, in recipes like our lamb-based zhajiangmian (page 115) and Lamb Wontons (page 179). But you don't have to just stick with lamb. Anything with a stronger flavor profile, like duck or any gamey meat, would really benefit from a hit of this blend.

2 tablespoons fermented lime powder, such as Black Lime from Burlap & Barrell

1 tablespoon ground green Sichuan peppercorns

2 tablespoons ground cumin

2 tablespoons gruond cinnamon

3 tablespoons cayenne pepper

2 tablespoons Chinese five-spice powder

1 teaspoon ground white pepper

DIRECTIONS: In a bowl, combine all of the ingredients and store in a jar or airtight container. It can be stored for months but is best enjoyed within 1 month.

PERSIMMON RED HOT SAUCE
Makes 1 pint (480 ml)

WE ALWAYS BUY A LOT OF PERSIMMONS WHEN THEY COME INTO SEASON IN THE FALL. One year, Trigg thought it would be fun to turn them into a jam to flavor a red hot sauce, giving it a little boost of sweetness. This became our unconventional topping for our Popcorn Chicken (page 165), which are boneless fried chicken morsels seasoned with five-spice and fried with some basil. Then we decided to add smoked trout roe to the dish for a sort of highbrow-lowbrow fried chicken combo. This Persimmon Red Hot Sauce acts as an adhesive, allowing you to place the orange bubbles of fish eggs on each fried chicken bite. It's all monochromatic golden-red in the end, and delicious. Even if you aren't making this particular dish, we think you'll love this hot sauce. Try it on chicken wings.

5 persimmons

2 tablespoons sugar

1 tablespoon mirin

1 tablespoon clear rice vinegar

2 cloves garlic

1 tablespoon Garlic Confit (page 256)

¼ cup (55 g) butter

¼ cup (60 ml) Frank's RedHot sauce

DIRECTIONS: Remove the stems from the persimmons and cut them into quarters. Place the quarters in a saucepan along with the sugar, mirin, and rice vinegar. Cook on a low simmer, stirring occasionally, until the persimmons have broken down entirely, about 8 minutes.

Let cool for several minutes before transferring the mixture to a blender or food processor. Add the raw garlic and garlic confit and puree until smooth.

Meanwhile, in a saucepan, gently melt the butter and remove from the heat as soon as it's almost fully melted. Stir in the Frank's RedHot. Combine the two mixtures. Keep refrigerated in an airtight container for up to 1 week.

SEA MOUNTAIN SAUCE
Makes 1 quart (950 ml)

THIS SAUCE IS POURED OVER A LOT OF SNACKS AND STREET FOOD YOU'LL FIND IN TAIWAN, LIKE *TIAN BU LA* (FRIED FISH CAKES ON A STICK) AND *O A JIAN* (PAGE 51), THE OYSTER OMELET, A REAL HIGHLIGHT OF TAINAN CUISINE. Its characters translate literally to "sea mountain sauce," which is a fitting name for one of the favorite sauces in Taiwan, a mountainous island surrounded by sea. It's ketchup-based and sweet and savory—think sweet-and-sour pork in a Chinese American takeout place, but with a little more slipperiness to its texture that's kind of irresistible. It glides onto your omelet and should cover the whole thing, so don't scrimp.

¼ cup (50 g) sugar

¼ cup (60 ml) white rice vinegar

¼ cup (60 ml) apricot preserves

¼ cup (60 ml) cold water

1 tablespoon potato starch or cornstarch

1 cup (240 ml) ketchup

¼ cup (60 ml) soy sauce

¼ cup (60 ml) Chinese black vinegar

DIRECTIONS: In a saucepan, whisk together the sugar, white rice vinegar, and apricot preserves over medium heat until bubbling and the sugar is dissolved. In a small bowl, stir together the cold water and the starch. While stirring, pour the water-starch slurry into the saucepan and bring it back up to a boil, continuing to stir as it thickens. Remove from the heat and let cool completely.

Whisk the ketchup, soy sauce, and black vinegar into the mixture. Keep refrigerated for up to 1 week.

SHRIMP POWDER
Makes about ½ cup (48 g)

DRIED BABY SHRIMP ARE SUCH A COMMON SEASONING IN TAIWANESE RECIPES. You'll typically find these tiny nuggets of concentrated shrimpy flavor in sticky rice, veggie bao like the Pan-Fried Chive Pockets (page 176), and much more. At Win Son, we turned it into a powder by dehydrating it and grinding it up to make a seasoning that was more pervasive throughout a dish, and invisible. I know it sounds like a weird extra step or a cop-out to accommodate diners who are wary of seeing baby shrimp in their food, but we just kind of liked how you could sprinkle a little here and there into dishes for a secret boost of umami, and how you don't have to get all that shrimpy taste in just one place at a time.

Also, it's become a sort of iconic ingredient in the kitchen at Win Son—it reeks when we're making it. Our former cook and recipe tester for this book, Rory, says it's "very Win Son" to walk into the kitchen one day with the whole place smelling like funky shrimp powder. So be prepared to open some windows when you make it at home. Or just go with dried baby shrimp, whole, for the Sticky Rice (page 136) or Danzai Mian (page 107). We also call for a pinch of shrimp powder in the

Guohua Street Salad (page 80), but if you're not shy of the whole critters, feel free to sub in a small cluster of them there, too.

---

1 cup (96 g) whole dried baby shrimp (can be found in Asian markets)

½ cup (48 g) dried anchovy

DIRECTIONS: On a sheet pan, scatter the dried baby shrimp and anchovy, and shake to distribute around in a single layer. Bake them at 200°F (90°F) for 7 to 8 hours. (Go with 7 if your oven runs hot or won't go as low as 200°F.) Let cool completely.

Transfer to a spice grinder or blender and pulse several times, until the mixture resembles the texture of sand. Keep in a jar in the refrigerator for months or even years. (But use it sooner for best flavor.)

SUPERIOR BROTH
Makes about 4 quarts (3.8 L)

THIS IS OUR ULTIMATE NOODLE SOUP BROTH, A SOUL-SOOTHING, CONCENTRATED TONIC OF CHICKEN, PORK, BONITO, AND KOMBU. It takes a long time to cook, but don't sweat it, as most of the process is hands-off. Ask your butcher for these pork neck bones and chicken backs and necks; if you can't find them, you can use other types of pork and chicken bones.

---

2 pounds (910 g) pork neck bones, in large, whole pieces or meaty bone chunks

2 pounds (910 g) chicken back and neck bones, in large, whole pieces

2 tablespoons neutral cooking oil, such as soybean

4 to 5 scallions, white and light green parts only (Save the green parts for garnish.)

4 to 5 cloves garlic

2-inch (5-cm) piece ginger, peeled and sliced

¼ cup (60 ml) Shaoxing wine

1 piece kombu (about 2 inches/5 cm in diameter)

1 cup (40 g) packed bonito flakes

DIRECTIONS: Preheat the oven to 500°F (260°C). Pat the bones dry with paper towels. On an oiled sheet pan, dry roast for 30 to 35 minutes, until well browned.

Transfer the roasted bones into a stockpot and add the oil, scallions, garlic, ginger, Shaoxing, and kombu. Cover with about 5 quarts (4.7 L) of water. (Your bones should fit into the pot comfortably without a lot of extra room. They should occupy about as much space as the pot will allow. The stockpot should be round and taller. If the bones only fill half the pot, only fill in as much water as needed to cover the bones.)

Heat over low heat and slowly bring the water to the gentlest boil possible; the stock should never reach a full simmer. Let cook like this for 16 to 24 hours—the longer, the better. It should reduce by 1 to 2 inches (2.5 to 5 cm) below the original water level and leave a little residue on the side of the pot so you can visually track reduction. If your heat is a little high and it reduces too much, add some more water and bring down the temperature. If the heat is too low and there's no reduction or bubbles, be sure to increase it.

Carefully strain the stock with a fine-mesh strainer or sieve. Immediately after straining, while the stock is still hot, add the bonito flakes. Let steep in the stock for 1 to 1½ hours, until the liquid has come down to room temperature. Strain again through a fine-mesh strainer or sieve. The stock can be refrigerated for up to 1 week, or frozen for up to 6 months. You can skim fat once it has been thoroughly chilled, if desired.

SWEET SOY DIPPING SAUCE
Makes 1 pint (480 ml)

THIS IS THE SAUCE WE SERVE WITH SCALLION PAN-CAKES AT WIN SON. One of our servers, Kat, started calling it "scake" sauce (short for scallion pancake sauce) and we use that name for it now at the restaurant. But it can be used for a lot of things other than scallion pancakes. Like Turnip Cakes (page 54) and just about anything else you want. Made with some oyster sauce and kecap manis, it has a bit more body than our other sauces so it sticks well onto the sauce vehicle. What is food, really, but a bunch of different vehicles for a bunch of different sauces?

½ cup (120 ml) oyster sauce

¼ cup (60 ml) kecap manis or Taiwanese soy paste

¼ cup (60 ml) House Chili Oil (page 258) or your favorite chili oil, such as Lao Gan Ma Spicy Chili (optional)

2 tablespoons mirin

2 tablespoons soy sauce

2 tablespoons Chinese black vinegar

¼ cup (60 ml) neutral oil, such as soybean

DIRECTIONS: In a medium bowl, place the oyster sauce, kecap manis, chili oil, mirin, soy sauce, and black vinegar and whisk to combine. Whisk in the neutral oil until emulsified. Dial it in to taste. It can be kept in an airtight container in the refrigerator for up to 2 weeks.

WIN SON ROMESCO
Makes 1 pint (480 ml)

At a halal beef noodle shop in Taipei, they serve a stir-fry of beef and peppers with crepes. The sweet peppers had a slight crunch and were so juicy and good that we started playing around with a pepper-based sauce on our own beef roll at Win Son (page 188). Ultimately, we decided to puree the peppers, creating an effect that is pretty close to the roasted pepper-based sauce romesco, which goes great with grilled beef. It's also really good whipped together with some mayo and slathered on a sandwich.

5 red bell peppers

¼ cup (60 ml) light soy sauce

¼ cup (60 ml) Chinese black vinegar

1 cup (240 ml) soybean oil

DIRECTIONS: Preheat the broiler. Lay the bell peppers on a sheet pan. Broil for 5 minutes, or until nicely charred on one side, then carefully flip over with tongs and continue to broil on the other side until the peppers are well blackened all over. Transfer the peppers to a large zip-top plastic bag and seal to steam them for 20 minutes.

Remove the bell peppers from the plastic and carefully remove all their skins. The skins should peel right off—if not, the peppers may need to be charred longer or they may be over-charred and too soft. (Live and learn, and it's OK if a few pieces of peel get in your sauce.)

Transfer the peppers to a cutting board and slice them open lengthwise. Place them seed pocket side up and cleanly slice away the seeds. Transfer the skinned, deseeded peppers to a blender or food processor and blend with the soy sauce and black vinegar until smooth. Stream in the oil, while blending, until fully incorporated and shiny. Keep refrigerated in an airtight container for up to 1 week.

RESOURCES

OUR FAVORITE PLACES TO FIND INGREDIENTS. We hope you make it to whatever Asian grocery is closest to you to find the bulk of the ingredients needed throughout these recipes. For everything else, fortunately there are some online sources that we've come to love. Here are a few of the places where we recommend seeking out Taiwanese ingredients, specialty butcher cuts, and more.

CANTON NOODLE, 101 MOTT ST.

Josh and his dad connected us to Richard, who they know from church and his family operation. We love them very much, even though we don't buy much anymore. I've spent a lot of time talking to Richard on the street about his family operation. The noodles and dumpling skins they make are incredible.

CARNATION BAKERY

A traditional, casual Chinese bakery, right next door to Gold City Supermarket.

FLY BY JING

(flybyjing.com)
This brand makes a great alternate to Lao Gan Ma's Spicy Chili Crisp and also sells some Chinese pantry goods.

GOLD CITY SUPERMARKET

A large Chinese grocery store in Flushing where we hand shop a lot of products and ingredients for the restaurant.

HERITAGE FOODS USA

(heritagefoods.com)
A distributor of heritage meats from small family farms that ships nationally.

THE JAPANESE PANTRY

(thejapanesepantry.com)
We found this retailer when sourcing Wadaman Golden Sesame paste, which is the best of the best. Rich Ho from Ho Foods showed me this product and we haven't looked back. They also have high-quality sugars, among other great pantry items.

LI CHUEN

A small but high-volume production kitchen, run by friend of Win Son Yula, that supplies restaurants and supermarkets with xiao long bao, scallion pancakes, and *mantou* (steamed buns). We opened with some of her products on our menu but have since taken over production ourselves.

THE MALA MARKET

(themalamarket.com)
A great source for dried chile flakes and other Sichuan ingredients.

MERCATO

(mercato.com)
Another great online grocery with fresh ingredients that has a pretty good selection of Asian products, including fermented tofu (aka *fu ru*).

MR. TU BAKERY

The bakery where we still purchase bolo bao for our Big Chicken Bun (page 155). It's also the first bakery our friend Mr. Tu opened. His old commissary is now our production kitchen, but when he was operating there, he showed us a lot of his techniques.

SAXELBY CHEESEMONGERS

(saxelbycheese.com)
Our favorite local cheesemonger, which also ships nationally. Thank you, Anne, for your personal and lasting touch. Love to your family.

WEEE!
(sayweee.com)
A vast online grocery specializing in Asian products, both fresh and pantry

WING HEUNG NOODLES, 144 BAXTER
Eric Sze put us onto these guys. Great noodles.

YUN HAI TAIWANESE PANTRY
(yunhai.shop)
An online shop for Taiwanese pantry products like soy paste, aiyu jelly, and more.

OTHER GREAT PURVEYORS THAT SHIP

BURLAP AND BARREL
(burlapandbarrel.com)
This is a great source for fair trade spices that are high-quality. Some of them are really unique too, like the fermented black lime powder and an amazing fermented white pepper. We also love their smoky pimenton.

REGALIS
(regalisfoods.com)
This importer is great for pantry goods and fresh ingredients, like prawns and other seafood. We get a lot of great mushrooms from them, and we use a smoked olive oil that they sell, which works really well with dishes like Danzai Mian (page 107).

SOS CHEFS
(sos-chefs.com)
This retailer for high-end pantry staples has everything—amazing spices, oils, and sauces, from the nicest granulated ginger to ginger vinegar. The diverse range of products is super helpful.

OUR FAVORITE BOOKS. To find out a little bit more about Taiwan, we recommend checking out the following additional reading:

A CULINARY HISTORY OF TAIPEI
BY KATY HUI-WEN HUNG AND STEVEN CROOK
Rowman & Littlefield, 2018

THE FOOD OF TAIWAN: Recipes From The Beautiful Island
BY CATHY ERWAY
Houghton Mifflin Harcourt, 2015

ISLAND IN THE STREAM: A Quick Case Study of Taiwan's Complex History
BY APRIL C. J. LIN AND JEROME F. KEATING
SMC Publishing, 2001

MISSION STREET FOOD: Recipes and Ideas from an Improbable Restaurant
BY ANTHONY MYINT AND KAREN LEIBOWITZ
McSweeney's, 2011

A NEW ILLUSTRATED HISTORY OF TAIWAN
BY WAN-YAO CHOU
(translated by Carole Plackitt and Tim Casey)
SMC Publishing, 2020

TAIWANESE HOMESTYLE COOKING
BY THE CALIFORNIA CHAPTER OF THE TAIWANESE NORTH AMERICAN WOMEN'S ASSOCIATION AND THE TAIWANESE AMERICAN CITIZENS LEAGUE, 2013

THINK LIKE A CHEF: A Cookbook
BY TOM COLICCHIO
Clarkson Potter, 2012

ACKNOWLEDGMENTS

FROM JOSH

This book would not be possible first and foremost without my mom. Your love and grace has imbued everything that is good within me. Thanks to my sisters, for their guidance and food ideas for when I've sought advice and when I haven't. And to my dad, for his support and enthusiasm.

To my partner, Trigg, for your camaraderie, support, and big chef energy, of which I could not be without. We've come a long way and I couldn't have asked for a more caring and complimentary partner to grow with. And of course, to your wife, Patty, who has been so supportive both at the restaurant and behind the scenes. I swear, I didn't give him that edible.

To our partner at Win Son Bakery, Jesse, for your trust, support, and belief in the work of our team.

To my dear friends and mentors in ancillary industries who have labored with and shown me everything I know in order to design, build, and maintain the restaurants: Jin Jiannan, Buddy, Brett Helms, Luft Tanaka, Shaun Kasperbauer, Nealon Kallok, Scott Schnall, Jeff Wong, and Romel Balchan.

To my cousin, Eric, who accompanied and guided us through our travels in Taiwan in search of delicious tastes. You are sincerely the greatest.

To my better half, Emily, who has cared for and centered me these past few years. I love you!

To all my friends and loved ones who have supported us in so many ways, I'm grateful. Your support has colored our place in ways that go beyond the business itself. Dom, Davy, Vira, Morgan, Jake, Simone, and Robin.

FROM TRIGG

First, I'd like to thank my wife, Patty, who cooked beside me during some of the best and hardest times, including on the line at Win Son before we had a core team. From station partners to parental partners, I'm up for all of life's challenges with you. And I love you, Juhee, Trigger, Ophelia, and Willie so much!

Thanks to my mom and dad and my brothers for always supporting me while I've gone down this strange cook's path.

To my partner, Josh Ku: without your confidence, support, and friendship, I wouldn't be where I am in my career and life. And to Josh's family—Auntie Leah, Eric, Tiger, Auntie Sophia, and Er Jojo—thanks for facilitating my education in Taiwan and for always treating me like family.

Thank-you to my Charlottesville people: Pei Chang, Ash Porter, Brooks Tanner, Steven Montelius, Mike Yager, and Craig Hartman.

Thanks to Paul Cruzer, who gave me my first restaurant job washing dishes and on the grounds that I was the only applicant to submit a resume.

Thank you Scott Leachman for the advice and support leading up to the opening.

Thanks to my brother Mac Murdock and the other Craft chefs I look up to and admire so deeply: Ed Crochet, James Tracey, and Damon Wise. Also big thanks to Carmen Salgado and Luciana Versuti for everything. My homies Nick Ugliarolo, Charles Lindsay, and Mitchell Willis—meat cowboys for life.

I'm also thankful to Corey Bennett. We hadn't spoken much since working at a restaurant together in college, but he enthusiastically joined before opening as the GM to help us set up the restaurant's strong front of house team.

Thanks to Romel Balchan for coming from a corporate restaurant group to help out us small potatoes.

Deep thanks to Julia Sung and Vinnie Cruz, and all my friends who have traveled from near and far to support and partake with us.

Thanks to Tom Colicchio for everything I learned and everyone I met through his institutional restaurants that were more like culinary schools for me.

Thank you to Katy Hui-Wen Hung for teaching me so much about Taiwanese food history.

FROM BOTH OF US

Our restaurant and bakery team, past and present, of whom none of this would be possible without. You've built the groundwork with us to create both an extremely fun and supportive place to work and we are so proud to work and have worked with you: Danielle Spencer, Calvin Eng, Isak Buan, Brian Girouard, Gabby Cambronero, Oscar Rojas, David Desimone, Stephan Godleski, Denise Beauchamp, Kat Norton-Bliss, Stephanie Auquilla, Kevin Bonora, Flavio Guzman, and Meliton Campis.

To the chefs, restaurateurs, and vendors that have paved a path for us and continue to inspire us to promote our understanding of Taiwanese culture and cuisine: Eddie Huang, David Chang, Danny Bowien, Rich Ho, Mr. Lin, Eric Sze, Moonlynn Tsai, Bin Chen, Lisa Cheng-Smith, Andrew Chau, Jeff Fann, Mr. Tu, Rich Eng, and Yula Chuen.

To our super-duper talented and kind friend Laura Murray, for all the times you've come to our rescue and photographed our menu and things.

To Cathy Erway, our coauthor, cheerleader, and engine who carried us through making this book. Your care and attention have been the pillars to our successful publication.

Thanks to Rory Campbell for testing all the recipes in this book.

Thanks as well to Massimo Mongiardo and Jackson Epstein. We're proud to incorporate your art into our restaurant and now this book.

Thank you to Rica Allannic for their support in making this book a reality.

Last but not least, thank you to our editor, Laura Dozier, and designer, Diane Shaw, for making this book possible and putting it together in such a visually stunning way.

INDEX

Editor: Laura Dozier
Designer: Diane Shaw
Managing Editor: Glenn Ramirez
Production Manager: Denise LaCongo

Library of Congress Control Number: 2022933594

ISBN: 978-1-4197-4708-3
eISBN: 978-1-68335-990-6

Printed and bound in Malaysia
10 9 8 7 6 5 4 3 2 1

Abrams books are available at special discounts when purchased in
quantity for premiums and promotions as well as fundraising or
educational use. Special editions can also be created to specification.
For details, contact specialsales@abrambooks.com or the address below.

Abrams® is a registered trademark of Harry N. Abrams, Inc.

ABRAMS The Art of Books
195 Broadway, New York, NY 10007
abramsbooks.com